SEE NO EVIL

Russian Literature and Thought
Gary Saul Morson, Series Editor

Dariusz Tolczyk

SEE NO EVIL

Literary Cover-Ups and Discoveries
of the Soviet Camp Experience

Yale University Press   New Haven and London

Designed by Sonia Scanlon
Set in Bembo type with Gill Sans display by dix!,
Syracuse, New York.

Printed in the United States of America.

Library of Congress Cataloging-in-Publication Data
Tolczyk, Dariusz.
    See no evil : literary cover-ups and discoveries of
the Soviet camp experience / Dariusz Tolczyk.
        p.   cm. — (Russian literature and thought)
    Includes bibliographical references and index.
    ISBN 0-300-06608-2 (cloth : alk. paper)
    1. Russian literature—20th century—History
and criticism.   2. Concentration camps in
literature.   3. Concentration camps—Soviet
Union.   4. Prisoners' writings, Soviet—History and
criticism.   I. Title.   II. Series.
PG3026.C64T65   1999
891.7'09355—dc21   98-50997
                              CIP

A catalogue record for this book is available from the
British Library.

The paper in this book meets the guidelines for
permanence and durability of the Committee on
Production Guidelines for Book Longevity of the
Council on Library Resources.

10 9 8 7 6 5 4 3 2 1

For my family

CONTENTS

ACKNOWLEDGMENTS

In writing this book I was fortunate enough to be able to share my ideas with many persons for whose help, advice, and criticism I am thankful. Jurij Striedter and Stanisław Barańczak advised me throughout my work on the first version of this book, and my gratitude for their intellectual mentorship cannot be overstated. My cordial thanks also go to Gary Saul Morson, whose comments inspired my work on the final text, and to Alexander Babyonyshev (Sergei Maksudov), Donald Fanger, Leonid Heretz, Alexis Klimoff, and William Mills Todd III, all of whom generously shared their criticism with me at different stages of the work. I cannot overstate my gratitude to Joseph Donohue, whose expert help made possible the timely conclusion of my work on the manuscript. I am also very grateful to Jonathan Brent of Yale University Press for his always thoughtful responsiveness. I thank in a special way my wife, Sharon, who not only bore the daily brunt of my work but was also my first critic and editor. My children, Adam and Aleksandra, born during the time of writing, became the most wonderful distraction and the most compelling reason for promptly finishing the project. And, finally, I send my heartfelt gratitude to my parents, Zdzisław and Krystyna Tołczyk, and grandparents, Henryk and Jadwiga Żochowski, without whose most meaningful support this book would not have been possible.

The research for this book was supported by a Charlotte Newcombe Fellowship, a Visiting Scholarship at the Kennan Institute for Advanced Russian Studies, a National Endowment for the Humanities Fellowship, and a Summer Faculty Research Grant from the University of Virginia. I wish to take this opportunity to thank these institutions for their generosity.

INTRODUCTION

In *The Origins of Totalitarianism,* one of the twentieth century's most influential books, Hannah Arendt describes concentration camps of totalitarian regimes in terms of gigantic laboratories. The purpose of the experiment carried out in these laboratories was—she states—to verify the fundamental belief of totalitarianism that human thoughts and actions can be controlled and shaped the way an engineer controls and shapes the natural world. If we look more closely at this historic experiment in its Stalinist variation, we can understand Hannah Arendt's metaphor in a double sense. On the one hand, the camps tested the assumption that a human being can, in fact, be reduced to a combination of predictable, and therefore controllable, reactions to such physical stimuli as hunger, fear, cold, pain, and so on. But besides this physical side, the totalitarian experiment conducted in the Gulag had its peculiar intellectual and spiritual side. I am talking here about concentration camps as a subject of consciousness of the victims and of the entire population of the totalitarian state, including the people who operated the camps.

This intellectual side of the camp experiment reflected a larger totalitarian attempt to control and program people's perceptions of the universe they live in, most especially their moral evaluations of the massive oppression imposed upon them by the regime. The Bolshevik leadership made efforts to prove that it could manipulate the consciousness of its population to the point of making people incapable of relying on their own experience as a source of knowledge. The importance of experience was to be undermined by ready-made, exchangeable versions of the reality, provided by the authorities in forms of words and images. In terms of this larger totalitarian experiment on the human mind it is hardly possible to find a theme more central to it than the theme of the camp. For if indeed it is possible to make people—outside and inside the camp—feel positive about experience so horrifying as life and death in the Gulag, then perhaps there is no limit to the totalitarian ambition of not only controlling the masses by means of physical oppression but also of controlling people's perceptions of the massive victimization imposed on the society in the first place.

This book is primarily concerned with this intellectual and spiritual aspect of the Soviet camp experience. The immediate focus is the changing image of the Soviet concentration camps projected by the official Soviet literature. Contrary to widely prevalent belief, the topic of state terrorism and its chief institution—the concentration camp—was not always absent from the official cultural and literary discourse of the Soviet state. Banishment of this element of Soviet reality to the sphere of the taboo, which began in 1937 and, with the exception of the brief Khrushchevian thaw, lasted until *glasnost'* in the 1980s, was a result of the regime's self-acknowledged failures in a series of experiments in manipulating the ethical terms whereby society viewed the camps. In these experiments, literature played an important, yet thus far largely unacknowledged, role.

The official Soviet literary image of the camp experience has received only sparse scholarly attention. This is all the more surprising considering the amount of critical work rightly devoted to the independent literature concerned with this topic, especially the works of Aleksandr Solzhenitsyn. The only comprehensive scholarly book on the subject of the official Soviet literary treatment of the camps is a study by Mikhail Heller, *The World of Concentration Camps and Soviet Literature* (1973), published in French, Russian, and Polish, but not in English. Heller, a historian, is primarily concerned with literature as a historical source, a mirror reflecting a historical reality that can be verified by other historical sources. Thus, Heller places the official Soviet camp literature in the context of the changing historical realities of the Soviet institutionalized terror and treats the ever evolving Soviet literary presentations of the camps as reflections of the evolution of the Bolshevik system of mass oppression. My book, while deeply indebted to Heller's, proposes a different approach to the problem at hand. It explores Soviet camp literature as a series of efforts inspired by Soviet ideology to challenge, redesign, and control moral perceptions of the camps by the Soviet public. The primary focus is on the official Soviet literary image of the camp experience, for the concentration camps of the Bolshevik regime epitomize the dual nature of the historic experiment conducted by this regime. On the one hand, the camps represent the most consequential and systematic form of the experiment subjecting human beings to total control and domination by a regime always ready to use any means of physical victimization and deprivation. On the other hand, the manipulation of people's perceptions of the camp experience, instituted by the Soviet regime with the help of writers, filmmakers, and other engineers of the human soul, is one of the most radical examples of the Bolsheviks' efforts to reprogram society's view of the politicized evil the regime was creating.

Life under the Bolshevik regime was subject to a peculiar

incongruity between the realm of people's experiences and the realm of public discourse. I do not mean the typical hypocrisy of many modern societies and governments engaged in activities fundamentally contradictory to the values officially preached. The Bolshevik project, motivated initially by millenarian hopes for the liberation of mankind, was inherently bound to the idea of accomplishing this goal by radically transforming society according to a blueprint for a better future. This required that the society become perfectly submissive as the object of this transformation realized ostensibly for the society's own good. So, in order to secure the full cooperation of people with the regime, their minds were supposed to be largely dispossessed of their capacity to identify and judge the historical reality around them in individualistic ways and made subject to programming by the regime. By tampering with the dynamics of human perceptions and evaluations of reality, the Bolshevik regime entered a realm traditionally explored by art and literature. And by attempting to reshape these dynamics, the Bolsheviks put themselves in a position of author of a fictional world in which readers—in this case Soviet society—were enticed to suspend disbelief. I call this process "totalitarian authorship."

The notion of totalitarian authorship differs from the traditional notion of authorship in its scope. Whereas literary authorship creatively transforms, questions, and shapes perceptions of reality, totalitarian authorship attempts to shape both the perception of reality and the reality itself, thereby eliminating the opportunity for other points of view to be expressed. With this self-endowed "creative freedom," totalitarian regimes attempt to shape the universe of words and perceptions independently of material reality and reserve the right to connect both realms by means of ideology. For inhabitants of totalitarian utopias-in-the-making, words and experience are to become irreconcilable unless they succumb to the regime's pressure to deny the world of experience for the sake of preserving the inner consistency of the world of verbal clichés generated by the regime. In the process of disconnecting the realms of words and experience, the Bolsheviks created a purely rhetorical basis for identifying human targets of the regime, by labeling them "class enemies," "enemies of the people," "kulaks," and so on. This provided the regime with unlimited license to victimize and exploit the population and marked life in the Soviet state with a characteristic sense of fear and unpredictability.

This book considers official Soviet camp literature as a product of the clash between the universe of experience and that of official words, which promoted unquestioned optimism and trust in the Communist leadership. The Soviet universe of public words and perceptions was dominated by the illusive security stemming from the simple logic and goal-oriented coherence of Bolshevik ideology. The essence of the Bolsheviks' attempt at mind control lay in their manipulative use of the temptation, perhaps inherent in the human condition, to turn away from the confusing universe of experience and toward the security of the clear-cut domain of words and ideas. The official Bolshevik word was to become the filter through which the horrors of experience were supposed to pass, thus resolving the tension between the human mind's desire to explore reality and to satisfy at all costs its own need for consistency.

The book discusses how Soviet literature created, out of ideological constructs, visions of Soviet reality intended to replace life experiences. One of the most important attractions of the Bolshevik design for literature is its solution to the problem, characteristic of modern culture, of the fragmentation of the world's perception. The nineteenth-century vision of the world's natural and historical order was exposed in the context of World War I as a mere fiction. New artistic and literary movements of the time seemed to be rapidly turning away from the assumption that there exists one, all-encompassing vantage point from which the world appears as a sensible whole. Instead, a new, pluralistic view of the world as the sum of many individual, biased, and mutually contradictory perceptions and truths was emerging in art and literature. This change stirred both hope for a less confining cultural climate and anxieties regarding the upcoming crisis—and possibly disintegration—of civilization. Bolshevism, in addition to the moral appeal of its promise of social justice, seemed to propose a new, all-encompassing vantage point that—as some were ready to believe—would allay these anxieties. Abandonment of the realm of experience for the sake of the ideological universe of Bolshevism was a way of restoring the possibility of reintegrating, both philosophically and structurally, the artistic perception of reality. One of the costs of this operation involved the adoption of new utilitarian ethics regarding the particularly disturbing elements of this reality, such as terror and concentration camps.

The Soviet attempt, unprecedented in modern history, to dismiss the value of common experiences and replace them with controlled verbal substitutes sheds light on the general question of human resistance and vulnerability to such extreme mind control. There are few phenomena as enlightening in this regard as the phenomenon of the Soviet literary treatment of the camp experience. The camps, which Hannah Arendt called "the testing ground of totalitarianism's attempt to fully control human behavior," were at the same time a testing ground of totalitarianism's control of people's perceptions of totalitarianism's own evil. For totalitarian literature, to present the concentration camps as a topic meant to take on the ultimate challenge of reality and present evil as good. This required creating artistic strategies whereby, under the impact of a literary work, the reader would be lured, pressured, or cajoled into the abandonment of basic ethical and cognitive prerogatives and into limitless submission to the new fiction in both literature and life.

The first of such literary strategies, introduced in the early 1920s, presents the Red Terror as a historical necessity. This convention reflects the ideologically motivated self-image of the Bolshevik regime as the positive side in the inevitable and final conflict between the forces of revolution (good) and those of reaction (evil). This positive self-image provided the primary basis for the justification of violence as a necessary means towards a noble end. It was reflected and refracted in numerous literary works, from those inciting revolutionary agitation to those attempting to comprehend the sources and nature of revolutionary violence. This variety was still possible in the 1920s, because the Bolsheviks' control over literary discourse was not yet complete. One can speak only about relative variety, however, since views directly critical of Bolshevik practice were quickly banned from Soviet literature.

Among these various literary approaches to the Bolshevik violence of the 1920s, I will examine more closely two literary conventions that provided ethical justifications of the Red Terror. The first was based on the nineteenth-century Russian Populist concept of the tragic moral contradiction between "necessary violence" and the traditional morality of the Ten Commandments. In the 1920s Ilya Ehrenburg, in his novel *The Life and Death of Nikolai Kurbov,* and Aleksandr Tarasov-Rodyonov, in *Chocolate,* readdressed this traditional theme through the inner conflicts of their protagonists. By presenting Bolshevik henchmen of the Cheka as tragic heroes, they romanticized and, ultimately, justified Bolshevik victimization. However, it was the other literary strategy that reflected the Bolshevik point of view more accurately. This strategy provocatively championed the notion of purely utilitarian, fully politicized "class ethics," totally independent of any traditional moral reservations. All means of action were allowed insofar as they served Bolshevik political goals. In fact, this approach reflected Lenin's fundamental admission of the political advantage of the "proletariat" as the only criterion of good and evil. Within this mode, a peculiarly bloodthirsty rhetoric of Bolshevik violence was developed in works by authors of varying caliber, from Vladimir Mayakovsky and Eduard Bagritsky to Vasily Knyazev, in his now forgotten *Red Gospel*. Through both the tragic convention of Ehrenburg and Tarasov-Rodyonov and the bloodthirsty rhetoric of Mayakovsky, Bagritsky, and Knyazev, these authors directly provoke, challenge, and assault readers on moral grounds, in circumstances allowing no possibility to retort. The traditional ethical categories applicable to the phenomenon of Bolshevik victimization are either questioned and relativized (within the tragic formula) or frontally attacked, ridiculed, dismissed, and automatically replaced by the utilitarian Leninist moral code.

These literary conventions had practically exhausted their inner purpose by the end of the 1920s. By that time, Stalin was laying the groundwork for the subsequent development of the terrorist potential of the Bolshevik state to its fullest degree. The systematic, highly institutionalized terror and slavery of the Soviet 1930s found their official literary representation in a convention that presented the chief institution of Soviet state terrorism, the concentration camp, as the locus of the reeducation and redemption of reactionary social elements on the way to a more just and humane future society. The main literary works in this new mode were Maxim Gorky's reportage "Solovki" (1929) and the collective volume *Belomorkanal* (1934). They are examined here as literary reflections of the evolving ideological self-image of the Bolshevik regime in the late 1920s and early 1930s. The focus on revolutionary conflict, characteristic of the literary justifications of the Bolshevik terror in the 1920s, is replaced here by a new focus on the unanimity and harmony allegedly representing current life under Communist rule. Thus, violence and oppression are absent from this new literary image of the camp experience. The topic of concentration camps is not associated with moral anxiety. On the contrary, the concentration camps are presented in positive moral terms as schools for a new, happier society. The alleged transformation of the universe (both the economic base and the intellectual superstructure) towards harmony here becomes the essence of the camp experience. A strategy of assault and challenge gives way to a manipulative assumption of ethical unanimity between the author(ities) and the reader (society). This strategy did not last long, however. It was abandoned by the Soviet regime in 1937 at the height of Stalin's Great Terror, when, for reasons to be discussed later, the topic of the Soviet concentration camps became taboo in official Soviet literature. From this point on, no new literary works focused directly on the topic of the camps could be published in the Soviet Union until 1962.

Literary testimonies to the Soviet camp experience, published in the Soviet Union in the brief period of Khrushchev's "late thaw," from 1962 through 1964, have all but been forgotten apart from Solzhenitsyn's *One Day in the Life of Ivan Denisovich*. Yet these works, all of them admittedly inferior to Solzhenitsyn's novella, document an extraordinary human condition. Georgy Shelest's *The Kolyma Notes*, Yuri Pilyar's *People Remain People*, Boris Dyakov's *The Story of What I Lived Through*, and Andrei Aldan-Semenov's *Bas-Relief in the Rock* portray the horrors of Stalin's camps as an unfortunate historical mistake, which does not lead to critical moral reflection upon the system of victimization created as a result of the Bolshevik experiment. These works represent a peculiar Soviet phenomenon: the camp experience addressed from the point of view of a prisoner who, though innocent, accepts punishment on ideological grounds. In order to protect the coherence of the Soviet regime's ideological vision (its verbal universe) from confrontation with the brutal Soviet reality, these authors seek to obscure any connection between the horrors of the camps and the ethical notions championed by Soviet Communist ideology. This phenomenon shows how earlier Soviet conventions for presenting Bolshevik victimization provided a screen through which some victims themselves admittedly perceived and presented their experiences. This phenomenon brings us to a more general question concerning the role of preconceived value systems and verbal strategies in the experience and relating of the extreme realities of totalitarian camps, Soviet and non-Soviet. An examination of these works by Shelest, Pilyar, Dyakov, and Aldan-Semenov in the context of literary testimonies to the Nazi camps by Elie Wiesel, Tadeusz Borowski, Primo Levi, and other authors sheds light on the peculiar functions played by the official word in the Soviet camp experience.

In the last chapter I examine the ultimate test to which Soviet literary strategies for presenting the camp experience were exposed after the publication of *One Day in the Life of Ivan Denisovich,* in November 1962. The uniqueness of Solzhenitsyn's account in the context of Soviet literature lies in his treating the camp as a moral problem, whose solutions are not provided by the author. The moral test that Ivan Denisovich Shukhov undergoes in the camp is a metaphor for the problem of Russia's moral response to totalitarianism. The ambiguity of the work provoked numerous contradictory interpretations, both in the West and in the Soviet Union. The debate among critics in the Soviet press following publication displayed virtually all the official strategies for presenting the camp experience that had been introduced in earlier Soviet literature. Readers and critics both supportive and hostile to Solzhenitsyn attempted to ascribe to *One Day in the Life of Ivan Denisovich* meanings hardly traceable in that work, in an effort to render it presentable within the conceptual framework of Soviet public discourse. The analysis of these various strategies of response exposes the ultimate limit of Soviet public discourse—its inability to face its own reality by any ethics other than the Leninist utilitarian "class morality" that provided ideological grounds for the Bolshevik abuses of power in the first place. The taboo that surrounded the subject of the Soviet camps again from the mid-1960s until *glasnost'* provides a natural closure to the problem of Soviet literary cover-ups and discoveries of the Soviet camp experience: having proved incapable of facing its own creations and reviewing its own projections, the Soviet totalitarian project entered the lengthy process of what we now see as its demise.

While examining official literary visions of the Soviet camp experience, I hope to elucidate some of the ideological, psychological, and cultural sources of twentieth-century totalitarian experiments and their attempts to replace traditional Judeo-Christian and humanist moral values with their own utilitarian substitutes. After all, the Soviet campaign in politics and literature to defeat experience with words, an echo, however distorted, of the fundamental dream of writers and poets to outweigh the shortcomings of material reality by the humanizing power of language, brought about results which proved only the peculiar capacity of rulers to turn even the most uplifting dreams into nightmares.

1

FICTION AND FEAR

Totalitarianism between Word and Experience

Soon after completing a journey through Russia in 1839, the Marquis de Custine published in Paris a travelogue, in which he wrote:

Despotism is never so fearful as when it claims to do good, since it can then excuse its most repulsive acts by their intentions, and there are no longer any limits to the evil it adopts as a remedy. Open crime can triumph for no more than a day: false virtues are what eternally mislead the spirit of a people.[1]

D
e Custine's book about Russia has stirred much controversy ever since. As an account of the empire of Tsar Nicholas I, it undoubtedly exaggerates the dark side of the autocratic Russian regime at the time. Yet, despite this exaggeration, or perhaps because of it, de Custine managed to accomplish something he himself could not have been aware of. He managed to describe, a hundred years in advance, the essence of the totalitarian society that the Bolshevik regime under Lenin and Stalin would strive to create in Russia in the twentieth century.

In his remarks de Custine repeatedly points to the political hypocrisy of a tyrannical regime that combines direct oppression of the people with efforts to skew the perception of such abuses of power by changing their ethical character. This tendency, ascribed by de Custine to the political regime of Nicholas I, to pass its own ethical transgressions through the filter of propagandistic rationalization and justification prefigures a key characteristic of Soviet totalitarianism—the complementary relationship between widespread victimization of the society and the constant attempt to reprogram and control the people's perceptions of it.

All the same, the similarity to de Custine's idea remains only partial. The radical ethical and cognitive assault mounted by totalitarianism defies analysis in de Custine's own terms. De Custine, a sensitive witness to the ethical contradictions and abuses at work in the Western world at a time of rapid disintegration of traditional values and their supplanting by the new agendas of the rising bourgeoisie, was intimately familiar with political hypocrisy. Yet political hypocrisy, a term that describes many ideas and actions in every epoch, does not sufficiently characterize the specific nature of the totalitarian attempt to redesign and control human ethics. A hypocrite, by manipulating the perception of his faults so that they meet commonly accepted ethical criteria (however shallow and fluid these criteria may be), acknowledges his essential dependence on them. In this respect, as we shall see, the reality of totalitarianism in Russia went much further than the prescient model depicted by the early French traveler.

Exactly a century after de Custine's journey, his prophetic remarks were subjected to empirical verification by another traveler in Russia, the Polish poet Aleksander Wat. In 1939, Wat was arrested by the Soviet political police (NKVD) in the city of Lvov, which was occupied by the Soviet Union following the Stalin–Hitler pact. As a result of his arrest, Wat spent over six years in the Soviet Union under Stalin. Unlike de Custine, he did not travel voluntarily, and the places he visited consisted of a series of Soviet prisons and several confined settlements. Twenty years after leaving the Soviet Union, he commented at length on his experiences in Stalin's empire:

Mass exterminations are not an exception; cruelty is part of human nature, part of society. But a new, third, dimension had been added that was more deeply and subtly oppressive: a vast enterprise to deform language. Had it been only lies and hypocrisy—lying is part of human nature and all governments are hypocritical. The rulers' hypocrisy can cause rebellion, but here any possible rebellion had been nipped in the bud once and for all. A lie is an infirmity, a disease of language. The natural function of language is to ascertain the truth, or truths. Lies, by their very nature partial and ephemeral, are revealed as lies when confronted with language's striving for truth. But here all the means of disclosure had been permanently confiscated by the police. The customary or even just the logical, natural connections between words and things, facts, had been taken from the individual, expropriated everywhere, and nationalized for good, so that now any word could mean whatever suited the whims of the usurper of all words, meanings, things, and souls. The viler the deed, the more grandiloquent the name. But if only this procedure were used just to mask criminal means and ignoble ends—that too had happened often enough in history, the history of wars, tyrannies, and annexations; Tacitus knew about all that. But in this case a coherent set of grandiloquent terms and the opposing monstrous reality were kept side by side, ostentatiously and with diabolical thoroughness and perseverance, and under threat of extermination a person was coerced into fully believing that the terms and the facts were identical. Such things had been anticipated and attempted in history's darker hours, but this was the first time that the "reforging of souls" was carried out by the police on such a colossal scale, with such speed and such logic. Collective farmers dying of starvation were herded to films in which the tables buckled under the weight of food; under threat of death they *had* to believe that these banquets, and not their wretched poverty, their collective farms, were true and typical. Young enthusiasts sang rapturously: "I know no other land / where a man can breathe so free" while their fathers perished in the camps.[2]

Wat chooses to extend his illustration only to this point. But the image of the children of Gulag victims praising the Soviet liberties can be further complemented. Like these "young enthusiasts," their fathers who perished in the camps were required to praise their own fate and their own oppressors. Amid the ordeals of slave labor in the camps, they were not only coerced to subject themselves to the official propaganda that skewed the image of the camps but also required to actively contribute to the creation of this fiction. Like the starving collective farmers who were shown films about happy Soviet collective farmers and were required to believe them, camp prisoners were shown "documentaries" about their own camps in which all the inmates burst with enthusiasm for their slave labor.[3] Required to prove that they were not lagging behind the prisoners shown on film, real prisoners were expected to voluntarily raise their own slave labor quotas and express in various forms their love of Stalin, the party, and slave labor. These forms included speeches, journalistic prose published in the inside press of the camps, theater performances, painting, sculpture, and so on. In the labor camps whose prisoners built the White Sea Canal in the early 1930s, for example, about 12,140,000 copies of camp newspapers and magazines were published by prisoners and for prisoners.[4] These were printed in many of the languages of Soviet nationalities, under the guidance and supervision of the political police and the central Soviet office of censorship (*Glavlit*). The most acclaimed among these periodicals, the daily *Perekovka* (The Reforging), alone was printed in 30,000 copies. Each of the paper's issues was filled with prisoners' enthusiastic praises of life and work in the camp.

No single serious complaint is to be found in this massive amount of material. Instead, the image of the prisoners, created by prisoners under the guidance of their Bolshevik "mentors," was that of zealous converts to Soviet Communism who found the purpose of their lives in overfulfilling the camp's work quotas and who were ready to put up with any possible deprivations for the sake of this. At the same time, prisoners' paintings were exhibited, showing glorious portraits of camp commanders, guards, and party officials, along with images of prisoners joyfully surpassing their work quotas. Enthusiastic songs and poems were composed, sung, and recited on camp stages. Prisoners at the Moscow–Volga Canal construction in 1934 even wrote and performed an operetta, *From Volga to Moscow,* which presented their slave labor in a cheerful convention with light music. The number of those who perished at these two canal projects alone is still difficult to establish. From numerous documents and testimonies we now know that for some prisoners contributing to this manipulative fiction was a form of saving their lives. Larger food rations received in return for such contributions saved many prisoners from starvation and additional abuse. One question, however, will perhaps always remain open: how many among these people, and at what point, started believing their own stories? This question defines the core of the experiment of mind control conducted by the Soviet regime in its chief human laboratory—the concentration camp.

In his comments on Stalinism Wat points to the uniqueness of the ethical assault carried out by the Soviet totalitarian regime: while not the first in history to bluntly rationalize and justify massive victimization, the Bolsheviks were pioneers in their ruthless attempt to systematically reprogram and control the human sense of truth and falsehood, good and evil. The Bolsheviks, in a way unprecedented for a political regime, attempted to enter the large sphere encompassing both the human mind, armed with its tools of perception and evaluation of the world, and the enigmatic world itself. This intrusion, according to Wat, was aimed at depriving the population of traditional values as well as personal cognitive and moral structures, thus creating an unbridgeable gap between the human mind and the reality the mind strives to penetrate and evaluate. Instead of maintaining and endorsing previously existing ways of defining and organizing experience, the Bolsheviks designed and imposed new, artificial ways on the population. The frightening, chaotic experience of life under totalitarianism was complemented by the depiction of a glorious, highly coherent verbal universe supposedly reflecting this life. Thus, the delicate balance between the desire of the human mind for consistency (expressed in the organizing functions of language) and the destabilizing impact of traumatic experience was upset through a process of intellectual manipulation conducted on a hitherto unknown scale. The basic activity of the human mind under the totalitarian regime was no longer to be the perception and analysis of reality according to the cognitive and moral concepts of truth versus falsehood and good versus evil, but rather the reconciliation of reality with an alleged verbal equivalent generated by the regime, reflecting the regime's ideological preferences.[5]

That Aleksander Wat was a poet says not a little about his sensitivity to the intellectual assault of totalitarianism. In challenging familiar human perceptions and evaluations of the universe by constructing a verbal substitution for existing reality, the totalitarian regime placed itself in a position analogous to that of an author. The dynamic between the organizing capacities of the human mind, replete with cognitive and axiological strategies, and the constant impact of experience constitutes the sphere that is examined, shaped, and reshaped by literature and art. Creating verbal refractions of experience, and so questioning or reshaping people's perceptions of reality and interactions with it, was a familiar function of literature—before it became the agenda of the totalitarian regime. For writers, challenging existing ethical norms can be a goal in itself or a step toward the further task of reshaping or reinforcing readers' ethical principles (as in moralistic or didactic literature). So it seems appropriate to describe totalitarian attempts to redesign human cognition and interaction with the world in terms applicable to the rhetorical strategies of literature.

Of course, the analogy must not be pressed too far. The fundamental difference between the position of an author as the communicator of a literary work and the special character of the "authorship" assumed by the totalitarian regime is important. What makes a totalitarian regime's creation of a verbal equivalent of reality different from analogous efforts in literature is not the blunt contradiction between the verbal refraction of reality created by the regime and reality itself. Nor is it the regime's simultaneous claim to full truth and objectivity. Both these tendencies can be observed in many literary utopias. What distinguishes the "authorship" assumed by the totalitarian regime is the new communicative situation of total univocality created by the regime through the exercise of such "extra-literary" techniques of influence as executions, prisons, concentration camps, and so on. In this new rhetorical situation, the verbal refraction of reality presented by the author-regime to the audience-population is designed to influence that audience and make it accept, logically and morally, the author-regime's self-endowed right to exercise this kind of authorship.

The creative power of literature to question and reshape human perceptions and evaluations of reality can play two quite opposite roles, depending on the rhetorical situation. Within the pluralistic universe of dialogical communication, this power serves to stimulate a variety of perceptions that complement and challenge one another. So it reaffirms the notion of the universe as an infinite reality embracing a number of perspectives and discourses, all of which engage with one another in dialogical relationships and none of which assumes an exclusive, definitive authority.[6] Totalitarianism represents a systematic, radical attempt to realize a second communicative model, the opposite of the one just described. This second rhetorical situation occurs as a result of the totalitarian regime's monopoly on one definitive point of view. In this case, the verbal refraction of reality championed by the regime claims to possess the sole legitimate, true image of reality, almost inevitably creating a conflict between the authoritative image of reality and the various human experiences of it, shaped by individual cognitive and moral options. This conflict can only be aggravated in a situation such as the Soviet one described by Wat, where a blunt contradiction emerges between life experience and its official verbal equivalent. Since there is only one truth in the authoritarian rhetorical universe, this conflict cannot be resolved. Instead, full allegiance must be given either to the subjective truth of the particular experience (which cannot be shared and verified outside itself) or to the authoritative version of this experience. What constitutes the essence of totalitarian "authorship" is its complex character: the regime creates the only true vision of the universe, while at the same time manufacturing a rhetorical situation in which this vision is supposed to assume an exclusive status. Under totalitarianism, verbal and physical means complement each other, constituting an unprecedented experiment in "authorship" in which a printing press and a concentration camp represent two sides of the same attempt to reshape the human relationship with the universe.

In this book, I examine a particular manifestation of these two key aspects of totalitarian "authorship": the situation in which the concentration camp becomes a prominent theme featured by the verbal refraction of reality espoused by the regime. Hannah Arendt wrote that "concentration camps and extermination camps of totalitarian regimes serve as laboratories in which the fundamental belief of totalitarianism that everything is possible is being verified."[7] Her words can be understood in a double sense. Stalin's concentration camps employed unlimited physical force and degradation as means of gaining total control over human beings, with a view to completely reifying them as mere instruments of state policy. At the same time, the inclusion of concentration camps—a monstrous encapsulating of totalitarian reality—within the sphere of the glorious verbal refraction of that reality was an attempt to verify in practical terms the totalitarian claim to total control over the human mind. Aleksander Wat characterized this control as creating an essential tension between "a coherent set of grandiloquent terms and the opposing monstrous reality . . . kept side by side, ostentatiously and with diabolical thoroughness and perseverance."[8] The measure of success of this mind control was the degree to which society could be made to believe in the paradoxical identity of these two separate, opposed universes.

To be sure, the existence of concentration camps, the epitome of totalitarian victimization, involved the inherent potential of provoking moral rejection of the totalitarian regime. To make this rejection impossible and to represent the camps in a positive light required a thorough reprogramming of the ethical terms by which the population viewed the world. In short, in totalitarianism evil must be turned into good by verbal means.

Official Soviet literature of this period comprises a series of works programmatically focused on the theme of the concentration camps. Though authored by a variety of writers, these works do not interest us as expressions of personal views of the reality of the camps. Each decision of the Soviet censorship to admit into public discourse a work devoted to a theme so politically charged verified the fact that the work was viewed by the authorities as promoting the regime's own point of view. In the 1920s this point of view was not always entirely clear and fixed, and a relative variety of viewpoints could coexist in Soviet literature. This situation changed at the beginning of the 1930s, when the now mature Soviet system of preventive censorship and literary bureaucracy became effective at securing an unprecedented degree of congruence between literary production and the ideological line of the day. This was especially true in the case of literature devoted to a topic as ideologically volatile as the camps. Since within a totalitarian rhetorical universe the only publicly existing point of view is supposed to be that of the regime, we are entitled to treat these works as reflections (actual, or assumed by the author or the censorship itself) of the point of view of the Soviet regime at different stages of its evolution. The evolution of official Soviet literary images of the concentration camps constitutes a prime case study in the dynamics of attempted totalitarian control of the human mind. Analysis of changes in the official verbal refraction of totalitarian evil intended to displace actual experience as a basis for human perception of the world serves to place these changes in the context of Bolshevik ideology, thus shedding light on the evolution of the Soviet regime's self-perceptions. At the same time, analysis of literary strategies for reprogramming perceptions and evaluations of the universe can be paired with examination of the strengths and limitations of literature as a medium of totalitarianism's self-realization. These literary images of the Soviet camp experience will be examined here primarily as products of particular correlations between ideological projections and the literary strategies employed. Attention will be paid to methods of applying these projections and strategies to certain aspects of common experience favored in the official Soviet camp literature, and inner inconsistencies in these methods resulting in the failure of formal conventions created for the purpose of addressing the topic of the camps will be emphasized.

Before embarking on the task of analyzing concrete literary material, however, it is important to examine the historical, ideological, and literary contexts in which this experiment of reprogramming human perceptions, epitomized in official Soviet camp literature, was conducted. First, it is important to understand what is meant by the general term "totalitarianism," to characterize its Soviet ideological and political parameters, and to place the problem of Soviet camp literature securely in this realm. Second, some attention needs to be paid to certain thematic and formal tendencies in Russian literature that provided favorable conditions for the new official Soviet camp literature becoming a medium through which the task of totalitarian reprogramming of human perceptions could be pursued.

Marxism Upside-Down

The term "Soviet totalitarianism" became a password among Western scholars in the 1950s, at a time when empirical research on the Soviet state and society was severely impaired by the secrecy and deception of the Soviet regime.[9] With the fall of this regime and the exploration of many hitherto secret or unavailable sources of Soviet history, the concept of totalitarianism has been tested in light of new historical evidence. New empirical research has obviously corrected many speculations about specific historical facts. Thus far, however, this new research has not, I believe, seriously challenged the concept of totalitarianism and its application to Soviet history and culture under Stalin. To engage in (or even summarize) the ongoing scholarly debate over totalitarianism would obviously transcend the limits of this book. The following passage from Andrzej Walicki's *Marxism and the Leap to the Kingdom of Freedom* eloquently illuminates what is also my understanding of the concept of totalitarianism in the context of this debate. Walicki states that:

the notion of totalitarianism should be preserved and used to explain two historical processes: that of totalitarianization and the reverse process of detotalitarianization. Such usage of the term *totalitarianism* historicizes its content and avoids the error of seeing totalitarianism as a stable system, a viable alternative to liberal democracy, let alone a system capable of effective control over everything and therefore immune from change. At the same time, it helps to distinguish and conceptualize different phases of the totalitarian movement: the phase of its revolutionary offensive, the establishment of a full-blown totalitarian state, the short period of its relative stabilization, and the long period of gradual detotalitarianization that paved the way for the final collapse of the system. Stalinism is, from this point of view, the closest approximation to the totalitarian model; the year 1956, in which communist mythology received a mortal blow, marks the beginning of a slow and convoluted, but nonetheless steady and continuous, retreat from the totalitarian ideal. It is therefore clear that this position differs from both the rival schools in American Sovietology. It differs from the totalitarian school because it rejects the view that totalitarianism survived in the countries of actually existing socialism until the Communist parties surrendered their political power. But it differs also from the revisionist interpretations of communism *before* Stalin and *under* Stalin. In this respect I endorse Kolakowski's view that Stalinism was a logical (though not inevitable) and ideologically legitimate result of Leninism. . . . Stalinism, as Kolakowski put it, "is not an incidental evil which somehow superimposed itself on an otherwise benign vision." [10]

An indirect definition of totalitarianism projected by Herbert J. Spiro in 1968 helps us understand the term as applied to the historical process of totalitarianization. Spiro sees the fundamental distinctive feature and moving spirit of totalitarianism in its all-permeating orientation toward goals imposed upon society by the totalitarian regime and pursued "without commitment to procedural stability."[11] The very process of the pursuit of the goal brings about other distinctive features of the totalitarian society, such as frequently experienced unpredictability and uncertainty of life, caused by this procedural flux. The unconditional priority given by the regime to the pursuit of the goal is reflected in the government's attempts to enforce universal participation of the society in this pursuit. In practice, this implies the use of direct and indirect coercion and violence. A special economy of human effort is created, aimed at the suppression of all activities not consistent with the principal goal and the destruction of all sources of resistance to the process of realizing the goal. These sources may be objective, as in the case of organizations and groups promoting activities contradictory to the principal goal. But they may also be identified as subjective sources of attitudes critical of the goal itself or of the process of its realization. In the situation, typical of totalitarian society, where violence, terror, and victimization become aspects of the process of realizing the goal, all ethical stands that evaluate these practices as evil become sources (actual or potential) of resistant attitudes. Consequently, these ethical stands must be destroyed and replaced by new ethics that will promote, not resist, the universal pursuit of the goal. Successful implementation of these new ethics is supposed to lead to internalization of the regime's will by the population, and to the creation of a new, quite voluntary basis of universal participation, in an instrumental sense, by the society in the process of achieving the goal.

The principal condition of such instrumentality is that all human reactions to the messages and stimuli generated by the regime be predictable and controllable. Hannah Arendt characterizes this stage as total domination of the regime over its subjects—the ultimate human effect of totalitarianism. "Total domination," she observes, "which strives to organize the infinite plurality and differentiation of human beings as if all humanity were just one individual, is possible only if each and every person can be reduced to a never-changing identity of reactions, so that each of these bundles of reactions can be exchanged at random for any other." [12]

This model of totalitarianism provides the first, general paradigm for the Soviet experiment of redesigning society's ethical and cognitive criteria through the complementary use of terrorist and literary techniques of influence. In order to understand the significance of the official Soviet cover-ups and disclosures of the camp experience, the general features of totalitarian procedure must now be viewed in the concrete form realized in Bolshevik Russia.

From its very beginning, the Bolshevik regime was marked by inner paradox: it took power in Russia, in 1917, in order to realize a social goal defined by the same ideology that asserted the futility of attempts to realize this goal under the conditions of Russia in 1917. From the ideological point of view, the "proletarian revolution," accomplished by the Bolsheviks as the fulfillment of the Marxist ideological program, "turned into something very different from what Marx had assumed it to be. Originally thought of [by Marx] as the act of taking over the mature industrial establishment created (and mismanaged) by capitalism, it now could take over nothing but a backward economy and culture; this led to the paradoxical conclusion that the proletarian state (a 'superstructural' phenomenon) will have to begin constructing its own economic 'base.' " [13] This conclusion, of course, is paradoxical in light of the principal Marxist belief that it is the economic base that determines the social and cultural superstructure (with its institutions, ideas, categories of human perceptions, communications, and value systems) and not vice versa. This inner inconsistency of Marxism–Leninism was described succinctly by Andrei Sinyavsky. "Marxism," Sinyavsky wrote,

> materialized [in Russia] despite its own teaching that the socialist revolution would occur first in industrially developed countries where the proletariat was a majority and where the economy was ready for the transition, and despite its own fundamental premise that existence determines consciousness and thus the idea, not the other way round. In practice, [in Bolshevik Russia] the idea transforms everything, dominates everything. . . . What is remarkable is that Marxism, en route to its realization, stood itself on its head and on this head the new society was built. Henceforth, consciousness determined existence. Ideology determined policy. And policy determined the economy. The scientific Marxist utopia materialized, but wrong side up, with its feet in the air.[14]

The paradoxical task of providing the already existing ideological and political "superstructure" of the post-revolutionary "proletarian" state with its own material "base" became the practical goal of the regime, which had to be accomplished before the pursuit of the Marxist utopia of the Communist society (the principal ideological objective of the revolution) could become the immediate issue. This task of creating something that, even from the Marxist point of view, could hardly be created, determined the core of Soviet totalitarianism: it became the goal whose realization, doomed from its very beginning, was nevertheless undertaken on an experimental basis, and with ruthless determination. The result was the establishment of a totalitarian government striving to create a totalitarian society. When the Bolsheviks seized power, they expected that successful proletarian revolutions in industrialized Western countries would help the new Soviet regime in Russia to create the necessary economic base for socialism. As these expectations failed to be fulfilled, the Bolsheviks were left with a task so immense that Lenin admitted the necessity, as Merle Fainsod quotes him, of "adopting dictatorial methods to hasten the copying of Western culture" and expressed his willingness to use "barbarous methods in combatting barbarism." "Restated in non-Leninist terms," Fainsod comments, "the historic burden that the Communists assumed was that of modernizing an underdeveloped country by dictatorial and totalitarian methods." [15]

The bridging of the gap between the ideological self-image of the Bolshevik regime as the first builder of a Communist industrial utopia on earth and its real position as a minority dictatorship in an underdeveloped country determined the inner dynamics of Soviet totalitarianism. On the one hand, it led towards the escalation and institutionalization of violence as the ultimate means of ensuring the population's participation in the task of constructing the economic "base" for the existing political "superstructure" of the Bolshevik state. On the other hand, all sources of resistance (actual, potential, or just imagined by the Bolshevik leadership) to the program of the universal pursuit of this goal had to be eliminated. This meant eliminating standards of perception and evaluation of reality that were either contradictory or impossible to utilize in the process of realizing the goal. The violence practiced by the Bolsheviks under Lenin and Stalin required ethical standards that would have identified this violence as negative, to be obliterated and replaced.

The first step in the ideological rationalization of terror was its pragmatic qualification as a necessary means of protecting the regime in the conditions of civil war. On 5 September 1918, after an unsuccessful attempt on Lenin's life, the Red Terror was institutionalized by force of law. "In the present situation it is necessary to secure our positions by means of terror," the new law bluntly states. It goes further than pragmatic necessity, however, when the source of the threat to the regime is specified. "It is necessary to defend the security of the Soviet republic by isolating its class enemies in the concentration camps," the decree goes on; "all persons involved in the White Guard organizations, conspiracies, and rebellions are to be shot."[16] The decree institutes punishment for two categories of people: the actual political opponents of the Bolshevik regime (who are to be physically eliminated) and those who have not committed any acts against the regime but can be defined according to Marxist ideological categories as members of social classes that, by definition, stand in the way of the proletarian revolution (who are to be confined in concentration camps).

The introduction of this second category of villains, defined as "class enemies" or "enemies of the people" and punishable by law, placed the Bolshevik approach to justice within the tradition of the "revolutionary justice" championed by the French Revolution. Clearly, the French revolutionary terror served as a direct model for the Red Terror. For instance, the very label of "enemy of the people," applied by the Bolsheviks to their victims under the pretense of an objective reason for punishment, was a direct copy of the French revolutionary invention. By adopting the model of "revolutionary justice" inherited from the French Revolution, the Bolsheviks rejected the rival notion of individual responsibility for proven crimes as the sole basis for punishment. The concept of responsibility to the regime transcended the realm of action to encompass the realm of birth, social origin, type of education, professional affiliation, and so on. By adopting the notion of the "enemy of the people," or its more Marxist version, the "class enemy," both of them extremely fluid terms totally dependent on ideological speculation, the regime created a practical groundwork for the potential victimization of any individual who could be identified by one of these labels. From the very beginning of Bolshevik rule, not real facts alone, but arbitrary ideological interpretation and verbal labels, became the basis of life-and-death decisions. Martin Latsis, deputy chief of the Bolshevik political police (Cheka) spelled it out in November 1918: "Do not look in materials you have gathered for evidence that a suspect acted or spoke against the Soviet authorities. The first question you should ask him is what class he belongs to, what is his origin, education, profession. These questions should determine his fate. This is the essence of the Red Terror." [17]

Originally, Lenin presented this self-endowed license of the Bolsheviks to exterminate and terrorize without proven guilt as a temporary and extraordinary measure, applicable only to a wartime situation. In 1918 he declared: "The dictatorship presupposes a state of contained war." In early 1920, he explained: "The use of violence is demanded by the task of eliminating the exploiters, of eliminating the landowners and capitalists; when this is done we will rescind all extraordinary measures." A year later, when the civil war ended with a Bolshevik victory and the enemy classes no longer existed in a socioeconomic sense, Lenin deferred indefinitely the date of rejecting violence as a method of governing: "The dictatorship is a state of exacerbated war. . . . So long as there is no definitive global result, this state of horrible war will continue. And we say: 'In war we act in a warlike way: we do not promise any freedom or democracy.'" [18] And since this "global result" was never achieved and the very existence of the foreign bourgeoisie never ceased to present a threat to the "homeland of the proletariat," Lenin's argument remained forever useful in justifying the regime's right to resort to "extraordinary" and "warlike" use of power.[19]

This self-perception of the Bolshevik regime as a besieged city provided a principal motive for the rationalization of violence and terror at various stages of the regime's history. As far as reality was concerned, the regime lost much in the way of objective grounds for seeing itself under direct threat of counterrevolutionary forces with the end of the civil war in 1921. All the same, this perception served well as a cover for another essential reason for maintaining the terror: namely, the management of the economy and the future construction of the material "base" for the Marxist–Leninist utopia. Violence and terror were not only the means of instituting the Bolshevik regime. Governing the country and realizing the ideological goals required human sacrifices as well. The Bolsheviks faced the reality of the economic collapse of Russia after the civil war, along with very little public enthusiasm for their economic program. Coercion and violence remained indispensable means of enforcing popular commitment to the chief goal of the Bolshevik state—the supervised construction of an economic "base" for socialism. Lenin admitted the point as early as 1918, in a conversation with Raymond Robins: "I will force to work at sufficient speed the number of people sufficient to produce whatever Russia needs."[20] And in the first draft of the regulation introducing compulsory labor in Russia, Lenin was even more specific: "Compulsory labor should be first imposed on the rich. . . . From compulsory labor of the rich, the Soviet authorities should move to applying the appropriate principles to the majority of employees, workers, and peasants."[21] In the context of the actual need of the regime for slave labor, everyone, in fact, was proven equal before the law. The proletariat, which in truth did not show sufficient enthusiasm for the construction of the utopia realized in its name, was to be forced to build this utopia anyway, if not for itself then for the sake of proving its own self-proclaimed "avant-garde" right.

With the exception of the ambiguous New Economic Policy (NEP) in the 1920s, when, after the disastrous period of War Communism, limited private initiative was allowed in the Soviet economy, the Soviet state under Lenin and Stalin failed to create an economic system in which slave labor and terrorist coercion did not play an important role.[22] By ending the NEP and enforcing the complete collectivization of farmland, the regime proved that it was determined to choose terror as a means of reaching its goals rather than compromise its own ideology and claim to power. In the early 1930s, the brutal collectivization of farmland, besides starving several million people to death, filled Soviet prisons, camps, and places of confined settlement with large numbers of dispossessed peasants punished for either protecting their property or simply not demonstrating sufficient cooperation in the process of their own dispossession. This "human material" was used in already existing small-scale labor camps— especially in the timber industry, which generated a vital Soviet export to the West and brought back hard currency in return. The overwhelming numbers in the custody of the police exceeded the needs of the existing slave labor system. In the face of these developments, a new, bold expansion of this system took place. Slave labor became a vital element in the development of the economic base of the Communist state. Prisoners were used in massive construction projects conducted under especially harsh conditions and without sufficient equipment or funding. By sending prisoners to these projects, the Soviet leadership could compensate for the lack of technology. Human lives were much less expensive than machines.

The practical need for regular replenishment of the slave labor pool was to be resolved by concentration camps run by the political police. Originally a means of isolating "class enemies," the institution of the concentration camp was soon transformed into a vital element in the system of coercion in the Soviet economy. The idea of turning concentration camps into slave labor camps was not a novelty in the 1930s. It was suggested by Felix Dzerzhinsky at the eighth session of the All Russian Central Executive Committee in 1919. Dzerzhinsky said: "I suggest that we keep the concentration camps in order to use the prisoners' labor. They will be populated by those gentlemen who live without employment and those who cannot work without being forced. . . . Let us create the schools of labor." [23] Thus the first pool of slave labor was to consist of "class enemies" and criminals who, unworthy of living in the proletarian utopia, were to be given a chance to redeem themselves in these "schools of labor." But as we have seen, identifying a "class enemy" as a member of the "enemy classes"—a landowner, a priest, a merchant, and so on—involved too narrow a yardstick, as a practical matter, to satisfy the constant need of the Bolshevik economy for a massive pool of slave labor in the 1930s. It was also too narrow and well-defined a strategy to provide a real element of threat for the entire population in order to force its participation in the effort to build the economic potential of the state. Concentration camps were intended to fulfill a dual economic function: to provide the regime with a massive pool of slave labor that could be utilized directly and, at the same time, to represent a threat to the entire population outside the camps and prisons. This latter function became a key disciplinary factor in maintaining Stalin's centralized economy. In order to subject the whole population to the system of concentration camps (either directly or by threat), the regime was in need of an ideological basis for punishment more flexible than that projected by a literal understanding of the "class enemy" label.

Mind Games

From the beginning of his political career, faced with the problem of how to represent the "proletariat" without asking for its approval, Lenin managed to make the category of "class enemy" hazy enough to manipulate according to political interests at any given moment. First of all, the definition of the "true proletarian" (the only type of human being who did not threaten the Bolshevik regime and, thus, was not subject to punishment) became a *tour de force* of rhetorical manipulation. A Soviet historian writes: "For V. I. Lenin workers were only those people who genuinely, through their life experience, internalized proletarian psychology." [24] Needless to say, the definition of "proletarian psychology" constituted secret knowledge, accessible only to the Bolshevik leadership. *"Proletarian psychology,* proletarian *class strength,"* Mikhail Heller commented on Lenin's rhetorical manipulation, "appears as some mystical, maybe magical, quality, something like the *state of grace."* [25] Only those endowed with the grace of "proletarian psychology" could be sure about their own class purity and, consequently, about their own innocence. The only judge capable of determining this state of grace was the Bolshevik leadership—the source of the grace itself. Thus, the key category of "class belonging," which defined who was to be condemned and who saved, and which replaced traditional ethical notions of guilt and innocence, was subject to total utilitarian control by the regime.

But even the "state of grace" conferred by the Bolshevik regime was not permanent. "By becoming the leaders of the poor, workers have not automatically become saints," Lenin argued; "they led the people forward but, at the same time, they frequently were infected with the diseases of the decaying bourgeoisie."[26] And in a different place he warned: "The proletariat is not free from the vices and weaknesses of the capitalistic society. The proletariat fights for socialism, and at the same time it fights against its own shortcomings."[27] The Bolshevik regime saw its role not only in securing the hegemony of the proletariat in an industrialist utopia built in an underdeveloped country, but also in purifying the existing proletariat and turning it into a "true proletariat." Only the regime itself was to enjoy the privileges of a "true proletarian" under the system of the "dictatorship of the proletariat." In other words, each individual was an actual or potential "class enemy." An individual did not have to be aware of his or her "crime" in order to become a "class enemy." Andrei Sinyavsky wrote:

> For Lenin, all opposition to Bolshevism, to his power, or to his point of view was an expression of bourgeois class or political interests. As a Marxist, Lenin did not recognize any individual ideology: everything was an expression of someone's class interests. Therefore, he lumped all his political opponents in the bourgeois camp which, he said, was bent on crushing the Bolshevik party and then Soviet power. Lenin salted all his articles and speeches with terms like "agents of the bourgeoisie," "agents of international imperialism," "social traitors," "traitors to the working class," and so on. A person's subjective honesty, his sense that he was neither bourgeois agent nor traitor, changed nothing in Lenin's view. Because what a person thinks of himself is not important, rather it's whose positions he expresses *objectively,* involuntarily. History's only laws are objective laws of class struggle.[28]

Thus, the definition of "class enemy" included everyone who was so named by the authorities, regardless of his thoughts, actions, and intentions.

This process of the institutionalization and rationalization of Bolshevik abuses of power shows how reality was subjected to the dynamics of rhetoric. The totalitarian universe that the Bolsheviks strove to create incarnated principles of consistency characteristic of the world of rhetoric, not of material reality. This practice, started by Lenin, reached its peak under Stalin. For Lenin an "agent of the bourgeoisie" meant someone who, perhaps involuntarily and without being aware of it, stands in the way of the Bolsheviks—enough to be punished.[29] As Sinyavsky observes, Lenin accused people of being "agents of the bourgeoisie" in a metaphorical sense. He did not think, for instance, that Mensheviks were literally paid by the world bourgeoisie to act on its behalf. They were "agents of the bourgeoisie" in the "objective" sense. Stalin, however, took these metaphors of Lenin's quite literally: for him an "agent of the bourgeoisie" meant an actual spy. "In this sense," Sinyavsky concludes, "the trials and executions of the thirties were nothing other than literal translations of Leninist metaphors. On Stalin's orders, the Soviet Chekists and investigators began torturing people arrested as agents of the Japanese, the Germans, or the English. The metaphor was taken to its real-life conclusion."[30]

For an individual, the experience of life in this world of confusion between verbal and material dimensions had far-reaching consequences, not only material but intellectual and psychological. In the ethical universe of the Bolshevik regime, where the proletariat struggles against its enemy classes, an individual is generally incapable of recognizing his "objective" position between the two poles of the struggle. He cannot be fully aware whose class interests he "objectively" represents at a given moment. The metaphysical "class

enemy" (defined by such abstract nouns as "world bourgeoisie") threatens the proletarian state not only from abroad
(Japan, Germany, England, and elsewhere) but also from
within, in the form of deficiencies in one's "proletarian psychology" or as an infection by "bourgeois microbes." The
only authoritative evaluation of the "objective" meaning of
one's actions is that provided by the authorities. So, for an individual, becoming an "enemy of the people" is always a potential fate. One does not choose it, and one is incapable of
either denying or overcoming it. The recognition of this fate
usually takes place precisely at the moment of hearing the
conviction. This fate means elimination from life, as the "class
enemy" has no place in the new, proletarian universe. The
elimination can take one of two forms: total damnation (and
sometimes execution) or a chance of redemption in the
"school of labor"—a concentration camp. In a society where
the "true" or "objective" identities of people are known only
to the authorities, not even to the people themselves, such a
prospect can become anyone's fate at any time. This unpredictability and insecurity of life was, according to Spiro, one
of the key features of the experience of totalitarianism:

> Unpredictability and uncertainty was the rule of life for
> ordinary men and for both high and low members of
> the dominant party under Hitler and Stalin. . . . Uncer-
> tainty meant, among other things, that the victims of
> liquidation might not know the reasons for their fate
> and, more important, that those who wanted to avoid
> liquidation in the future had no rational means for
> doing so. They could escape from the dilemmas of un-
> certainty neither by withdrawing from politics nor by
> mouthing the current party line, because that would
> expose them to condemnation for merely mechanical

commitment. Repeated executions of chiefs of the secret police can serve as a paradigm for this process.[31]

Given these elements of uncertainty, threat, and coercion,
life under totalitarianism was a life in which anyone could be
labeled and re-labeled as anyone else on a purely verbal basis
and then suffer the material consequences of these verbal op-
erations. Such a universe, where principles of common sense
do not function as a basis for relative predictability, and in
which objects and people are not unconditionally identical
with themselves, is normally represented in dreams and
nightmares rather than in everyday experience. A world in
which people's identities change according to some obscure
verdicts that imply severe punishment for crimes they never
committed and thoughts they never entertained clearly resembles a nightmare universe. If there is one thing common
to many varieties of nightmares, it is the overwhelming urge
to escape to a world of some consistency and clarity. This
urge of the human mind for consistency greater than that
provided by direct experience was characterized by Hannah
Arendt as a key psychological response invoked by totalitarianism. In 1951 she wrote:

> while it is true that the masses are obsessed by a desire
> to escape from reality because in their essential home-
> lessness they can no longer bear its accidental, incom-
> prehensible aspects, it is also true that their longing for
> fiction has some connection with those capacities of
> the human mind whose structural consistency is supe-
> rior to mere occurrence. The masses' escape from reality
> is a verdict against the world in which they are forced
> to live and in which they cannot exist, since coinci-
> dence has become its supreme master and human be-
> ings need constant transformation of chaotic and

accidental conditions into man-made patterns of relative consistency.[32]

In this light, the essence of the Soviet totalitarian experiment, defined by Aleksander Wat as an attempt to impose upon the human mind the duality between "a coherent set of grandiloquent terms and the opposing monstrous reality . . . kept side by side, ostentatiously and with diabolical thoroughness and perseverance,"[33] can be seen as psychological manipulation on a massive scale. In this respect, the Soviet experiment of mind control can be described as an attempt to provide the population with a mental path of escape from the frightening reality, which leads into a trap of mental dependence on the authorities. While creating a reality dominated by unpredictability and insecurity (the environment from which the human mind strives to escape in search of "man-made patterns of relative consistency"), the Bolsheviks introduced a verbal equivalent of this reality, but one entirely different from the reality itself: if reality was experienced as a chaotic, dangerous world of inconsistency and unpredictability, the supposed verbal equivalent of the same reality appeared as a highly organized cosmos, characterized by unbending consistency. Having imposed on society the reality of victimization and insecurity, the Bolsheviks strove to fuel "those capacities of the human mind whose structural consistency is superior to mere occurrence" and that long for consistent fiction instead of chaotic and accidental reality. At the same time, they took upon themselves the task of providing the population with this fiction: they "conjured up a lying world of consistency which [was] more adequate to the needs of the human mind than reality itself."[34] Thus, for the human mind, unsettled by the experience of the totalitarian reality, a remedy was offered: this reality should be approached as a reflection of the Bolshevik verbal universe of "man-made patterns of consistency."

The Order of All Things

The verbal universe designed by the Bolsheviks as the mental antidote to the horrors and dangers of reality was to become the cognitive filter through which reality was to be perceived and evaluated. As such, it retained a certain dependence on two factors: the doctrinal and the pragmatic. The doctrinal factor consisted in using the language of Marxism as the lexicon whereby reality was defined. At the same time, the verbal universe of the Bolsheviks in its pragmatic role projected perceptual, ethical, and even aesthetic terms of human interaction with reality intended to preclude any resistance to, or lack of cooperation with the totalitarian project. In this way, "the interpretation of Marxism–Leninism–Stalinism [was kept] in a condition of continuous flux controlled only by [the ruler] himself." [35] Only those elements of the original ideology that were amenable to the pragmatic priorities of the current verbal interpretation of reality by the regime were admitted as formative elements of the verbal equivalent of that reality. These combinations of ideological and pragmatic factors changed at different historical stages, and will be analyzed later.

Notwithstanding the changing interrelationships of specific ideological and pragmatic priorities, conditioned by changing political, ideological, and formal contexts, a general principle of the Bolshevik verbal refraction of reality can be identified as a principle of *teleology,* or goal orientation. Teleology, the key characteristic of the Marxist utopia and, at the same time, the principal ideological ground for totalitarian violence, became the link between the ideological and pragmatic factors that combined in creating the Bolshevik verbal universe. Because of its teleological nature, the most characteristic feature of this universe is its apparent inner wholeness and completeness: the purpose of existence of each object within the Bolshevik verbal universe is determined by this object's relevance to the ultimate goal. Because the goal of history is Communism, everything that exists must be seen in its relation to the task of building Communism. Reality as it is at the moment, however terrifying and unpredictable it may be, must not be seen as an end in itself, but always as a stage in the universal transformation of the world leading to the ultimate goal. In short, within the Communist vision of the world, the present is a function of the future. And it is their presumed knowledge of the laws of successful transformation of the present into the future that makes the Communist authorities' point of view definitive. This notion of the present as a function of the future has fundamental epistemological, ethical, and aesthetic implications.

To be able to perceive the present reality as a function of the Bolshevik idea of the future, one must subject one's cognitive standards to some radical adaptation. The focal point of one's cognitive perspective becomes reserved for those elements of the present experience directly relevant to the future goal. Elements whose relation to the goal cannot be determined, or whose very existence contradicts the goal, are relegated to the fringes of the cognitive range of vision. In more radical cases the refocusing of cognitive criteria reaches a point where there is a direct contradiction between the basic empirical data drawn from experience and the image of that experience projected by the teleological, authoritative point of view. The hungry collectivized peasants, after watching the film showing the happy collectivized peasants surrounded by plenty, are expected to dismiss the empirical testimony of their own stomachs and acknowledge that what they saw on the screen was the truth. This was what Stalin called "the dialectical method." What is most important to this dialectical method, Stalin proclaimed, "is not that which is stable at present but is already beginning to die, but rather that which is emerging and developing, even if at present it does not appear stable, since for the dialectical method only that which is emerging and developing cannot be overcome."[36] What is actually "emerging and developing" is known only to the authors of the "dialectical method"—namely, the Bolsheviks. The real is not what exists, but what the Bolsheviks say should soon come into existence.

Ethically, within the view of the present as a function of the future, basic moral categories become subject to the teleological, utilitarian principle. In short, "good" and "evil" are respectively definable as "contributing to the goal" and "obstructing the realization of the goal." In this respect, as in many others, the Bolsheviks proved to be particularly zealous and radical implementers of ideas with which the Western world had already, in fact, been experimenting (although usually in more cautious, or at least more covert, ways) for centuries. It should be noted that the Bolshevik concept of ethical utilitarianism was a peculiarly radical echo of the well-known Jesuit idea.[37] In the practical terms of the Soviet regime, the self-proclaimed avant-garde leading proletarian society to its destined goal, the concept of ethical utilitarianism was spelled out by Lenin in 1920: "Our morality is entirely subordinate to the interests of the class struggle of the proletariat. . . . We say that morality is what serves the destruction of the old exploitative society and the unification of all workers around the proletariat, which is creating the new society of Communists. . . . We do not believe in eternal morality."[38] This Leninist ethical view is reflected in the idiosyncratic monolog of Volodya Makarov, a character from Yuri Olesha's novel *Envy* written in 1927:

The revolution was . . . well, what? Of course, very cruel. Ho! But for the sake of what was it malicious? It was magnanimous, right? Was good—for the whole dial. . . . Right! One has to take offense not in the space between two divisions but in the whole circle of the dial. . . . Then there is no difference between cruelty and magnanimity. Then there is only one: time. The iron, as it's said, logic of history. And history and time are one and the same, doubles. . . . I say: the main feeling of man must be the understanding of time.[39]

Given the Bolshevik regime's view of itself as the sole master of time (history) and the only agency capable of charting the path to the future, the utilitarian ethical principle achieves a direct political application: "good" means useful for the regime, and "evil" means useless or contradictory to the regime's current policy.

This goal-oriented nature of the Bolshevik project has its impact on aesthetic concerns as well. Aesthetic matters are never considered apart from epistemological and ethical considerations. Aesthetics are just one more area in which the object's relation to the universal goal is articulated. This dependence of aesthetic values upon the larger teleological concerns places them, along with cognitive and moral values, in a domain controllable by the sole agency capable of defining their relevance to the future goal—that is, the regime. The question of beauty becomes the question of the role of the aesthetic object with respect to the policy of the regime. An example of the direct application of this principle was provided (once again) by Yuri Olesha. In 1936, during a well-known propaganda campaign against the music of Shostakovich, Olesha confessed at one of the writers' meetings in Moscow:

When I like some artist or other, I tend to exaggerate his merits and to forgive him for everything, as if believing he cannot be wrong. That is exactly how I felt about Shostakovich. Suddenly, I read in *Pravda* that Shostakovich's opera is "muddle instead of music." This was said in *Pravda,* the voice of the Communist Party. What should I do with my attitude towards Shostakovich? If I was delighted with Shostakovich, and *Pravda* said his opera was muddle, then either I am wrong or *Pravda* is wrong. The easiest thing of all would be to say to myself, "I am not wrong," and to reject, internally, the opinion of *Pravda.* In other words, having been left with the conviction that, in a given case, the Party is saying untrue things, I would allow the possibility that the Party is wrong. What does all of this lead to? Very serious psychological consequences.[40]

Here, Olesha represents the point of view of someone who has internalized the teleological principle as the foundation of consistency in the universe. He has to choose between contradictory testimonies of his own experience and the party's word—a choice between the subjective and uncertain world of experience and the consistent verbal world of Bolshevik teleology. The choice of consistency over experience makes sense only if the source of the consistency is infallible. And, since the aesthetic standards reflect the teleology that is the source of the Bolsheviks' exclusive infallibility in matters of epistemology and ethics, the Bolsheviks represent exclusive authority in aesthetic matters as well.

The integration of all three aspects of the human experience of the world—epistemological, ethical, and aesthetic— within the Soviet teleological model makes for a conceptual framework of quite unusual consistency. Plato's ideal triad of

Truth, Goodness, and Beauty, which continued to pose so many philosophical and artistic problems over the course of the history of Western thought, here appears reunited: the basic elements of present reality, considered by the regime as instrumental in taking society to its future goal—Communism—are by definition true, good, and beautiful.[41] This conceptual framework, as in the case of any ideology, is projected by the regime, in order to satisfy "the need for a cognitive and moral map of the universe, which . . . is a fundamental, although unequally distributed disposition of man. . . . By placing at its center cosmically and ethically fundamental propositions, [this framework] brings to those who accept it the belief that they are in possession of, and in contact with, what is ultimately right and true."[42] The particular "cognitive and moral map of the universe" projected by the Bolsheviks was, in comparison to many ideologies, additionally ambiguous, so that the "contact" of the believers "with what is ultimately right and true" could be only indirect: it had to be mediated by the party. This was the case because the nature of truth and value is not apprehensible by any individual other than one in the peculiar "state of grace" conferred on him by the regime. It is this peculiar state of inner harmony with the regime that Lenin called "proletarian psychology."[43] Thus, the verbal world of consistency projected by the totalitarian regime in Russia is a place where the human mind, unsettled by the reality of Bolshevism, is tempted to find the Bolshevik regime itself the sole source of its security.

This creation of a verbal world of consistency and its location as a cognitive and axiological filter of reality had a double function: it served as the basis for reprogramming and controlling the minds of the population and, at the same time, provided the authorities themselves with a frame of reference reflected in the programming and evaluating of their own actions.[44] Under totalitarianism, both society and the regime (especially its lower branches, which had to prove their ideological correctness to their superiors) were constantly required to translate reality into ideological terms. For this purpose they had to refer to models that literature and art were to provide. This task required radically "creative" methods, owing to the radical contradictions between life experience and the conceptual framework of Soviet ideology. The data of life experience had to be selected and filtered through the official cognitive and axiological criteria without any outright admission of the anti-empirical nature of the operation. Of many methods proposed and tested in the 1920s, it was Maxim Gorky's that finally achieved the status of the party's official artistic style, known as socialist realism. "A fact," Gorky proclaimed, "is still not the whole truth; it is merely the raw material from which the real truth of art must be smelted and extracted—the chicken must not be roasted with its feathers. This, however, is precisely what reverence for the facts results in—the accidental and inessential are mixed with the essential and typical. We must learn to pluck the fact of its inessential plumage; we must be able to extract meaning from the fact."[45]

What is "essential" and what "accidental" within the Bolshevik epistemology has already been illustrated by Stalin's definition of the "dialectical method" for extracting the truth. As for the "typical" (the other crucial attribute of Gorky's concept of truth as the object of art), it is, according to Georgy Malenkov's definition formulated at the Nineteenth Congress of the Communist Party, "not what is encountered the most often, but what most persuasively expresses the essence of a given social force. From the Marxist–Leninist standpoint, the typical does not signify some sort of statistical mean. . . . The typical is the vital sphere in which is manifested the party spirit of realistic art. The question of the typical is always a political question."[46] Thus, as Boris Groys puts it, for a true Soviet artist or writer

> the portrayal of the typical refers to the visual realization of still-emerging party objectives, the ability to intuit new currents among the party leadership, to sense which way the wind is blowing. . . . Thus what is subject to artistic mimesis is not external, visible reality, but the inner reality of the inner life of the artist, who possesses the ability to identify and fuse with the will of the party and Stalin and out of this inner fusion generates an image, or rather a model, of the reality that this will is striving to shape. . . . The mimesis of socialist realism is the mimesis of Stalin's will, the artists' emulation of Stalin, the surrender of their artistic egos in exchange for the collective efficacy of the project in which they participate. The "typical" of socialist realism is Stalin's dream made visible, a reflection of his imagination.[47]

To deny the value of empirical data, however, in favor of ideological consistency (or the narrative consistency of Stalin's dreams) in the realm of philosophical debates and artistic experiments is an entirely different matter from disregarding such empirical data as blood, hunger, and pain, key elements of the totalitarian experience in its most complete form—the concentration camp. In the general context of "extracting meaning from the facts," providing a model for the replacement of the experience of totalitarian victimization at its worst—the experience of the concentration camp—with an ideological equivalent was the greatest challenge of all for Stalinist literature.

The World Broken into Pieces and Glued Back Together

Translating experience, individual and social, into "man-made patterns of consistency" is, by definition, what literature does, confronting the chaos of experience with the order of language. In order to be able to generate ideologically inspired refractions of reality, despite striking contradictions between reality and its official ideological interpretations, literature as a medium had to demonstrate a certain readiness, formal and philosophical, to accomplish the task. "Every ideology—however great the originality of its creators—arises in the midst of an ongoing culture," Edward Shils wrote. "However passionate its reaction against that culture, it cannot entirely divest itself of important elements of that culture. . . . There are, therefore, always marked substantive affinities between the moral and cognitive orientations of any particular ideology and those of the outlooks and creeds which prevail in the environing society and which affirm or accept the central institutional and value systems." [48] For Russian literature, creating verbal strategies for replacing the concentration camp experience with its ideological image meant, on the one hand, selectively adapting already existing strategies and thematic focal points by reworking them according to the new principles of consistency governing the Bolshevik refraction of reality. On the other hand, writers involved in this literary experiment had to relate to some cultural and philosophical climate, represented in Russian literary tradition, favorable to the task of the ideological refraction of experience according to the Bolshevik recipe.

The task of implementing the Bolshevik refraction of reality in literature required, first and foremost, the readiness of this medium to accept the very core of the Bolshevik world view—the monolithic, authoritarian vision of the universe.

This meant either denying or challenging the dominant direction in the evolution of the vision of the universe inherent in modern literature. If the cognitive, ethical, and aesthetic aspects of the Bolshevik vision were bound to violate existing ways in which reality was perceived at the level of particular human experience, the monolithic nature of the universe projected in that vision likewise contradicted the perception of the universe represented in modern literature, both in its direct statements and in the evolution of modern literary forms. For the vision of the universe projected in evolving modern literary forms was anything but the integrated, sensible whole conceived in the mind of the ideologue-ruler (Bolshevik or otherwise) who dreams about the radiant future and pronounces his vision in a monolog to be repeated by everyone.

To illustrate the new awareness of the universe projected by modern literature, an awareness contradictory to the basic premises of the Bolshevik world view, a passage from Konstantin Fedin's novel *Cities and Years* (1924) can be usefully glossed by some general remarks by Jurij Striedter on post–World War I developments in the novel. Fedin's two protagonists, Andrei Startsov and Kurt Wahn, meet in Moscow in 1918. Wahn, a German artist and currently a Soviet revolutionary, relates to Startsov his experiences of World War I and the revolution:

> If I had sat out this time somewhere in a workshop, perhaps the world would seem something whole to me, as it did before, as we said and understood before—humanity, the world, looking from above. But I sat below, under the floor, I saw how everything was arranged. In short, it's a theater. Nothing is whole. Humanity—is a fiction. . . .

Before, everything was complete, like a company on the march. Man was fitted to man like board to board in a door. Now everything has disintegrated. There are cracks between the boards. Even a blind man can see that everything's fallen apart. . . .

Once I thought that novels are written the way boxes are made. Every board must fit the other boards on all sides. That, at least, is how novels were written before the war. Now, it's probably impossible in a novel, too, to bring more than two people together at a time. The glue is no good, it doesn't hold.

That's my story and those are my conclusions. The boards that still hold must be separated, perhaps smashed, because they are glued together artificially and because people can't be glued together into humanity with that kind of glue. But that, after all, is our aim.[49]

Wahn's monolog about the new perception of the universe and its presentability in the novel could have been echoed by "many of the protagonists, novelists and critics of Kurt Wahn's generation," Jurij Striedter comments:

In this framework, the novel, more than any other genre, is supposed to mirror "the world" in regard to a given society. The emphasis, however, is on the point of view (from where this world is viewed) and on the *structural* analogy between the novel and the world it represents. Such an analogy implies that any kind of fiction—even a novel containing pronounced social criticism—committed to the artistic ideal of formal completeness or wholeness, implies a belief in a whole, or complete world—a belief unmasked by world war and revolution as a mere fiction. . . . Hence, what is proclaimed or deplored as "the crisis of the novel" (a complaint almost as old as the genre itself, but nevertheless particularly characteristic of the period under consideration) can really be regarded as a reflection of a general political, social and cultural crisis.[50]

Kurt Wahn's discovery that the world can no longer be represented in one all-encompassing, integrated vision ("looking from above") is not so much a reflection of some sudden disintegration of the universe itself, or of human perceptive and evaluative capacities, as it is an acknowledgment of the collapse of the "utopian pretension" that "*one* voice can represent reality as univocal, noncontroversial world."[51] "The unmasking of such pretensions of the 'novelistic *word*,'" Striedter comments, "can shift into the unmasking of those corresponding utopian pretensions in the surrounding social and political reality which claim to represent the only valid, univocal world."[52] In short, the evolution of literary forms (the novel is especially representative because of its structural analogies to the world it presents) indicates a significant evolution in the very perception of the structure of the world presentable in literature. The crisis of the novel is a crisis of authority. With the absence of one acknowledged, authoritative presentation of the universe, each point of view, being questionable and relative, becomes an object of potential irony: the greater its claim to authority, the larger the gap between its pretension to exclusivity and its inevitable subjectivity and relativity. Consequently, the rhetorical universe implied by the direction of the structural evolution of the modern novel is entirely opposite to the rhetorical universe inherent in the Bolshevik world view.

The perception, characteristic of the modern novel, that, as Fedin's protagonist puts it, "nothing is whole" and "the glue . . . doesn't hold" can lead in two opposite directions. At one end of the spectrum stands the author, who accepts the novel's fragmented universe of many subjective truths as an adequate representation of the actual state of humanity.[53] At the other end is the author who views this fragmentation as a temporary anomaly, an illness in need of a cure. In the eyes of the former, the "crisis of the novel" is not a crisis at all, but rather an opportunity to reinvigorate the genre. Having abandoned its utopian pretensions to authority, the novel now proves to be more in tune with its own generic nature. For, as Gary Saul Morson notes, in the novel, as opposed to the utopian narrative, "each truth is *someone's* truth, qualified by what might be called an 'irony of origins'—that is, by our knowledge that it reflects a particular person's (or character's) experience and a given set of personal and contextual circumstances. They are consequently understood to be *partial*—that is, both limited and biased—even if we (or the author) are inclined to share that partiality."[54] The novel, whether formally univocal or polyphonic, always testifies to the polyphonic nature of the universe. As Striedter points out, the "polyphonic" type of novel

> reflects, in its own structure, the polyphony of the cultural and social context. It organizes its own controversial voices and views into an intrinsic dialogue, which is also a dialogue with the respective voices and views articulated in the ongoing discourse of the given society (including its tradition). The "monophonic" or "univocal" type intends, or pretends, to represent *one* world in *one* voice. But even this type enters, explicitly or implicitly, into a dialogue with the context, with other controversial voices in the cultural discourse, referring to the same topics from other points of view, and in other verbal patterns.[55]

Thus, at the time when the "crisis of the novel" (which we understand as a crisis of authority) was emerging, the new, more adequate mode of implementing the structural analogy between the novel and reality was found to lie in the polyphonic type of novel. In the domain of social and political reality, unmasking the utopian pretensions of authoritarianism meant admitting pluralism as the only adequate expression of an intrinsically controversial world in which many points of view were in dialog. If we look at this problem in the context of Bolshevik Russia, pluralism and polyphony, sociopolitical and, in consequence, literary, constituted precisely the perspective that the Bolsheviks struggled to rule out of their world. Hence, the interpretation of the pluralistic fragmentation of the world as this world's natural condition was a way of thinking not allowed in the context of providing the Bolshevik regime with an ideological refraction of reality.

What proved more useful for the Bolshevik regime was an alternative interpretation of the world's fragmentary condition. According to this interpretation, the dialogical state of the universe was perceived as a temporary crisis in need of remedy. This general view was formulated in numerous intellectual and artistic statements and was popularized in many clichés in the context of the *fin de siècle* and the revolution. Aleksandr Blok's remarks in his essay "The Collapse of Humanism" exemplify the timbre and atmosphere of these formulations. Generalizing about the European culture of humanism and its crisis, Blok defines the essence of that crisis as "division amidst a general striving for unity." "The fundamental feature of contemporary society is its scattered quality, its lack of any stable unity," Blok explains; "in all layers of society we observe an uncommon anxiety, a kind of morbid unrest and a searching for something." In another passage Blok comments:

The variety of phenomena of Western European life in the nineteenth century cannot hide from the historian of culture, but, on the contrary, underlines for him the special feature of all European civilization: its lack of unity, its fragmentation. . . . We observe the same phenomenon of fragmentation, while vain efforts go on to restore the lost wholeness, in all fields. . . . In its attempt to enrich the world, civilization overloaded it. The building of civilization is often compared to the building of the tower of Babel. . . . All was multiplicity, disunity, and the cement necessary to unify was lacking. "The feeling of discontent with oneself and with one's surroundings leads to *exhaustion,*" as the historian declared. "We have the right to use Pascal's words in speaking of ourselves: man flees from himself. This is the illness of our age, and its symptoms are very obvious to every thinking individual as the physical premonition of a coming storm."[56]

Under the premise exemplified by Blok's remarks, acknowledgment of the fragmentary and pluralistic condition of the universe was tantamount to acknowledging the collapse of the European, humanistic principles that, earlier, had generated a more unified, coherent world view. A need for reintegration based upon some new, more adequate unifying principles had now emerged. The very core of the old civilization—individualism—is described by Blok as the main source of the chaotic disintegration (philosophical and social) of the universe of that civilization into many subjective, isolated universes. Kurt Wahn, who discovered that the "glue" of the traditional value systems that had established the prospect of an integrated universe "doesn't hold" anymore, concluded that "the boards that still hold must be separated, perhaps smashed, because they are glued together artificially and because people can't be glued together into humanity with that kind of glue."[57] Blok speaks of a premonition of the upcoming storm. In both cases, the state of polyphony is acknowledged as a condition of growing chaos that the universe cannot tolerate. The crisis, the climax of the process of disintegration, leads to a resolution that can be either catastrophe or a new integration. The "artificial" (that is, the old) integration must be replaced by the "true" (the new) integration. In both the social and the literary universes the challenge of the new integration requires finding new cognitive and axiological principles to define the new authoritative, final vantage point from which the universe can appear once again as a whole. At the moment of crisis, the universe of both the ideologue and the author stands in need of a new consistency and a new authority.

Bolshevism, with its all-encompassing teleology and claim to exclusivity, offered (to those unsettled by the vision of the dialogical world) a potential substitute for both the consistency and the authority necessary for the reintegration of the universe in a political as well as literary sense. The point of view from which reality could be perceived in its totality, as a coherent whole, was the point of view of the Bolshevik regime. The writer ready to undertake the task of reintegrating the universe according to the Bolshevik gospel had to forsake the concept of individual authorship involving a subjective representation couched in the language of a particular experience of reality and join in a more ultimate sort of authorship, entailing the objective, finalizing view of reality generated by the regime. If this operation required choosing between the data of life experience and an ideological view contradictory to that experience, ideology had to be given priority over experience. In other words, literature had to express "those capacities of the human mind whose structural consistency is superior to mere occurrence."[58] In the case of aspects of reality so appalling as the totalitarian concentration camps, the kind of consistency needed most was moral consistency. And to find a moral consistency such that concentration camps would assume positive significance required internalizing the Bolshevik point of view from which the existing, present experience could be addressed as a function of the future envisioned in the ideology.

Tyranny and Authorship

Since the universe of the novel (in which "each truth is *someone's* truth," both limited and partial) is incompatible with the Bolshevik universe of one absolute truth represented in the ideology, the literary genre naturally suited to accommodate the structure of the Bolshevik universe was not the novel but—quite obviously—the literary utopia. In utopias, in contrast to novels, the social observations of the authors—or delineators, to use Gary Saul Morson's term— "are designed not to portray the complex psychological ambiguities of a personal opinion, but rather to exploit the dramatic power of a truth revealed." While "novels are . . . well suited to convey a skeptical or ironic point of view, utopias, by contrast, are used to make the sort of categorical claims about ethics, values, and knowledge that novels do not admit."[59]

What the utopia shares with the novel is the common element of fictionality. The fictionality of the utopia, however, is employed in pursuit of a goal quite different from that of the novel. The main purpose of the utopia is to commit the reader to an ideological project of transforming the real society to which the reader belongs, according to a blueprint provided by the author. Fictionality becomes a device aimed at achieving a goal identified as extra-literary. What the author of a literary utopia tries to achieve through his use of the conventions of fiction is a classical artistic seduction of the reader's imagination. Having, as Gary Saul Morson puts it, "traded metaphysics for genre and principles for conventions," the author induces the reader to follow his lead to a point that Plato warned against in addressing the subject of the theater in his *Republic*. This is the point, Morson explains, when "actors and audiences may become 'infected with the reality' . . . that the dramatic fiction represents, and so reverse mimesis." "Utopia's aim," Morson comments, "is just such an 'infection' of its audience with the 'reality' of its fiction. In this particular sense, the genre is magical, seeking to make the representation of a nonexistent state of affairs the means for its realization." [60]

The author of a literary utopia may feel in possession of the definitive remedy for curing all the problems of humanity, but in the world, where he does not have the absolute political power necessary to apply this remedy, he must usually focus on converting others to his project. Hence he must depend on the seductive powers of his fiction in the hopes of winning his readers' assent. More often than not, in searching for a means to attract and command the reader's attention, he chooses to turn to the arsenal of novelistic conventions. He uses these conventions in order to compromise the very world implied by the novel as a genre: the world of many personal truths. It is on the ruins of this world that the authoritarian world of utopia can be established.

The most influential literary utopia in pre-revolutionary Russia, Nikolai Chernyshevsky's *What Is to Be Done?*, was particularly keen to use novelistic conventions in its struggle against the pluralistic world represented by the novel. "Like so many Russian nihilists, Chernyshevsky saw the novel as a doomed Babylon's last flower, exquisite in its unnecessary luxury and fascinating in its distracting design," Morson observes.

The duplicitous strategy of his work is to encourage the readers' fascination with novelistic plots and themes, and then to reproach them for that very fascination. . . . Like most utopian writers, Chernyshevsky divides his readers into two groups, a larger one whom he "reviles" and a smaller one whom he flatters. In Chernyshevsky's case, this division probably derives not only from earlier utopias, but also from apocalyptic writing—a tradition on which utopias frequently draw for both millenarian imagery and prophetic rhetoric. In both utopias and apocalypses, the explicit division of the audience functions as a provocation to choose one side or the other. The logic of both traditions is that of the excluded middle: there can be no innocent bystanders at the apocalypse, no disinterested contemplators of the revolution.[61]

The author of *What Is to Be Done?* resembles (though only superficially) the author of the biblical Book of Revelation, in that he too appears to be in possession of the ultimate revelation of history's final destiny. The source of the truth revealed in *What Is to Be Done?* is a socialist ideology that projects the futuristic vision of a happy collectivist society as both an optimistic and inevitable resolution of history. The road to the realization of this vision leads, typically enough, through the abolition of private property, the source of all evil. In the absence of God, the socialist destiny, according to Chernyshevsky (quite unlike the sacred destiny envisioned by St. John), must, in order to be realized, be enacted by its subjects themselves. The speed of this process is highly dependent on the enlightening power of the literary utopia itself. The enlightened ("infected") reader who accepts the revelation is supposed to respond—not only in words but also in action—to the question: What is to be done? Thus, the borderline between fiction and reality must be crossed, leading to the realization of the utopia in real life.

Yet, not withstanding its fervor for transforming historical reality, *What Is to Be Done?*, along with other literary utopias, was *just* a work of literature—a voice among other voices within the broader public discourse. In the rhetorical situation of relative pluralism (the presence of different coexistent views) characterizing cultural discourse in nineteenth-century Russia, the success of a literary utopia depended on the verbal effectiveness of its vision as measured against other visions functioning in the cultural discourse. Whereas the universe projected by Chernyshevsky's utopia assumed the existence of only one, exclusive, unmistakable point of view, in the pluralistic rhetorical situation into which the utopia entered, this authorial claim to the ultimate knowledge could be only proposed to—not imposed on—the audience.

The most famous example of Chernyshevsky's implied reader was one who actually lived, Lenin. The fact that the chief designer and strategist of Bolshevism read *What Is to Be Done?* as a political instruction to be acted out in reality is of more than anecdotal significance.[62] As if following the model of the author represented in Chernyshevsky's utopia, Lenin put himself in the position of an author of sorts, whose point of view—based on supreme knowledge of a deterministic and "scientific" ideology—transcends human limitations and makes him both fully objective and morally right. But Lenin's way of erasing the line separating the verbal from the material universe was much bolder than that of his favorite writer. He decided to overcome the limitations of literature and to exercise the authorial claim to omniscience and ethical infallibility in both verbal and material universes *at the same time.* Bolshevik totalitarianism, realized in its mature form through the institution of the concentration camp, can thus be seen as an attempt to create a totally univocal rhetorical situation in which the expression of the Bolshevik vision of the universe would not be challenged by any other point of view. If the author of *What Is to Be Done?* had to rely on his literary skills in hopes of seducing the reader's imagination away from other, competing visions, the author of the Soviet utopia in power freed himself from this constraint by simply attempting to eliminate all potentially competitive points of view, physically coercing his population-audience to subscribe to the only vision remaining—his own. So, in the history of utopias, literary seduction was replaced by rape at gunpoint.

Thus, whereas the author of the traditional literary utopia was an artist of the word who shaped and reshaped his verbal universe in hopes of influencing his reader, the Bolshevik regime became the ultimate artist whose material was the universe of words along with the real universe inhabited by the addressees of these words. The Bolshevik design invoked total "artistic" freedom of the regime in its efforts to transform the chaos of the old life into the Communist cosmos. This new cosmos was to include all human ideas and activities, harmonized according to the all-encompassing design. In the process of accomplishing this transformation, the regime (the supreme artist) had to overcome all resistance of the "human material" and make it perfectly malleable so that it can assume the desired shape. Boris Groys who, in his book *The Total Art of Stalinism,* described Soviet totalitarianism in terms of an artistic experiment, argued that what enabled the Bolsheviks to champion such an experiment was, first and foremost, their profound axiological relativism.[63] Only their belief that each thing and each value that people deem stable, everlasting, and unchangeable can in fact be reshaped and transformed gave them faith that their experiment would succeed. Moreover, the position of the artist in full control of his material, once assumed by the Bolsheviks, made them immune to criticism. "Since critics occupy only a particular position in society," Groys writes,

> they do not have the overarching view of the whole that only power can provide. Their criticism, therefore, can only arise from remnants of the old social order in their thought or from one-sided views incapable of grasping the artistic whole of the new world. Here the perspective of power and aesthetic distance coincide. If, as Nietzsche assumed, the world as it is can only be justified aesthetically, then it is even more true that only such a justification is possible for the building of the new world.[64]

This artistic experiment was to be conducted simultaneously by the members of the monopolized creative unions and the functionaries of the police state, both under strict control of the party leadership.

The notion of art as a transformation of the existing world assumed an especially prominent position in Russian high culture in the decade preceding the establishment of the Bolshevik regime. The notion was championed most radically by avant-garde movements that associated the artistic revolution with the social revolution and almost instinctively offered their services to the newly established Bolshevik regime. Groys illuminates the crucial parallelism between the logic used by Russian avant-garde artists and Bolshevik politicians:

> Traditional artists who aspire to re-create various aspects of Nature can set themselves limited goals, since to them Nature is already a completed whole, and thus any fragment of it is also potentially complete and whole. Avant-garde artists, on the other hand, to whom the external world has become a black chaos, must cre-

ate an entirely new world, so that their artistic projects are necessarily total and boundless. To realize this project, therefore, artists must have absolute power over the world—above all total political power that will allow them to enlist all humanity or at least the population of a single country in this task. To avant-gardists, reality itself is material for artistic construction, and they therefore naturally demand the same absolute right to dispose of this real material as in the use of materials to realize their artistic intent in a painting, sculpture, or poem. Since the world itself is regarded as material, the demand underlying the modern conception of art for power over the materials simply contains the demand for power over the world. This power does not recognize any limitations and cannot be challenged by any other, nonartistic authority, since humanity and all human thought, science, traditions, institutions, and so on are declared to be subconsciously (or, to put it differently, materially) determined and therefore subject to restructuring according to a unitary artistic plan. By its own internal logic, the artistic project becomes aesthetico-political. Because there are many artists and projects and only one can be realized, a choice must be made: this decision is in turn not merely artistic but political, since the entire organization of social life is dependent upon it.[65]

The fact that the avant-garde itself became a victim of the Soviet cultural policy of the 1930s, which favored socialist realism, should not obscure the fact that in suppressing the avant-garde the Soviet regime followed the avant-garde's own logic. "If the principal characteristic of totalitarianism is that it proclaims its ideological doctrine as both uniquely true and universally obligatory," Igor Golomstock comments in *Totali-tarian Art,* "then it is the artistic avant-garde of the 1910s and 1920s who first elaborated a totalitarian ideology of cul-ture."[66] Since the primary goal of avant-garde art is the trans-formation of the world in the direction envisioned by a particular artist or movement, then any other attempt by a dif-ferent artist or movement must be contradictory to the for-mer inasmuch as the two visions of the future are different. Therefore all competition must be discredited as not truly progressive. Following a similar logic, Lenin discredited all his political opponents as perhaps unintentional and unaware but nevertheless counterrevolutionaries and reactionaries. Stalin adopted this way of thinking in regard to avant-garde artists themselves, among others. The avant-garde artists had to ac-knowledge that their status under the Soviet regime was, in fact, analogous to that of the rest of the human material in the hands of the ultimate artist—the Communist leadership and Stalin himself. Many of those artists found themselves subject to transformation. They were sent to laboratories established by the ultimate artist, where the human material was to be transformed according to the overall artistic plan. These labo-ratories were the concentration camps.

Morality Seen from Horseback

This relationship between the regime-author and the popu-lation-audience-material, odious from the point of view of Judeo-Christian and humanist ethics, becomes quite natural when approached within the ethical framework of Bolshevik teleology. In the Leninist view of "morality subordinate to the interests of the class struggle of the proletariat," victimiza-tion assumes a positive ethical value if carried out by the Bolshevik regime (the avant-garde of the proletariat).[67] For literature, assuming the new, all-integrating point of view represented by the Bolsheviks required embracing this teleological morality.

In so doing, a Soviet writer committed to the Bolshevik point of view could employ structural analogies between the Bolshevik teleological universe and numerous currents of Russian literary and ideological tradition in which the present was addressed in terms of the future. One of the principal motifs in this pre-revolutionary tradition was that of Russian national and cultural identity perceived as a projection of a futuristic idea, rather than as the tangible reality of the present time. Pushkin's figure of the leaping horse in *The Bronze Horseman* and Gogol's galloping troika in *Dead Souls* metaphorically exemplify the Romantic sources of this tradition. Inspired by Johann Gottfried Herder's Romantic myth of Slavs as the "race of the future," the tradition approaches the present Russian reality as chaotic, amorphous matter striving for ultimate form.[68] The identity of contemporary Russia is presented in a state of becoming. The focus is on a dynamic, goal-oriented process rather than on something fixed and stable. So Russia can be described by first defining its ideal goal and then placing the present reality in the context of this goal. In *The Bronze Horseman* Pushkin embodies this puzzle of Russian historic destiny in a literary figure built upon the motif of St. Petersburg's equestrian monument of Peter the Great:

How awesome in the gloom he rides!
What thought upon his brow resides!
His charger with what fiery mettle,
His form with what dark strength endowed!
Where will you gallop, charger proud,
Where next your plunging hoofbeats settle?[69]

Gogol's figure of Russia from the last paragraphs of *Dead Souls* echoes this dynamic concept:

Oh, you *troika!* . . . Is it not like that, that you, too, Russia, are speeding along like a spirited *troika* that nothing can overtake? The road is like a cloud of smoke under you, the bridges thunder, and everything falls back and is left far behind. The spectator stops dead, struck dumb by the divine miracle: is it not a flash of lightning thrown down by heaven? What is the meaning of this terrifying motion? And what mysterious force is hidden in these horses the like of which the world has never seen? . . . Russia, where are you flying to? Answer! She gives no answer. The bells fill the air with their wonderful tinkling; the air is torn asunder, it thunders and is transformed into wind; everything on earth is flying past, and, looking askance, other nations and states draw aside and make way for her.[70]

Within the pattern of thinking about Russia exemplified by these literary figures, the question of Russian identity and destiny was a question of the goal towards which the present reality heads. In *The Bronze Horseman,* however, Pushkin provided his key figure with an element of inner tension: between the goal of fulfilling society's (the nation's) historic destiny, represented by state power (the figure of Peter), on the one hand, and the lives and needs of its individual members, on the other. The relationship between these two is portrayed in terms of the relation between the horseman and the horse:

Oh, Destiny's great potentate!
Was it not thus, a towering idol
Hard by the chasm, with iron bridle
You reared up Russia to her fate?

In one of the crucial scenes of *The Bronze Horseman* the figure of Peter the Great and Pushkin's "little man," Eugene, driven to despair by the death of his fiancée during a flood, face each other in ambiguous confrontation:

> And furtively with savage scowling
> He eyed the lord of half the earth.
> His breath congealed in him, he pressed
> His brow against the chilly railing,
> A blur of darkness overveiling
> His eyes; a flame shot through his breast
> And made his blood seethe. Grimly louring,
> He faced the haughty image towering
> On high, and fingers clawed, teeth clenched,
> As if by some black spirit wrenched,
> He hissed, spite shaking him: "Up there,
> Great wonder-worker you beware! . . ."[71]

This confrontation is a result of Eugene's own personal catastrophe, which can be seen as a "side effect" of realizing the grand historical goals of state power. Here, the direct issue is the construction of the state capital, for strategic reasons, in a place not safe enough to protect its inhabitants. This represents a more general problem of a contradiction between the grand destiny of the society as a whole (embodied in the symbol of state power) and the modest human needs of individuals. In Pushkin's work the figure of the Bronze Horseman (Peter the Great) triumphs over the "little man," driving him to fear, insanity, and destruction. The truths revealed in this work are marked by a tragic duality of purpose between the individual and society. The historic process of fulfilling the grand destiny of the state determines the fate of the individual, whose personal goals are sacrificed for the sake of the superior goal.

Facing this contradiction between the destiny represented by state power and individual goals, nineteenth-century Russian literature tended to assume the side of the "little man," Eugene. In order to overcome the tragic contradiction between state goals and individual goals, Chernyshevsky in his literary utopia conceived an ideological vision in which the poor and downtrodden were to become masters of destiny. In the utopian vision described in *What Is to Be Done?*, Chernyshevsky cancels out the tragic contradiction, claiming that it is not state power but the "little men" who represent the grand historic destiny. For, according to Chernyshevsky, the goal of history itself is consistent with the goals of the "little men" (which, in turn, are almost identical for each individual "little man"). In order to realize this destiny, the "little men" must acknowledge the analogy between their own goals and history's and then take the rule of history from the representatives of state power.

About half a century after the publication of *What Is to Be Done?,* the Bolsheviks were bringing this basic ideological premise to life. Their knowledge of real "little men," however, was greater than Chernyshevsky's. Facing the apparent apathy of the "little men" who were slow in appreciating the alleged analogy between their own goals and the goals of history (defined by the Bolsheviks themselves), the Bolsheviks set out to realize these goals in spite of the "little men." In the process of fulfilling this grand historic destiny, they were ready not only to accept, but also to cause, "necessary" casualties, also among the "little men." For the majority of Russian writers and intellectuals at the time of the Bolshevik revolution this prospect was odious and unacceptable. For those who longed for ideological consistency in Bolshevism, joining in the new totalitarian authorship meant introducing a radical ethical novelty into Russian literary tradition. In order to reintegrate the universe according to the Bolshevik blueprint, the new Soviet literature was expected to ally itself with power and destiny, and against the "little man," who apparently did not pass the test of knowing what was good for him. Soviet literature had to take the side of the Bronze Horseman against Eugene. Now, in confrontation with the Bronze Horseman, Eugene was supposed to accept the official vision of destiny as the only consistent view of the world. He had to accept his own dispensability in the fulfillment of history's grand goal and to involve himself in this process. The role of the Bronze Horseman—"Destiny's great potentate"—was now taken over by the Bolshevik regime. As for the modern Eugene, his destiny depended on whether or when his masters decided to call him a "class enemy." If he was given that label, he faced the alternatives of either total damnation (execution) or a chance of redemption through labor (the concentration camp). Whether, or when, one of these two alternatives would materialize as the ultimate destiny of the new Eugene depended on factors beyond his influence. The new Soviet literature had to be ready to present each of these experiences from the point of view of the new Bronze Horseman looking down at his new victim before, during, and after trampling him.

2

FROM TRAGEDY
TO FESTIVAL

Revolutionary Violence and Ethical
Experimentation in the 1920s

Man:

My Paradise is for everyone

except the poor in spirit

.   .   .   .

Come unto me

all you who have calmly stabbed the enemy,

and then walked away from the corpse

with a song on your lips!

Come,

unforgiving one!

You have first right of entry

into my kingdom . . .

—Vladimir Mayakovsky, *Mystery-Bouffe* (1918)

For the Good of the Cause

When challenged with the task of presenting Bolshevik violence through the prism of Bolshevik ideology, Soviet literature managed to come up with a series of literary conventions that served this goal at different historical stages. Particular modes of reconciling Bolshevik oppression with the Bolshevik claim to ethical superiority varied. So, undoubtedly, did the personal motivations of particular writers involved in this moral and literary experimentation. This was especially true of the initial Soviet period of the 1920s, when Bolshevik control over literature was only superficial, and the outcome of revolutionary violence was still a matter of prediction. To draw distinctions between a writer's mere opportunism and ideological blindness on the one hand and his or her genuine effort to comprehend the new reality of Bolshevik violence on the other is a matter of speculation that transcends the limits of this book. What must be emphasized, however, is that in numerous presentations of the Bolshevik point of view on violence in the 1920s, we are dealing with a peculiar ambiguity. On the one hand, there are clear, direct literary endorsements of Bolshevik violence. On the other hand, Bolshevik justifications of violence are often embodied in literary designs without clear signs of either authorial support or rejection. Quite frequently, the author's assumed endorsement of, or ambiguous distance from, the Bolshevik discourse of violence is a matter of the individual reader's interpretation of a particular work. However, regardless of the frequent impossibility of discerning authors' attitudes toward revolutionary violence (and in many cases this ambiguity of attitude reflected the authors' hesitant efforts to comprehend the new reality), many of these diverse literary presentations have one common feature. In order to present the Bolshevik philosophy of violence in a non-negative way (as an article of faith on the author's part or simply as a potentially valid discourse among other discourses), the writer had to find a means of undermining the age-old Russian literary tradition (to use Dostoevsky's phrase) of "the insulted and the injured."

This tradition of moral commitment of literature to the weak and downtrodden became so central in nineteenth-century Russia that it hardly needs exemplification. What calls for special notice, however, is that, besides focusing on the poor, helpless, and unjustly oppressed, this literary tradition was notable for its particular concern with prisoners. These were not only political prisoners and victims of false accusation (conventional subjects of a larger European philanthropic tradition in literature), but also criminals whose guilt was never in doubt. Their punishment in prisons, hard labor camps, and places of confined settlement was viewed as just and lawful; and yet, instead of giving rise to a dominating emotion of satisfaction at this victory of law and order, it tended to evoke compassion for these convicted criminals. This view of prisoners, exemplified in Dostoevsky's *Notes from the House of the Dead,* Mamin-Sibiryak's *Siberian Stories,* and Chekhov's *Sakhalin,* among many others, reflects a characteristic Russian popular tradition in which convicts were referred to as *neschastnye* (the unfortunate ones, the miserable ones).

It is important to remember that, faced with the realities of the Bolshevik takeover, the majority of Russian writers and intellectuals remained faithful to this ethical tradition. Their voices were soon silenced or marginalized, however, within the new Soviet cultural discourse. A much more prominent position in the formation of this new discourse was granted to authors who searched for terms in which to

present the Bolshevik point of view on revolutionary violence in a non-negative light. In the 1920s, for a short time,
these new ethical terms were either presented as authorial
interpolations or included in more dialogical literary designs.
Yet, both modes of presentation implied a search for literary
conventions capable of undermining, or at least relativizing,
the tradition of the "insulted and in'ured." One of the
sources that proved useful in the creation of such conventions was a particular version of the Russian pre-
revolutionary tradition of ideological debate and literary
presentation of the moral problem of "violent means and
noble ends." It was natural for early Soviet literary presentations of the Bolshevik terror to be placed in the context of
preexisting intellectual and literary patterns for justifying
revolutionary terrorism. Vasily Grossman comments on the
specific ethical characteristics of the Russian revolutionary
tradition:

> Throughout the whole history of the Russian revolu-
> tionary movement, such qualities as love of the people,
> inherent in many of the revolutionary intellectuals,
> whose meekness and readiness to endure suffering
> seemed unequaled since the epoch of the first Chris-
> tians, mingled with diametrically opposite attributes,
> and these, too, were inherent in many Russian revolu-
> tionaries—contempt for and disregard of human suffer-
> ing, subservience to abstract theories, the determination
> to annihilate not merely enemies but those comrades
> who deviated even slightly from complete acceptance
> of the particular abstraction in question. Sectarian de-
> terminism, the readiness to suppress today's living free-
> dom for the sake of an imaginary freedom tomorrow
> and to violate universal canons of morality for the sake
> of the world to be—all these aspects were evident in

the character of Pestel, Bakunin, Nechayev, and in some of the statements and actions of the Narodnaya Volya [People's Will] disciples.[1]

In this general climate of ethical ambivalence surrounding the question of "necessary violence" in Russian revolutionary tradition, the Russian Populist terrorists of the People's Will (Narodnaya Volya) were among the most vocal proponents and ideologues of the terror, and they set a pattern of thinking about this issue reflected in later revolutionary movements. Isaiah Berlin characterized the Russian Populists' approach to the moral issue of "violent means and noble ends" thus:

> If violence was the only means to a given end, then there might be circumstances in which it was right to employ it; but this must be justified in each case by the intrinsic moral claim of the end—an increase in happiness, or solidarity, or justice, or peace, or some other universal human value that outweighs the evil of the means—never by the view that it was rational and necessary to march in step with history, ignoring one's scruples and dismissing one's own "subjective" moral principles because they were necessarily provisional, on the ground that history herself transformed all moral systems and retrospectively justified only those principles which survived and succeeded.[2]

This Russian Populist view of the ethics of revolutionary terrorism played an important role as a point of reference for Soviet literary approaches to this issue. These approaches varied from attempts to conditionally embrace the moral anxiety projected by this Populist view to instances of directly rejecting it in favor of purely utilitarian ethics. For it must be said that the Bolshevik idea of class morality formulated by

Lenin is in fact far removed from the Russian Populists' attempts to justify revolutionary violence (acknowledged verbally by some Populist leaders and writers though not necessarily followed by all terrorists of the People's Will).[3] Russian Populist ethics leave a revolutionary who commits violence with at least two ethical dilemmas. First of all, the question has to be raised of the actual necessity of the violent act each time the act is committed. This question has no definitive answer. The only answer possible is purely hypothetical, because no one can foretell the future and say what would happen if the violent act were not committed. Second, the revolutionary must be entirely sure that the ultimate effect of the violent act will, in fact, "outweigh the evil of the means." This issue, like the previous one, can be dealt with only hypothetically. Again, in order to have the certainty necessary from an ethical point of view, one must have a clear view of the future consequences of one's present actions. This view is given to the revolutionary in the form of ideology, which implants in his mind a present idea of the future and obliges him to believe in the upcoming incarnation of this idea. The degree of faith one has in the idea then determines one's readiness to act in a way that history will validate. The fundamental difference between Russian Populist ethics and Bolshevik ethics lies in the fact that the Russian Populists assigned individual ethical responsibility in the case of a revolutionary who made a mistake and committed violence unnecessarily, whereas Bolsheviks exculpated their henchmen from such responsibility by requiring blind belief in the ideas proclaimed by the party leadership. From the vantage point of Russian Populist ethics of revolutionary terrorism, ethical anxiety is almost bound to torment those who choose to resort to violence in hopes of effecting good. The revolutionary terrorist must live with a sense of moral uncertainty, hoping that there was no other way of acting and that the good achieved at the expense of violence will eventually outweigh immediate evil.

The Russian Populist legacy of ethical ambivalence towards the issue of revolutionary violence was a lasting one, which found literary expression in, among other works, a semi-autobiographical novel *That Which Wasn't,* written in 1912 by a prominent Russian Socialist-Revolutionary terrorist, Boris Savinkov, under the pseudonym Viktor Ropshin. In his novel Savinkov presents moral dilemmas of revolutionary violence through the thoughts of the protagonist, whose experiences are based to a considerable degree on the author's own: "When I joined the Party, I thought I had it all figured out. . . . Almost everyone thinks that. Violence? In the name of the people, even violence is permitted. Lies? In the name of the revolution, lies are permitted. Fraud? In the name of the Party, fraud is permitted. Now I see it's not that simple. . . . Can the end justify all means? Can everything really be permitted?" Savinkov's novel belongs to a category of literature that does not stop at posing questions but attempts to provide them with direct answers. The answer given by Savinkov to the question of ethical justification of immoral revolutionary actions is tragically ambivalent: "Yes, you have to lie, kill, but you don't have to say that this is permitted, justified, that this is fine. You don't have to think that by lying you are sacrificing yourself, that by killing you are saving your soul. No, you have to have the courage to say: this is evil, cruel, terrible, but it is unavoidable . . . yes unavoidable. . . . Terror is not only sacrifice, but also lies, blood and shame." [4]

Savinkov's literary hero (and his ideological *porte parole*) is trapped between two irreconcilable moral codes. On the one hand, he displays a sense of absolute, timeless morality that says "Thou shalt not kill" and "Thou shalt not steal" without regard to the intentions of the person. On the other hand, he relates to the idea of ethics as historically conditioned, relative, and dialectical. On ethical grounds, he rejects the social status quo as unjust and thus immoral. Furthermore, he takes upon himself responsibility for bringing about a better, more just world, and he is ready to endure sacrifices, both material and moral, in order to meet this self-imposed responsibility. This striving for ethical maximalism on the part of the revolutionary, who attempts to satisfy two hardly reconcilable moral codes, puts him in a tragic position. The contradiction between the two contrary moral bases for action literally destroys him; for this contradiction, in Savinkov's view, cannot be reconciled within the person embodying it other than by this person's sacrificial death. Only the heroic sacrifice of the revolutionary's own life can eliminate his perpetual moral anxiety and the sense of guilt generated by the mutually exclusive alternatives of two equally strong moral bases. In Savinkov's book, an example of the literary formulation of the ethical legacy of the Russian Populists, the moral dilemma of the revolutionary reflects a conflict essential to tragedy, a conflict between two equally compelling, yet mutually exclusive, moral bases that destroys the uncompromising hero.

Executioners as Tragic Heroes

This tragic formula of revolutionary terror, exemplified in literary visions such as Savinkov's, found reflections in early Soviet literature dealing with moral justifications of Bolshevik terror. Revolutionary terrorist characters from previous periods found equivalents in early Soviet literary works in the characters of official terrorists of the regime. The mass experience of the Red Terror was often presented in these works from the point of view of those who signed death sentences, carried out executions, and took hostages. These new protagonists, the Bolshevik henchmen, have the aura of tragic heroes of the revolution, torn apart by conflicting moral codes, just as their literary predecessors were. Such are the Chekist Aleksei Zudin in Aleksandr Tarasov-Rodyonov's novel *Chocolate* and Ilya Ehrenburg's Nikolai Kurbov in *The Life and Death of Nikolai Kurbov*.[5] Both send people to death without much thought about their guilt or innocence, and so represent countless actual Bolshevik terrorists. Both authors present these characters in realistic terms, and in order to match the requirements of verisimilitude, they have to introduce certain modifications to their models of tragic heroes. In reality, the sheer quantity of killings and other violent acts committed by the Bolsheviks had no precedent in the history of Russian revolutionary movements. Bolshevik terror, in contrast to the pre-revolutionary terror of the People's Will and the Socialist Revolutionaries, dealt not with individual targets and accidental victims but with masses of people. So it could not be approached by an author in a realistic way without addressing the psychological impact of this quantitative aspect on the Bolshevik protagonist. In fact, early Soviet works introduce psychological modifications compared with pre-revolutionary models.

The daily routine of the Chekist Zudin includes executions of both convicted "enemies" and, occasionally, accidental hostages. Zudin himself is presented as a soldier of the revolution who does not avoid the heaviest responsibilities in his fight for the good cause. Placed by history in the role of an executioner, he is not unaware of the basic moral dimension of his actions. After ordering the execution of a hundred hostages in retaliation for the death of one of his fellow Chekists in a battle with a counterrevolutionary group, Zudin says: "I killed a hundred hostages and I never wondered if they were guilty of anything. What is guilt? Is a bourgeois guilty of being a bourgeois? Is a crocodile guilty of being a crocodile?"[6] This seemingly radical violation of the old moral code of revolution (as exemplified by Savinkov's tragic hero) does not, however, immediately destroy Zudin. With respect to the descriptions of Zudin's actions alone, the reader of *Chocolate* would have good reason to perceive this character as morally illiterate and a compulsive murderer. But nothing could be further from the truth. Zudin is a loving husband and father, and his selfless service to the cause of the revolution makes him suffer at the thought of his wife accepting a gift of some chocolate for their children. As the chief of the local Cheka, he feels that he should remain absolutely pure and stay away from anything even slightly resembling a bribe. But killing enemies, actual and potential, is quite another matter: it is his duty.

Tarasov-Rodyonov strives to create an aura of moral complexity that would put the traditional, Judeo-Christian moral categories relevant to Zudin's crimes in question. Psychological overtones are instrumental in creating this aura of ethical ambiguity. While appearing on the surface as a cold, fanatical bureaucrat-executioner, Zudin has, in fact, a psychological "second layer" that reveals his tragic inner split. Faced with the revolutionary task of violence, Zudin must adjust psychologically in order to carry it out. It is not true that he is devoid of a sense of absolute, timeless morality; this sense is merely suppressed and pushed into the subconscious, while the only conscious motivation of his actions remains the dialectical ethics of a historical process, according to which the end automatically justifies the means. Only occasionally does his conscious "I" become aware of the clash between these two irreconcilable moral bases for action. This is the clash that tears him apart, as his irrational, emotional side emerges from beneath the tight lid of ideological self-control. For instance, Zudin cannot reconcile his personal identity as a father and husband with his ideological identity as a revolutionary executioner. "How good it would be if workers didn't have children," Zudin muses.[7] It is the existence of children and family that, according to him, produced situations in which "one would sometimes feel shame, and one would take back his hand raised and ready to strike." It is the growing split between Zudin's irrational (subconscious) and rational (conscious) sides that leads inexorably to the final moment in the novel—his self-destruction. Zudin, the pure, ruthless soldier of the revolution, feels some confused sympathy for the beautiful, spoiled Elena Waltz, a former ballerina who also turns out to be involved with an English spy. Zudin believes in Elena Waltz's willingness to reform herself in the new society and gives her a job in the Cheka. Like Robespierre and Felix Dzerzhinsky, Zudin never compromises his revolutionary purity. He successfully resists Elena's erotic overtures, but his revolutionary alertness fails him and he is unable to uncover a major extortion for which she is responsible. Fortunately, other Chekists make up for Zudin's shortcomings and arrest Elena along with the astonished Zudin. Zudin understands that his lack of knowledge about Elena's activities cannot excuse his unforgivable failure, and accepts his punishment by death. During his trial, the issue of the hundred hostages shot by Zudin is briefly mentioned. Neither the prosecutor, nor the judges, nor the defendant admit anything inappropriate in it.

Ultimately, Tarasov-Rodyonov follows Savinkov's footsteps in presenting the tragic fate of the revolutionary undermined by the inner contradiction between two motivations neither of which he is capable of compromising. Moreover, the Soviet writer goes further in creating the tragic aura around his Bolshevik hero: Zudin's death at the hands of his fellow revolutionaries adds a strong element of tragic irony to his already solemn portrait. Yet, while awaiting his execution, Zudin feels relieved. His moral dilemma is soon to be resolved in the only possible way. At the same time, he does not lose his revolutionary faith: he has a vision of the future Communist paradise that, despite everything, he has helped to bring about.

The protagonist of Ilya Ehrenburg's *Life and Death of Nikolai Kurbov,* the Chekist Kurbov, represents yet another embodiment of the romanticized figure of the Bolshevik henchman as tragic hero. The key conflict between the requirements of revolutionary ethics and a sense of personal morality tears him apart in a way reminiscent of Zudin. Here a love theme serves as the primary means of realizing the conflict between a conscious commitment to the revolution and a subconscious allegiance to the simple and quite traditional human sense of right and wrong. Kurbov becomes aware that the woman he is in love with does not know his actual identity and that it is she who plots to assassinate the infamous Cheka executioner Nikolai Kurbov. He knows that her arrest would lead to her inevitable execution, and he cannot bring himself to order it. This conflict, just as in the case of Zudin, destroys Kurbov, who commits suicide. Like Zudin, he does not lose faith in the future glory of Communism even when he is about to shoot himself, convinced that his own weakness is what prevents him from serving the revolution with sufficient ruthlessness.

Both Tarasov-Rodyonov and Ehrenburg, by employing elements of the approach to revolutionary violence developed previously by the Russian Populist and later pre-revolutionary terrorist ideologies, worked out a formula for presenting the Bolshevik oppressors as ethical maximalists who have taken upon themselves the historical task of transforming the world for the better, and who sacrifice themselves and others in the process. This approach, represented in the pre-revolutionary novel by Savinkov and reintroduced, with modifications, by Tarasov-Rodyonov and Ehrenburg, suggests that the relationship between revolutionaries committed to turning history in the "right" direction and history itself is, in fact, tragic. Tragic irony is hardly avoidable in a literary vision in which the supposedly "conscious" Communist revolutionaries, who claim to possess sole objective knowledge of history's goals and behave as if they are taking control of the destiny of the whole population, become victims of their own incapacity to control their still deeper psychological motivations. It is history that, in fact, takes control of them and determines their fate. Ultimately, their vantage point on current reality does not differ much from that of their victims: they too are subject to human fallibility and doubt. The authors are persistent in reassuring their readers that the final outcome of history will be what the Bolshevik regime promises—the happy, triumphant era of Communism revealed to their literary heroes in their moments of ultimate crisis. Meanwhile, however, the large masses of history's sacrificial victims consist of both the executed and the executioners, and the future happy society is unlikely to remember who was who at the time of the hecatomb.

"To Hell with Your Morality!"

Literary visions of Bolshevik victimization, presented from the point of view of executioners draped in the cloaks of tragic heroes, express a fundamental belief in the inevitability of revolutionary violence and in the ultimate justification of this violence as the only pathway to a better future. Nevertheless, the functionality of these visions as means of reprogramming people's perceptions of the Bolshevik violence was limited. True, they challenged traditional ethical standards, according to which the massive Bolshevik oppression was likely to be seen by the population as a destructive wave of hatred and crime. In these literary presentations, traditional standards of Judeo-Christian "absolute and timeless morality" were put in deadlock opposition with a set of seemingly equally substantial ethical concepts supporting revolutionary violence. The point is, however, that tragedy was not the frame through which the Bolshevik regime viewed itself and its own violence. In Bolshevism, given its unconditional teleology, even tragedy had to be optimistic.[8] For the Bolsheviks, the figure of the Communist revolutionary was to be presented as a didactic model to be emulated in life, not a tragic hero (who was hardly attractive as a life model). In the teleological order proclaimed by the Bolsheviks there is, indeed, hardly any place for tragic heroes. In this world, all moral conflicts that appear irresolvable when viewed from a point of view confined by the here and now can be resolved when seen from the point of view of someone aware of the ultimate goal of all things. This means that every conflict and contradiction of values becomes transparent for the true Bolshevik whose faith is strong enough to overcome the limitations of the here and now. Those who doubt and make mistakes do not represent the true Bolshevik position. Lenin himself made this clear in rejecting all moral notions except purely utilitarian ones.

In light of Leninist ethics, the lofty, tragic views of revolutionary terror presented in works inspired by pre-revolutionary traditions such as Tarasov-Rodyonov's *Chocolate* and Ehrenburg's *Life and Death of Nikolai Kurbov* could be taken as little more than reflections of ideological confusion between correct (dialectical and utilitarian) and incorrect ("eternal") moral codes. The moral dilemmas that turn revolutionary protagonists into tragic heroes, when approached from a Leninist moral standpoint, are bound to be perceived not as results of irreconcilable, tragic contradiction, but as objectively just punishment inflicted by history upon those whose "class instinct" fails and permits weakness. Lenin, once again, made the point clear, stating that "sentimentality is no less a crime than speculation in time of war." [9] According to these ethical notions, moral anxieties tormenting revolutionaries are negative phenomena that interfere with revolutionary action and thus delay the ultimate victory of the revolution, which is the only truly moral resolution of all conflicts in history. The people who dare to take responsibility for bringing about this ultimate moral resolution can be judged only on the basis of their effectiveness. Passivity and hesitation caused by ethical self-doubt are among the cardinal sins of the Bolshevik moral code.

Anatoly Lunacharsky expressed this ethical position in his article about Vladimir Korolenko, an outstanding spokesman for the traditional moral values of the Russian intelligentsia who openly opposed Bolshevik violence after the revolution. After Korolenko's death in 1921, Lunacharsky wrote: "Righteous men are appalled by the blood on our hands. Righteous men are in despair over our cruelty. . . . The righteous man will never understand that 'love demands expiatory victims,' that it is a question not only of self-sacrifice (this he understands), but also of the sacrifice of others." [10]

It is highly significant how the tragic view of revolutionary violence, outwardly rejected by Lunacharsky, nevertheless provides him with a lofty rhetorical vocabulary full of catchy associations. While defying any sense of morality other than a purely utilitarian, revolutionary one, Lunacharsky is considerably dependent on a high rhetorical style that generates a vague aura of solemn mystery surrounding the issue of Bolshevik violence ("love demands expiatory victims," "sacrifice," "self-sacrifice," "blood on our hands"). The protagonists in this mystery (the Bolsheviks themselves) appear, by sheer consequence of stylistic appropriateness of word to referent, as high, lofty characters. Thus, somewhat independently of the message of Lunacharsky's statement, the style itself creates verbal dynamics that generate associations between the Bolsheviks and some vague yet lofty moral position. This position appears as a sort of super-morality which calls for victims and which is inaccessible to the profane. If we remove these stylistic ornaments, Lunacharsky's message appears as just one more declaration of Bolshevik ethics, which can be evaluated as simply and briefly as did Andrei Sinyavsky: "I don't know if Lunacharsky suspected what he was saying here: that the new man should be stained with blood, the blood of others, as the supreme symbol of righteousness. This reduces the moral code of the revolutionary to that of the executioner and informer. . . . Bloodstained hands were no longer the exception but the rule—a historical, even psychological necessity."[11]

Direct defiance of any view of morality other than Leninist moral utilitarianism constituted a new literary approach to the phenomenon of Bolshevik violence. The element of moral shock on the reader's part is included in this literary strategy. Direct methods of dealing with this assumed moral shock varied, however. The poet Vasily Knyazev, for instance, presents an extreme case of what has already been found in Lunacharsky's rhetoric—namely, a vague application of highfalutin evaluative verbosity as the mode in which Bolshevik violence is presented. Knyazev, unlike Lunacharsky, is quite explicit about the ethical basis of his apotheosis of cruelty, murder, and vengeance. His long poem *Red Gospel* of 1918 can be analyzed in the context of Lenin's remarks on "eternal" and "dialectical" morality. Knyazev's preference for the latter seems absolutely unconditional: in fact, his poem is an extensive, lofty sermon on how the "confusing" sense of human compassion should be rejected for the sake of the revolutionary "class morality."

Hey, you! blind from birth!
Firm moralists!
Isn't it about time to regain your sight?!
> Your morality?
> Ha!
To hell with your morality!
The revolution means death to your morality!

The new morality, bound to replace the old, is proclaimed in terms pompous enough to make it appear as no less sacred than traditional Judeo-Christian morality:

This is the Second Christ's behest:
Take swords into your hands,
Throw out of your hearts
The seeds of worn-out truth.
Until the last obstacle falls down,
And disappears like smoke,
Blessed are those who do not know mercy
In the struggle against their enemies!

In the process of elevating the new ethical utilitarianism to the level of the sacred, Knyazev's lyrical persona functions as its prophet and formulates moral instruction:

People, heed the words of the prophet:
Stay away from the path of treachery!
In battle, there is no disgrace more deadly
Than mercy.
The enemy should be offered no mercy.
He fell. . . . He is still alive? Stab him!
Only he who knows how to hate
Will reach the Earthly Kingdom.
. . . .
Do not have mercy for your enemies:
Death to those who stand on the other side!

Take no prisoners:
Put bullets through the heads of those loyal to the
   throne![12]

Unlike Tarasov-Rodyonov and Ehrenburg, Knyazev does
not surround the theme of Bolshevik violence with an aura
of moral complexity and ambivalence. On the contrary,
Knyazev reverses the traditional negative moral categories
applicable to violence and presents them as totally purified
by the instrumental role they play in the revolution. Thus
justified, victimization and killing present no ethical problem. Moreover, they become ethically positive if done for the
sake of the universal justice of the Bolshevik future—the goal
attainable only through the ultimate victory of the revolution. An unquestioning faith in the revolution as salvation lies
behind the explicit assertion of a reversal of basic moral notions. Knyazev writes about faith as the driving force of the
revolution, accomplished against the will of the majority of
the population:

Our hearts sing the glory of the only faith.
We are few but it does not matter!
We will force to follow us
The flocks accustomed to whips.
We know the only straight path to Paradise.
Death to whoever dares
To bar our way![13]

This fragment is an accurate, if lyrical, illustration of practical Leninism: it presents the totalitarian idea of coercing the
popular participation of the population in the effort to realize the goals of those who "know better" where the road to
the future paradise lies.
    Eduard Bagritsky's poem "TBC" echoes these basic no-
tions of Bolshevik ethics:

The century waits for you on the road,
Like a sentinel—all focused.
Go, don't be afraid to join him.
Your solitude is just like his.
You look around: enemies are all around you.
You grope around: there are no friends.
But if he tells you, "lie," then lie.
But if he tells you, "kill," then kill.[14]

In these visions of Knyazev and Bagritsky the only essential ethical dimension of violent action is definable by its relevance to the historical goal revealed through the "voice of
the century," or the ideological inspiration of the "Red Evan-
gelist." This voice is identical with the voice of the Communist Party leadership. What is significant is that both Knyazev
and Bagritsky avoid euphemisms in their endorsement of
Bolshevik atrocities. On the contrary, they insist on calling
killing, torture, and lying by their proper names. As in the
case of Savinkov, their literary strategy is based on a direct,
non-euphemistic admission of the violent, repulsive character of the revolutionary terror when judged by traditional
moral standards. For Bagritsky, as for Savinkov, a lie does not
stop being a lie, murder does not stop being murder, even if
committed for an apparently good cause. But in Bagritsky's
view, lies and murders are not only morally permissible but
required of the faithful Bolshevik. This projects an element of
moral provocation as an important factor in the reader's assumed response to the text. In the face of such a blatant assertion of the ultimate morality of killing and lying, any
moral protest on the part of the reader becomes simply irrelevant, because it must be based on the traditional ethical
concepts that set negative connotations for the words *lie* and
murder. So by reacting negatively the reader places himself
among those who "do not understand" the fundamentally

new basis for ethics and against whom the poems by both Bagritsky and Knyazev are written. The new mode of reader response projected in these works should be seen in the larger context of the Bolshevik anti-religious campaign, in which physical terror and the desecration and confiscation of churches, synagogues, and mosques were accompanied by the derision and ridicule of religious values. All those inclined to argue for an "eternal" morality, according to which lying and killing are wrong by definition, tended to be seen as confused representatives of an outdated religious mentality that was to be eliminated from the new world. From the point of view of the "conscious" Bolshevik (the only point of view seen as not confused), the moral connotations of the words *lie* and *murder* should depend only on whose class interest they serve.

This literary approach to the phenomenon of revolutionary violence, perhaps closest to the actual point of view of the Bolshevik leadership, soon became a widespread cliché of literature written by Bolshevik partisans and sympathizers, and not only in the Soviet Union. Bertolt Brecht embraced it in his 1930 play *Die Massnahme* (The Measures Taken):

> What base act would you not commit, to
> Eradicate baseness?
> If, at last, you could change the world, what
> Would you think yourself too good for?
> Who are you?
> Sink into filth
> Embrace the butcher, but
> Change the world: it needs it! [15]

If Ehrenburg's Nikolai Kurbov and Tarasov-Rodyonov's Aleksei Zudin struggled with the old world's sense of "eternal morality," a Chekist named Bezais in Viktor Kin's 1928 novel *On the Other Side* seems already free of such limitations:

The world was simple for Bezais. He believed that the world revolution will take place, if not tomorrow then surely the day after tomorrow. He did not struggle with himself, did not write diaries. When they told him in the club that the merchant Smirnov was shot at night on the other side of the river, he said, "Well, that is the way it should be," because he did not see any other use for merchants. . . . Bezais somehow ended up reading Dostoevsky's *Crime and Punishment*. Having finished the whole thing he was surprised: "My God, so much talk because of one mere old woman!"[16]

In Soviet literature of the late 1920s, the formula that automatically justifies revolutionary violence by noble goals appears as an already abused cliché, as it is in Yuri Olesha's *Envy* (1927), where a soccer player, Volodya Makarov, an energetic and active young man but hardly an intellectual beacon, presents his ethical view of the revolution and proclaims "no difference between cruelty and magnanimity" in the light of "the iron, as it's said, logic of history."[17]

By the time *Envy* was written, the Leninist ethical formula of revolutionary violence had become so much of a commonplace in Soviet cultural discourse that it had lost its shocking edge, and even characters of questionable intellect such as Olesha's Volodya Makarov are capable of reciting it without hesitation.

Classes and Species

What is quite common and highly significant in many literary presentations of the Leninist view of revolutionary violence is the tendency to resort, in addition to the seemingly rational, anti-sentimental argument, to motifs of verbal dehumanization of victims. Nikolai Kurbov, the protagonist of

Ehrenburg's novel, who eventually fails to perform his revolutionary duty, is eager to justify his violence according to the Leninist formula of utilitarian ethics, which he translates in his mind into a language of metaphoric images. Ehrenburg offers readers an insight into the imagery found in Kurbov's mind. This is how Kurbov's routine activity of signing death sentences appears to him as related through the narrative technique of the *erlebte Rede:* "He signed these things many times and with confidence. It was simple: he weeded the gigantic garden, pulling out various kinds of weeds." [18] Ehrenburg's metaphor of "weeding the garden" has at least triple significance. As a device for dehumanizing the victim, it obscures the direct, tangible reality of killing a human being. Kurbov's mind no longer deals with the realia of the particular act of killing, but with the metaphoric image of "weeds" being removed. Furthermore, the very image of a garden being weeded evokes associations with the organizing, purposeful, nurturing, and cleansing character of the activity to which the image refers. Finally, by referring to the biblical tradition of the metaphor, the image provides an association with the Last Judgment described in the Gospel in the parable of separating the wheat from the chaff. [19] The Last Judgment is the goal of history as formulated in the New Testament: it is the ultimate point in the future, when all moral dilemmas and all conflicts of history will be definitively resolved by the ultimately just Judge. Within the associative dynamics triggered by this motif in Kurbov's mind, the role played in the New Testament version of the Last Judgment by Christ, who judges in the name of his Father, is assumed by Kurbov and his Cheka comrades, who judge and condemn in the name of history.

The phenomenon of verbal dehumanization of the victim is common among psychological patterns accompanying human aggression regardless of the particular cultural setting.

It is aimed at eliminating the sense of compassion that could either directly undermine the aggressive motivation or create feelings of guilt and remorse associated with an already committed violent act. Such feelings could prevent violent acts from being repeated. What is particularly significant in the patterns of verbal dehumanization of the victims of Bolshevik violence in literary presentations of this violence from the Bolshevik point of view is their apparent redundancy in the context of the Bolshevik ideology. On the one hand, the Bolsheviks proclaimed the theory of moral utilitarianism, which was supposed to resolve all potential doubt. On the other hand, as if not trusting the power of their own argument, they tended to "reinforce" their rational point of view using devices of irrational manipulation such as the dehumanization of victims. These devices included likening the victim to a weed in a garden, imagining the victim as a wild beast, an insect, and so on.

Bolshevik literary heroes tend to indulge in this verbal dehumanization of their victims while attempting to rationally justify their own terrorism in Leninist terms. The most typical technique for doing this is to use dehumanizing motifs as illustrative metaphors that, on the surface, only illustrate the rational argument but, at a deeper level, create a protective semantic substitute that replaces the physical reality as the object of direct attention of characters and readers. When Zudin, the hero of Tarasov-Rodyonov's *Chocolate,* consciously justifies his order to execute a hundred hostages, he spells out the Leninist credo of "class ethics": for him, the idea of guilt and innocence is simply irrelevant to the world of Leninist ethics. His hostages simply belong to the wrong class: they are bourgeoisie the way crocodiles are crocodiles. An illustrative comparison between the bourgeois and the crocodile enables Zudin to perceive the representatives of a different social class in terms of a different species, no longer "fellow humans" (and, according to Lenin's logic, a "socially alien element" can be anyone other than the leadership of the Communist Party). The revolution—the epitome of the class struggle—is viewed in this light as a struggle between different species. It assumes the character of a quasi-zoological phenomenon to which human ethical notions such as guilt, crime, justice, and compassion no longer apply. To make this chain of associations even more appealing to the irrational sphere of basic natural fears and instincts, Tarasov-Rodyonov makes Zudin associate "class enemies" with a species as formidable and frightening as the crocodile. The very idea of coexistence between humans and crocodiles in a shared environment seems hardly imaginable. The only real issue raised by application of this type of dehumanizing imagery to the "class enemies" is who is going to eliminate whom.[20]

One of the most persistent patterns of dehumanization of victims noticeable in these literary works is based on the rhetorical dynamics established by the abstract ideas that constitute the theoretical core of the Bolshevik ideology. The Bolshevik vocabulary of abstract notions such as "class," "historic process," "class struggle," "revolution," and so on served many writers as a screen through which concrete, material situations could be perceived and presented. These concrete events, persons, and so on are approached as representations of general ideas embodied in history—hence the potential for obscuring the direct, physical reality of the victimization by translating it into the language of abstract rhetoric. In his justification of the killing of the hundred hostages in retaliation for the death of a Chekist killed in a battle, Zudin argues: "The capitalistic organization killed Katzman. They struck at an individual because they don't understand the laws of society. I knew them and that's why I struck at the class as a whole. I killed random members of their organization, whoever I could get first, nothing more, nothing less."[21]

In other words, as Mikhail Heller comments on this passage, "they" killed a human being (an individual) and thus committed a crime, while "I" took revenge on "them" by "striking at the class"—an abstract construct, devoid of physical and psychological qualities such as pain, suffering, blood, fear, and so on.[22] It is a "class," an immaterial, inhuman monster, that killed a man—Comrade Katzman. The struggle between "us" and "them" is, once again, a struggle between people and monsters (either crocodiles or invisible entities such as "classes").

Vassily Grossman's novel *Forever Flowing* addresses the issue of the verbal dehumanization of victims by the Bolsheviks and sees in it an inspiring motive for historic victimization in Bolshevik Russia. One of the secondary characters of the novel, Anna Semenovna Mikhaleva, recollects the collectivization of 1933:

> And nowadays I look back on the liquidation of the kulaks in a quite different light—I am no longer under a spell, and I can see the human beings there. But why had I been so benumbed? After all, I could see then how people were being tortured and how badly they were being treated! But what I said to myself at the time was "They are not human beings, they are kulaks." And so I remember, I remember and I think: Who thought up this word "kulak" anyway? Was it Lenin? What torture was meted out to them! In order to massacre them, it was necessary to proclaim that kulaks are not human beings. Just as the Germans proclaimed that the Jews are not human beings. Thus did Lenin and Stalin: kulaks are not human beings.[23]

In light of these dehumanizing devices and their peculiar combination with ideological arguments, we must notice the duality of the Bolshevik approach to the theme of the Red Terror in its early stages. This is a mutually complementary duality of ideological and psychological appeal. While the Leninist ideology of purely utilitarian ethics provided a rational framework for the justification of Bolshevik violence, the rhetoric of dehumanization aimed at making this violence digestible on the level of semi-conscious, psychological responses.

Rhetoric and Moral Illiteracy

These verbal strategies of presenting the Red Terror as a morally justifiable practice were introduced at a time when Russian public discourse was permeated by a new, peculiarly casual attitude to violence. This attitude could be seen, on the one hand, as a psychological response to the prolonged period of war, revolution, and civil war. On the other hand, the new, more casual discourse on violence was instrumental in the hands of the Bolsheviks, for whom social hatred and conflict were a necessary means of achieving power.

In the short story "A Letter," in Isaak Babel's cycle *Red Cavalry,* this casual discourse on violence is presented in a singularly compelling form. A young illiterate, Cossack Kurdyukov, dictates to the narrator a letter to his mother. In the letter, he tells his mother how his father, a White Army soldier, murdered one of his sons, Kurdyukov's brother, only to be murdered by another son. In Kurdyukov's words, the killing of his father and brother seems to belong to the category of daily business. He does not proceed to describe them in his letter until after he addresses seemingly more urgent matters such as his horse and his occupation as a distributor of the Bolshevik propaganda—"the *Izvestia* of the Moscow

Central Executive Committee, the Moscow *Pravda,* and our own merciless paper the *Red Trooper,* which every fighting man in the front lines wants to read, and after that with heroic spirit he chops up the Poles." Only afterwards does Kurdyukov proceed to describe the scene in which his father murders his brother:

> Dad was then with General Denikin, commanding a company. . . . And they took us all prisoners because of that treason and my brother Theodore came to Dad's notice. And Dad began cutting him about, saying: "Brute, Red cur, son of a bitch," and all sorts of other things, and went on cutting him about until it grew dark and Theodore passed away. . . . Only I soon ran away from Dad and managed to get to my unit under Comrade Pavlichenko. And our brigade was ordered to the town of Voronezh to have its numbers made up, and we got reinforcements there, also horses, knapsacks, revolvers, and all we ought to have. About Voronezh I can write to you, Dear Mother, that the town is a jolly fine one, a bit bigger than Krasnodar. The people in it are very good-looking, the river is all right for bathing. They gave us two pounds of bread a day, half a pound of meat, and the right quantity of sugar so that we drank tea with sugar when we got up and the same in the evening and forgot about hunger, but for dinner I used to go to brother Simon's place to eat pancakes or goose.

After a lengthy description of the wonders of Voronezh, Kurdyukov proceeds to the murder of his father, caught by the Red Army and killed by Kurdyukov's other brother, Simon:

Simon turned to us all and said: "And what I think is that if I got caught by his boys, there wouldn't be no quarter for me.—And now, Dad, we're going to finish you off."

The letter ends on an upbeat note:

After that we were quartered in the town of Novorossiysk. About that town it can be said that there isn't any dry land on the other side of it but only water, the Black Sea, and we stayed there right till May, when we left for the Polish front, and now we're making the *pans* shake in their shoes.[24]

Kurdyukov's point of view is that of a moral illiterate. His very young age and daily exposure to the atrocities of war provide psychological and circumstantial explanation of his casual approach to family tragedy. Additional explanation can be found through the analysis of the language that he adopts as the medium of his report. His letter is evidence of an extraordinary stylistic confusion: his attitude to the facts described is dictated by the inner dynamics of different styles. Among these styles, revolutionary rhetoric mingles with the casual, matter-of-fact style of an uneducated Cossack youngster, to which he adds traditional, ritualistic phrases from his village culture. These styles clash, and the confusion resulting from this clash deprives Kurdyukov of any consistent moral categories in terms of which the atrocities could be viewed. Edward Brown examined this merging of revolutionary rhetoric and casual folk style as a factor contributing to an amoral attitude to the revolutionary atrocities related in literary works of that time. He commented on Babel's *Red Cavalry*: "The stories are studded with such phrases as 'no more masters,' 'heroic revolutionary army,' 'all are now equal,' 'the teachings of Lenin,' 'the revolutionary consciousness of the mass,' and so forth. . . . In Babel's stories they are always given in mangled, misunderstood form by a moral illiterate who has just performed some needless piece of violence, such as killing an old Jew or shooting a woman in the back." [25] This peculiar combination of moral illiteracy and revolutionary rhetoric was grasped in Blok's "The Twelve," a long poem profoundly ambivalent in its attitude to the horrors and early hopes of the revolution. In the words of Edward Brown, Blok's poem presents "the world at the mercy of twelve Red guards who kill and plunder to the tune of revolutionary songs and slogans. The hopes and fears of the reformers, idealists, and revolutionaries of the nineteenth century, in *Konarmia* [*Red Cavalry*] as well as in 'The Twelve,' find distorted utterance in brutish mouths." [26]

This newly emerging casual attitude to violence and death was, however, not only a product of the stylistic and moral confusion caused by the collapse of the social structure and the prolonged exposure of simple people to the atrocities of the revolution and the civil war. It had literary roots as well. In his long poem of 1920, *150 000 000,* Vladimir Mayakovsky wrote:

> Fly more densely, bullets!
> Cover the whole shy crowd!
> *Parabellum,* blast
> Those who are running for cover!
> . . . .
> We
>   will finish you off
>   world—the romantic!
> . . . .
>   Instead of faith
>   in our souls

                     there is electricity

                                 steam.
        Instead of poverty
               bag the wealth of all worlds!
        Old men—kill them!
                         make ashtrays out of their skulls![27]

This is one of many examples of Mayakovsky's rhetorical provocation, achieved by charging his lyrical expression with violent hyperbole, projecting the dehumanizing dynamics so useful in the Bolshevik view of revolutionary victimization. In order to see the connection, one must read this rhetorical excess not just in the context of the Cubo-Futurist formal revolution, but in that of the historical realia of the political revolution endorsed by the text itself. For within the context of revolutionary and post-revolutionary violence, this hyperbole acquired new, perhaps unintentional, realistic connotations. As distinctions between rhetorical and literal understanding of verbal devices became blurred under the Bolsheviks, rhetoric like this was potentially useful as the source of a new convention of presenting Bolshevik violence in a positive light. This rhetoric should be seen in the context of the casual attitude toward violence emerging as a psychological response to the prolonged period of revolution and civil war.

The heroes of Savinkov, Tarasov-Rodyonov, and Ehrenburg struggle with their own deep sense of morality while annihilating innocent people in the name of abstract progress and abstract "historical" justice. The lyrical protagonists and literary personages of Knyazev, Mayakovsky, Bagritsky, and Babel imply or directly express an attitude entirely "free" of such inner hesitation. In fact, the rhetoric of Knyazev, Mayakovsky, and Babel's character Kurdyukov reveals that execution itself can be presented as a quite casual, even jocular, activity. This verbal and, consequently, psychological potential of turning violent horror into a festival of sorts found its poetic reflection in Maximilian Voloshin's poem "Terminology," in which a simple enumeration of contemporary "nicknames" for execution suffices as a commentary on the relationship between language and the reality of violence in the context of the revolution:

> They "target practiced," they "stood you against the wall,"
> "Wrote you off:"
> That's how subtleties of life and language
> Kept changing from one year to another.
> "To bang," "to whack," "to send for spanking,"
> "To send to General Dukhonin's staff," "to waste."
> You can't talk simpler and sharper than that
> About our bloody thrashing.
> They pulled the truth from under fingernails,
> They jammed explosives into throats,
> They "sewed epaulettes," they "cut stripes,"
> They made "one-horned devils."
> How many lies were necessary
> To rouse and pit against each other
> Armies, classes, nations.[28]

"Two Worlds in a Deadly Battle"

These expressions of Bolshevik attitudes toward revolutionary violence, spoken, thought, or written by characters who may or may not represent the point of view of their authors, share a common ground. Each of them represents an ideological vision of the universe whose principal structural dominant is the opposition, the conflict, between the old and the new. In this conflict one side can survive only by destroying the other, and direct violence is inevitable and necessary for bringing about a resolution of the conflict. Knyazev writes:

Stop dreaming of reconciliation,
It is impossible now:
Only in a deadly battle
We will reach the gates of Paradise.
The enemy must fall. He must fall forever,
Like an idol toppled by life!
And let rivers of blood flow:
They will drown the old world.
. . . .
It is pointless to dream about returning to the past,
The river does not flow backward,
Two worlds are in a deadly battle,
And he who trembles will die!
. . . .
This struggle is not a joke,
If they defeat us, rivers of blood
Will extinguish the fire for many years.
If we win, the old world
Will fall forever into ashes.[29]

In this universe, revolutionary violence is presented as such, without attempts to conceal its bloody, irreversible aspects. It is viewed as a necessary means of self-protection on the part of a regime that represents a new world; at the same time, it is seen as positive because it aims at the ultimate triumph of the positive future over the negative past. This general context of revolutionary violence is made more precise by placing it in the ideological framework of Marxism-Leninism. The struggle between the forces of the past and the future is the fundamental dynamic of the Marxist historical universe. Within this view of history, socialist revolution occurs the moment these contradictory forces enter into direct conflict and engage each other in the ultimate fight without possibility of reconciliation. One side wins by destroying the other. In this situation, with direct force as the only means of resolution, the only question remaining is, whose violence will prove more effective, and, consequently, which way will history move? Will the new, promised world of universal justice and plenty unfold, or will society slip back into the world of enmity, confusion, and exploitation? Thus, writers presenting Bolshevik violence from the regime's point of view do not search for ways to conceal the bloody horrors of Bolshevik violence, but treat them as a quite natural, inevitable, and, in an ultimate historical view, positive phenomenon. Bertolt Brecht, himself a faithful follower of the Bolshevik ideology at the time, put it briefly:

> We
> Who wished to prepare the ground for friendliness
> Could not ourselves be friendly.

And:

> Where violence rules
> Only violence helps.[30]

Getting this fundamental ethical view of revolutionary violence across requires no less than a direct challenge to, or plain dismissal of, human notions of right and wrong other than the utilitarian "dialectical morality" of Lenin. The expressions of this view examined above challenge the assumed "eternal morality" of the reader and introduce in its place a new, politicized sense of ethics. Just as the old world and the new oppose each other in these works, so the ethics championed by their authors challenge the ethical universe of their assumed readers. (Of course, this interpretation should not be applied to those authors who present the Bolshevik approach from a distance.) The "tragic heroes" of Tarasov-Rodyonov and Ehrenburg challenge the reader's traditional ethics by portraying the alleged necessity of immoral actions on the part of the Bolshevik regime. By introducing the motif of the tragic duality of two opposed ethical universes, these authors undermine traditional moral notions as relative in the context of the new ones. At the same time, casual or lofty invocations of state terrorism, as found in works by Knyazev and Bagritsky, directly defy the reader's traditional sense of morality. Thus, the opposition between the new and old, between revolution and reaction, is not limited to the world presented in these literary works as their subject matter, but is extended to include the rhetorical sphere where the encounter between the reader and the text takes place. The reader is directly challenged by these works and presented with the antagonizing option of either remaining faithful to a traditional sense of right and wrong or accepting the ethical justification of Bolshevik horrors and thereby abandoning his original moral sense. The choice is hardly fair, since remaining faithful to traditional ethics and rejecting the new stand is tantamount to admitting that one belongs to the forces of reaction. It means admitting something inadmissible in Soviet public discourse.

If the universe presented in these works is characterized by the impossibility of reconciliation between the two sides of an inner conflict, the opposition between the author committed to Bolshevik morality and the reader committed to traditional moral values exhibits the same irreconcilable polarity. The way of resolving the opposition between the points of view of the author and the reader leads, by analogy with the revolutionary situation, through challenge, assault, and subjugation, not through dialog and reconciliation. The universe reflected by Knyazev and Mayakovsky is revealed from a point of view involved in the central conflict and is colored by an intense partisan attitude. It seems quite logical that, in a universe whose fundamental structure consists of inner conflict, there is no place for a finalizing, definitive point of view beyond it. The mere admission of such a possibility would mean that the conflict could be neutralized, relativized, or reconciled within the scope of some larger vision beyond the reach of the immediate participants in the struggle. The revolutionary universe presented here does not need such an "absolute" point of view located outside the conflict, because it is precisely one of the adversarial points of view engaged in the struggle that is bound to provide the ultimate resolution to this central opposition by simply annihilating the other side and assuming sole authority. The Bolshevik point of view is presented as subjective "in the short run," but it is this very point of view that is bound to become the only definitive, objective position from which all history, including the present time, will be viewed. This will happen when the enemies of the Bolsheviks are destroyed. "During the period of revolution," Leon Trotsky wrote in 1924, in *Literature and Revolution*, "only that literature which promotes the consolidation of the workers in their struggle against the exploiters is necessary and progressive. Revolutionary literature cannot but be imbued with the spirit of social hatred, which is a creative historic factor in an epoch of proletarian dictatorship." [31]

3

THE GLORY
OF THE GULAG

Stalin's Camps as Social Medicine

Life has become better, comrades, life has become
gayer.

—Joseph Stalin (1934)

The honored guests, Comrades Kaganovich,
Yagoda, and Berman, arrived at Lock No. 3. (Their
portraits hung in every barracks.) People worked
more quickly. Up above they smiled—and their
smile was transmitted to hundreds of people down
in the excavation.

—Y. Kuzemko, *The Third Lock* (1935)

The final end of any revolution is the restoration of
power. Otherwise it would finally lead to chaos.

—Diary of Joseph Goebbels

Struggle, Victory, Labor, Harmony

The Bolshevik ideology that in the 1920s inspired the Soviet cultural discourse justifying Bolshevik victimization was the same ideology that rendered this discourse dysfunctional towards the end of the decade. Bolshevik violence, coercion, and terror, according to the prevailing Soviet cultural discourse of the time, were deemed necessary in a revolutionary universe dominated by the struggle of the two irreconcilable forces of revolution and reaction. This was the "truth" for the 1920s, especially for the early years of the decade. Within the Marxist–Leninist universe, however, each truth was subject to the dialectical principle of historical relativity. This included the "truths" created or adopted by the regime in order to explain the Bolshevik use of violence and terror at different stages of Soviet history.

According to this dialectical mode of thinking, once the final victory of the revolution was accomplished, revolutionary violence was prone to gradually lose its status as a "necessary" factor in the protection of the new regime. As class enemies were defeated, the "spirit of social hatred" that inspired revolutionary struggle would become increasingly obsolete as the principal attitude towards social problems both in life and in literature. It would be expected that after the victory, the "spirit of social hatred," along with its actual embodiment—Bolshevik terror—would gradually wither away, and a new, more harmonious spirit would begin to dominate the minds of the inhabitants of this post-revolutionary utopia-in-the making.

Trotsky, who proclaimed the rule of the "spirit of social hatred" in the literature of the revolution, expected a natural transition to a more harmonious world after the revolutionary victory. He wrote: "Revolutionary art which inevitably reflects all the contradictions of a revolutionary social system, should not be confused with Socialist art for which no basis has as yet been made. On the other hand, one must not forget that Socialist art will grow out of the art of this transition period." Trotsky wrote these words in 1924. At that point, he made a prediction concerning the nature of the new attitude toward life that was to dominate post-revolutionary Russia: "Socialism will abolish class antagonisms. . . . Under Socialism, solidarity will be the basis of society. Literature and art will be tuned to a different key. All the emotions which the revolutionists, at the present time, feel apprehensive of naming—so much have they been worn thin by hypocrites and vulgarians—such as disinterested friendship, love for one's neighbor, sympathy, will be mighty ringing chords of Socialist poetry." [1]

Toward the close of the 1920s, as the new social order created by the victorious revolution was entering its second decade, the days of common "disinterested friendship," "love," and "sympathy" were still to come; yet it was becoming more and more urgent for the Bolsheviks that at least some progress toward these goals should be acknowledged and identified as part of current Soviet reality. It was the promise of a better, harmonious society that constituted the ideological and political basis for the Bolshevik claim to legitimacy. Ten years after the October revolution, the confrontation of the promise with reality was natural, not only for the population (increasingly muffled), but for some of the revolutionaries themselves. Yet, despite the inherent logic of the ruling ideology, the "natural" withering away of the Bolshevik terror was not about to happen. On the contrary, after the initial success in subjugating the society, followed by the ambiguous period of the NEP, the revolutionary regime was to embark on a series of ambitious projects expected to result in the construction of the much-needed economic base for the Marxist–Leninist superstructure already in place. The speedy and complete collectivization of farmland was among the most urgent new tasks of the regime, and only someone extremely naive could expect to accomplish it without the extensive use of terror. This new wave of terror needed new rationalization, both for the population and for the Bolshevik functionaries themselves. Further use of the argument of the "inevitability" of violence as a necessary means of protecting the revolutionary regime naturally led to a question: Was the revolution truly victorious, since a decade after its seizure of power it must still rely on force in order to survive? Such questions came close to evoking revisionist answers, but revisionism was not what Stalin, then establishing himself as the new Soviet dictator, was prepared to tolerate.

Despite repeated mouthing of slogans concerning the continuous threat posed to the Soviet state by the world bourgeoisie, the verbal formulas of the 1920s that justified Bolshevik victimization as a necessary means of self-protection were becoming more and more obsolete from the pragmatic, political point of view as well. These attitudes to violence were useful when spontaneous aggression was unleashed during the revolution that brought the regime to power and, later, whenever psychological aggression was used against some targeted group of the population (kulaks, "Trotskyites," engineers, doctors, and so on). On the other hand, when viewed from the vantage point of the established and now powerful totalitarian regime, these violent and immoral attitudes presented an element of unpredictability, and unpredictability of social behavior was close to the last thing the maturing Soviet regime was willing to cope with. The political functionality of the formula "necessary violence," quite high in the period of the civil war and initial revolutionary terror (as well as in the cyclical waves of controlled public hatred orchestrated later by Stalin), was rather low in the system of institutionalized, disciplined terror in the labor camps that was about to become a stable element of Soviet reality. The idiom of destructive violence, useful for assuming power and eliminating political competition, had fulfilled its role in the 1920s and now needed to pass into history (which, in the Bolshevik case, meant into oblivion). When Bertolt Brecht spelled out a moral justification of Bolshevik violence in *Die Massnahme* (1930), he did it a bit too late: both the Communist party of Germany (KPD) and Moscow "reacted angrily to *Die Massnahme*—because communists [did not] *say* things like that [any more], not in public anyway." [2]

What the Bolsheviks needed at the beginning of the 1930s was a convention reconciling the population with the new face of Soviet totalitarian victimization—the "constructive" violence of slave labor and its chief institution, the concentration camp (renamed labor camp). This was a new type of violence: systematic, controlled, oriented toward a goal, disciplined, and ultimately justified by the great achievements promised in the future. For while the general public might not have been aware of it, the Soviet state was moving toward the admission of terror and slavery as inalienable elements of the Soviet socioeconomic system. Slave labor and terror were to become indispensable means of constructing the Marxist utopia in Russia.

By 1929, the year called by Stalin "the great turning point," this direction of the development of the Soviet state was becoming more and more apparent. The NEP was stopped and replaced by the first Five-Year Plan, which centralized the economy in order to forcefully industrialize the country in a speedy fashion. The final decision on the collectivization of farmland was announced by the end of the year. [3] Soviet cultural life was soon to be directly and officially subject to the control of the Communist Party. [4] All these and other similar changes in Soviet social and economic life were presented by the regime as indications of the growing consolidation of the whole society in its collective effort to build a better future under the leadership of the Communist Party. In other words, they were supposed to reflect progress on the route towards what Trotsky had imagined as the world of collective harmony, "disinterested friendship," "love," and "sympathy," in which the remnants of the historic conflicts of the age of revolution were soon to fade away. The leaders of the party encouraged writers to acknowledge this progress, and so instructed them at the meeting of the Central Committee in August 1928: "You should emphasize the positive aspects of our work. . . . You should pay more attention to a thorough selection of facts, and present genuinely positive examples."[5]

Besides ideology and domestic politics, an important factor in this change in the official image of Soviet terror and violence was Soviet foreign policy. As hopes for immediate world revolution diminished in the 1920s, Stalin was gradually developing the ostensible image of his regime as a "normal" state, ready to engage in international trade and ready to cooperate with moderate Western governments in containing the radicalism of the Fascist, Nazi (after 1933), and other ultra-right regimes. As socialist and Communist sympathies became more widespread among Western intellectuals after the economic crash of 1929, the Soviet leadership won a receptive audience in the West, an audience that could become an important ally or a tool of Soviet policy. It was humanitarian concerns that steered many Western intellectuals towards Communism, and if the Soviet regime wanted to influence them, it would have to present itself in a more humane light. An image of the Soviet system as the only alternative to Fascism, the bourgeois liberal democracy being identified as morally bankrupt and hopelessly outdated, was cultivated by the Stalinist regime for the consumption of Western audi-

ences until Stalin's surprising pact with Hitler in 1939. After
the German aggression against the Soviet Union in 1941,
these notions were soon revived and proved highly influential with the Western left during and long after World War II.

Meanwhile, at home, political developments at the end of
the 1920s and the beginning of the 1930s opened the way
for a new, easily predicted massive wave of Soviet state terror
against those slow to accept the forced dispropriations of collectivization, of both the land and the minds. Terror and victimization were on their way to becoming a long-lasting
feature of life in the Soviet Union—Stalin's way to socialism.
If the revolution, along with its "spirit of social hatred," was
over, and a new order of harmonious, collective solidarity
was to become a reality, the foundations of this new order
would have to be built by millions of terrorized slaves and
semi-slaves in militarized factories, collective farms, places of
confined settlement, and concentration camps, whose number and population were to grow rapidly at the turn of the
1930s.

Neither the tragic overtones projected by Tarasov-
Rodyonov nor the bloodthirsty rhetoric of Knyazev were
useful as normative attitudes toward this new type of violence that was to cast its shadow over Soviet life in the near
future. Besides, the violent, immoral, and casual attitude toward violence, projected in many literary works of the 1920s,
came dangerously close to becoming identifiable as a revelation of pure, unmitigated crime—evil without any ethical
disguise. And, as the Marquis de Custine noted in 1839, "*open
crime can triumph for no more than a day.*"[6]

The Bolsheviks were in the business of building a long-
lasting order of the future. They were doing it supposedly for
the sake of the population they ruled. Their method was to
terrorize the population in order to make it construct its
own better future. In the process, as some among the Bolshe-

viks hoped, the population would become aware of the advantages to come, and the element of terror would become obsolete and slip into oblivion. Thus the elements of terror and brutal coercion could be treated as irrelevant in terms of the future. Those who were to populate the better world to come would become "new people," too content with their lives to regret the paths that had led them thither. Those who did not survive the process would not be heard from anyway. The vision was optimistic, constructive, and, in its own way, highly ethical. Its literary expression had to exhibit the same features.

A Sentimental Journey of Maxim Gorky

The year 1929, called by Stalin "the great turning point" on the Soviet way towards socialism, also witnessed the firm establishment of a new literary convention, created in order to justify the new forms of institutionalized terror already developing in the Soviet state. This new literary strategy, different from the formula of "revolutionary morality" of the 1920s and its shocking literary visions, was to reflect the new, post-revolutionary, "constructive" mode of Soviet life. This new convention was to replace the revolutionary discourse of terror, vengeance, and class-cleansing with the pedagogical discourse of reeducation and resocialization through compulsive labor. As a matter of fact, this new discourse was not entirely new. As mentioned before, in 1919 Felix Dzerzhinsky postulated turning the civil war concentration camps into "schools of labor," where hard work would successfully discourage the former "class enemies" from opposing the new proletarian regime, to the point of transforming these former parasites into true proletarians. Almost at the same time, the pedagogical concept of the resocialization of criminals, especially juvenile offenders, was championed and tested in Soviet Russia by a Communist educator, Anton Makarenko. In 1920–1927 Makarenko founded and directed a corrective colony for juvenile offenders near Poltava, named in honor of Maxim Gorky, and in 1927–1935 a similar colony in Kharkov, named in honor of Felix Dzerzhinsky himself. In these colonies inmates engaged in collective labor and study were expected to develop a positive sense of self-respect and social responsibility. Makarenko, who presented his humanitarian pedagogical concepts in the highly publicized novel *The Pedagogical Poem* (1933–1936), became one of the most venerated figures of official Soviet culture.[7]

The first fairly large-scale concentration camp of the 1920s, on the islands of Solovki, began integrating Dzerzhinsky's idea of the "schools of labor" with a rhetoric of re-socialization that sounded much like Makarenko's highly humanitarian way of addressing the topic of juvenile offenders. Thus the vision of a humane, benevolent concentration camp became possible, and Soviet propaganda began to create and implement it. In 1927–1928 a propaganda film was made by order of Stalin's political police (OGPU) about the successful resocialization of the prisoners in the Solovki camp.[8] However, it was not until 1929 that this new, "humanitarian" vision of the camps became the principal convention of Soviet literature, determining the ways in which the topic of the camp would be approached in the period of its highest visibility in Soviet discourse. The literary beacon of this convention was the reportage from the Solovki camp written by Maxim Gorky after his visit to the camp on 20–23 June 1929.

Before turning to Gorky's work a few words should be said about its direct subject, the Solovki concentration camp. Despite their remote location off the shore of the White Sea, the Solovki islands were very well known throughout pre-revolutionary Russia, because of a large, important monastery and fortress established there in the Middle Ages. Throughout its history, the Solovki monastery was not only a center of Russian Orthodox spirituality, but also a crucial military stronghold, a manufacturing center, and a place where political prisoners were sent by the Russian tsars. The Bolsheviks destroyed all these functions of the Solovki monastery except the last. In 1920 the monastery itself was closed, and on 6 June 1923 the first prisoners were sent to the Solovki camp, many of them from smaller concentration camps at Arkhangelsk, Kholmogora, and Pertominsk. The growing population of the camp consisted of, besides criminals, former officers of the Imperial Army and White Guards; former civil servants; clergy; participants, supporters, and sympathizers of anti-Bolshevik peasant insurrections; businessmen and speculators; and members of all political parties other than the Bolsheviks (and, later on, Bolshevik victims of Stalin's purges).

These prisoners, along with many accidental victims, were subject to forced labor, hunger, terror, and numerous deprivations. Solzhenitsyn in *The Gulag Archipelago* cites a few disciplinary measures used customarily in the Solovki camp (many witnesses confirmed these facts):

> Poles the thickness of an arm were set from wall to wall and prisoners were ordered to sit on these poles all day. (At night they lay on the floor, one on top of another, because it was overcrowded.) The height of the poles was set so that one's feet could not reach the ground. And it was not so easy to keep balance. In fact, the prisoner spent the entire day just trying to maintain his perch. If he fell, the jailers jumped on him. Or else they took him outside to a flight of stairs consisting of 365 steep steps. . . . They tied the person lengthwise to a "balan" (a beam), for the added weight, and rolled him

down (and there wasn't even one landing, and the steps were so steep that the log with a human being on it would go all the way down without stopping). . . . Or they might put the prisoners on a sharp-edged boulder on which one could not stay long either. Or, in summer, "on the stump," which meant naked among the mosquitoes. . . . Or they might drive a person into marsh muck up to his neck and keep him there. And then there was another way: to hitch up a horse in empty shafts and fasten the culprit's legs to the shafts; then the guard mounted the horse and kept on driving the horse through a forest cut until the groans and the cries from behind simply came to an end.[9]

Amidst this terror and deprivation, the Bolsheviks found it fitting to create and sustain the image of "life as usual" in the Solovki camp: camp newspapers were edited by prisoners; the ethnographic society, the amateur theater, and musical ensembles were run by prisoners; and in front of the main OGPU headquarters there was a flower bed in the shape of an elephant with letters spelling SLON (which in Russian means "elephant" and, at the same time, stands for the abbreviation of the Solovki Special Purpose Camps—*Solovetskie lageria osobogo naznacheniia*—SLON).[10] One may find it thought-provoking to compare this early Soviet phenomenon to a later one, in the Nazi camps, where mass murder and slavery were accompanied by music played by prisoner orchestras. In some of those camps flower beds and paths were kept spotless, and prisoners sometimes played soccer next to gas chambers in full operation.[11]

Established long before the rapid development of the Soviet slave labor camp system in the 1930s, the Solovki camp served as a laboratory for testing various methods of terror that, later on, were either adopted or dropped, according to their usefulness. One of the most peculiar Soviet inventions tested in Solovki was the "prisoners' self-organization." Under this system, prisoners who collaborated with the regime in supervising and guarding others were rewarded with significant, sometimes life-saving, advantages, such as the shortening of their sentences, not to mention lighter work and better access to such camp "benefits" as food and clothing. In fact, the Soviet political police succeeded in creating in Solovki a system considerably dependent on breaking prisoners' solidarity and thus turning many of them into collaborators with the regime. This and other methods of transforming victims into instruments of victimization became, later on, a hallmark of the Soviet camps.

The Solovki camp had been in operation for a long time before forced labor was recognized by the Soviet regime as a vital part of the country's economy. In the 1920s the status of forced labor in the Solovki camp was determined by two factors. On the one hand, it was officially recognized as a way of transforming people's identities from parasitic class enemies into Soviet people, according to Dzerzhinsky's formula of the concentration camps as "schools of labor." On the other hand, whenever this ideology was put into practice, it tended to change the nature of labor from an activity oriented toward a goal to just another form of punishment. As such, it was executed without much concern for the results of the actual work. Solzhenitsyn notes:

[I]t would seem that in the first years of Solovki both slave-driving the workers and allotting back-breaking *work norms* took the form of periodic outbursts, transitory anger: they had not become a viselike *system*. The economy of the whole country was not based on them, and the Five-Year Plans had not been instituted. In the first years of SLON there was evidently no firm external economic plan. Yes, and for that matter there was no very careful calculation of how many man-days went into work for the camp as a whole. This was why they could suddenly switch with such frivolity from meaningful productive work to punishment: pouring water from one ice hole into another, dragging logs from one place to another and back. There was cruelty in this, yes, but there was also a patriarchal attitude. When slave-driving became a thought-out *system,* pouring water over a prisoner in subzero temperatures or putting the prisoner out on a stump to be devoured by mosquitoes had turned into a superfluity and a useless expenditure of the executioners' energy.[12]

In 1929, the year Gorky visited Solovki, the Solovki camp was evolving from an experimental concentration camp to a system of production-oriented slave-labor camps, of a type that, in a few years, would be copied and further perfected all over the Soviet Union. The masters of the camps were already beginning to think in economic terms, and to think big. With the camp population rapidly growing, Nogtev, the new chief of SLON appointed in 1930, reported that in 1926 Solovki provided the Railroad Timber Trust and the Karelian Timber Trust with 63,000 rubles' worth of timber; in 1929 it turned out 2,355,000 rubles' worth; and in 1930 the amount tripled.[13]

This was the camp that Gorky visited on 20 June 1929. His reportage, "Solovki," appeared in print as part of a longer cycle of travel sketches written in 1928 and 1929 and published in six subsequent issues of the Soviet journal *Nashi dostizheniia* (Our Accomplishments) in 1929 under the title *In and About the Soviet Union*.[14] Gorky's approach to the Soviet terror and victimization evidenced in the concentration camps set a new standard for the presentation of this topic in

Soviet literature and public discourse in general. Gorky's strategy, first implemented in "Solovki," was further developed in 1934 by a group of thirty-six Soviet authors (under Gorky's editorship and with his contribution), in the fullest ever literary presentation of the Soviet world of concentration camps seen from the point of view of the Bolshevik regime—a thick volume entitled *Belomorsko–Baltiiskii Kanal imeni Stalina: Istoriia stroitel'stva* (The Joseph Stalin White Sea–Baltic Sea Canal: History of Its Construction), better known by its abbreviated Russian name, *Belomorkanal*. The book was dedicated, on behalf of the newly created Soviet Writers' Union, to the Seventeenth Congress of the Communist (Bolshevik) Party, and to Stalin personally. In what follows, the ideological assumptions and literary strategies employed by Gorky in 1929, and by his followers in 1934, will be analyzed, in order to describe what became the most radical design in Soviet, and perhaps world, literature of a literary medium employed to reprogram people's perceptions of their own victimization.

The story of the creation of Gorky's first reportage from the Soviet concentration camps begins, not on a June day in 1929, on the shores of the White Sea, but in Gorky's villa "Il Sotto," in the distant Italian resort of Sorrento where, on 10 October 1927, Gorky wrote to the editors of Gosizdat in Moscow: "I feel like writing a book about the new Russia."[15] It had been six years since Gorky left Russia and settled abroad. The main reason for Gorky's leaving Russia precisely at the moment of the Bolshevik victory in the civil war was customarily explained by Soviet sources as the writer's poor health and the necessity of seeking treatment abroad. While there is some truth to this, another, perhaps more important, factor—a political factor—seems to have played a major role in Gorky's decision. Gorky, a Bolshevik supporter before the revolution, personally befriended by Lenin, was outraged by

Bolshevik revolutionary violence. He publicly condemned the Bolshevik terror in the Left Menshevik newspaper *Novaia zhizn'*, and when the newspaper was closed down by order of Lenin in July 1918, he republished his critical comments abroad in a volume entitled *Untimely Thoughts*.[16] Lenin neither reprimanded nor took revenge on Gorky. He apparently never ceased trusting Gorky and considered him an important ally of the Bolsheviks. In fact, Gorky wavered between moral acceptance and rejection of the Bolshevik regime. "I intend working with the Bolsheviks as a free agent," he wrote in a letter to his first wife, Ekaterina Peshkova.[17] At the same time, he believed that his open criticism of the Bolsheviks would help to alleviate their oppressive measures, especially those against the Russian intelligentsia. Gorky found himself in the position of an influential spokesman for Russian writers. His interventions, made possible by his personal relationship with Lenin, quite often received a positive response from the Bolshevik leadership. However, the presence of such a demanding and critical confidant of Lenin was becoming increasingly troublesome to Bolshevik officials who came in contact with Gorky. Lenin himself seemed well informed about Gorky's self-assured "special status," and it was Lenin who, under the guise of concern about Gorky's health, kept prompting him to leave the country.

On 20 October 1920, Lenin insisted in a conversation with Gorky: "You are doing nothing to look after your health, . . . and it has completely gone to pieces. Push off abroad, to Italy or Davos. . . . If you won't go, then we'll have to send you."[18] And on 9 August 1921, he wrote to Gorky: "Here, there are no opportunities to work in a sensible way, nothing but futile political agitation."[19] As Lenin's insistence grew, so Gorky's special influence on the Bolsheviks gradually diminished. His attempts to secure the Soviet government's permission for the ailing Aleksandr Blok to leave the country and seek treatment proved futile. Blok died while waiting for his exit visa. Just three weeks later, another intercession proved unsuccessful: the poet Nikolai Gumilev, charged with conspiracy, was executed despite Gorky's pleas for his life. Finally, on 8 October 1921, Gorky, undoubtedly disillusioned, left Soviet Russia. Lenin commented on Gorky's departure: "He has delicate nerves. . . . He is an artist, after all. It's better if he leaves, gets some treatment and rest, and takes another look at all this from far off. Meantime we shall sweep our streets and then we shall say: 'Things are tidier here now, we can even invite you our artist.' " [20] And Lunacharsky added: "And so Alexei Maximovich, hounded by his illness and the necessity of saving his life, which we all so valued, . . . was separated from us by distance. But this did not break our ties. A thread through which blood flowed, a vessel leading to the heart of Alexei Maximovich, remained." [21]

Lunacharsky's words were proven right. Once abroad, initially in German and Czech spas and then in his luxurious villa in Sorrento, Gorky strayed from his Bolshevik loyalty to the point of almost severing his ties with the regime once and for all. Yet, this severance was never complete, and Gorky kept wavering between anti-Bolshevik and pro-Bolshevik sentiments. In the summer of 1922 Gorky wrote in an emigré newspaper: "With others of his kind, Lenin, an amoral person who regards sufferings of the people with aristocratic indifference, a theoretician and dreamer with no acquaintance with real life, carried out a planetary experiment, and it has failed." [22] Gorky's correspondence with Vladislav Khodasevich, his fellow-editor of the emigré journal *Beseda,* reveals some of Gorky's thoughts at the time. On 4 July 1923, Gorky wrote to Khodasevich from Gunterstahl: "The letters I get from Russia are far from good. There is some quagmire of fatigue and depression in them." One year later, on 13 July 1924, he wrote to Khodasevich from Sorrento: "Here, almost every day we have fireworks, processions, music, and folk festivals. 'And in our country?' I think. And, forgive me sir, I feel like crying and anger overwhelms me. There is so much envy, anguish, shame, and everything else in me." And on 5 September 1924, Gorky added, "I swear that when I am alone with myself, at night, I feel so disheartened that if this act were not so banal and ridiculous I would shoot myself in the head." [23]

Gorky did not kill himself. Instead, he took a no less astonishing step: he decided to go back to the Soviet Union. His return was a gradual process, which started from his conspicuous reconciliation with the Soviet regime. Exactly when and why Gorky decided to return is far from clear. One can observe a gradually emerging pattern of behavior leading to Gorky's acceptance of the Bolshevik regime with all the moral qualities that Gorky had despised just a few years earlier. The KGB archives contain copies of letters sent to Gorky from the Soviet Union that describe the reality of growing terror and oppression in the Soviet state. Gorky, sensitive to such voices just a few years before, now began turning a deaf ear to them. Moreover, he started rebuking and ridiculing them in the Soviet press. He publicly dismissed his correspondents for not signing their letters with their real names, as if unaware of the consequences these authors would face, as their letters were regularly opened and copied by the political police. Today, these letters are known only because copies survived in the police archives.

This turnaround in Gorky's attitude to the Soviet regime coincided with Lenin's death, and one may speculate that Gorky, having lost his ultimate protector, had to choose between the fate of a political emigré and the still possible prospect of literary fame in the Soviet Union. Gorky could not be sure whether he could manage to win the favor of the new Soviet dictator, Stalin. He must have remembered that, back in 1917, after the publication of his anti-Bolshevik criticism in *Novaia Zhizn'*, Stalin himself wrote in *Rabochii Put'* that Gorky "some day may easily end up in the camp of people rejected by the revolution." [24] Bitter letters from the Soviet Union did not turn Gorky away from his new path back to the limelight of the Soviet literary stage. The new Soviet leadership under Stalin seemed to lure Gorky back by inciting his sense of personal grandeur. The official Soviet cult of Gorky started well before the writer set foot on Soviet soil again after his voluntary exile. Gorky's sixtieth birthday provided an opportunity for widespread, officially arranged celebrations. On the very day of Gorky's birthday, 29 March 1928, an anonymous Russian scholar wrote to Gorky:

> I consider such celebrations to be equally offensive to you, our greatest living Russian writer, and to us, as scholars and representatives of the Russian intelligentsia which always attributed serious value to similar celebrations only if they were a free expression of public sympathy and emotion. . . . From your fine distance, enjoying complete freedom and independence (if under the protection of the Fascist government and blessed sky of Italy), inhabiting a superb villa with no limits on your living space, you repeat, after the official lying press of Soviet Russia, what those who have lived through the last 10 years in Russia itself know to be falsehoods—untruths that cannot be justified by any, even the highest, goals and ideals. You do so, moreover, before the eyes of the entire civilized world. . . . I know that you will throw this letter into the waste basket with a contemptuous smile as one more anonymous, pitiful and feeble outpouring of an enemy of the prole-

tariat etc. . . . You can harass us without any fear of reprisal. You cannot hear anything from us in reply: our hands are bound and the Soviet gag is forced into our mouths. But knowing this, do you suppose that you are acting as a champion of the free world? . . . I do not wish to believe, as many are saying, that you are knowingly writing falsehoods or that you have sold out to the Soviet authorities. If I thought that, of course, I would not have written to you. Yet I cannot fathom why you take on yourself the right to judge so hastily that which you do not know, have not seen and are not yourself experiencing.[25]

Flattered and praised in Soviet propaganda, Gorky seems to have ceased to pay attention to anonymous warnings sent to him in private letters. His return to the Soviet Union effectively began in 1928, with a series of cautious "reconnaissance" trips, and was finally concluded in 1933. Consistent with his expectations, Gorky assumed the post, prepared for him by Stalin's regime, of central authority on Soviet literature.

Although the motives underlying Gorky's return present a series of ethical and psychological questions, one thing is certain: Gorky was not unaware of the moral nature of the Soviet system. By choosing to assume the highest post in the Soviet literary hierarchy, he clearly consented to fulfill the political obligations attached to it. His blatant attacks in the Soviet press on the defenseless authors of anonymous letters of warning can be seen as a public message by the self-exiled writer to the Soviet leadership, confirming his readiness to serve the Bolshevik regime and to comply with Stalin's rules of the game. Gorky was signalling to the Soviet authorities that his period of rebelliousness was over and that he could be relied upon politically. Then, in 1927, Gorky took the next step. He decided to visit the Soviet state for the first time since his departure in 1921. He was ready to write a book about Soviet reality and to make it his passport back to the favors of the Bolshevik regime. The image of the Soviet Union in this book constituted a response to the political and ideological needs of the Soviet authorities.

This was the moment when Gorky wrote his letter to the Soviet publishing house, Gosizdat, in Moscow. Having stated his desire to write a book about the "new Russia," Gorky continued: "I have already collected a lot of interesting material for the book. I must now go incognito to factories, workers' clubs, villages, beer taverns, construction sites; I must see Komsomol members, students, rural correspondents, and worker correspondents; I must go to schools and to colonies for socially dangerous children; I must have a look at women-deputies, and Muslim women, and so on. It is a serious matter. Whenever I think about it, I get extremely excited." [26]

Gosizdat responded positively to Gorky's suggestions, and on 28 May 1928, Gorky arrived in Moscow. In July, he started his travels around the new Russia, in search of—as he put it—first-hand materials for the book. Gorky's itinerary reflected his priorities as spelled out in his original letter. In the summer of 1928 he visited, among others, the industrial centers and construction sites of Baku, Donetsk, Dneprostroi, Makarenko's corrective labor colony for minors, museums of Kazan, and the towns of Tbilisi, Yalta, Simferopol, Erevan, Nizhny Novgorod, and Leningrad.

The mode of Gorky's "writer's journey" was far from what he had suggested in his letter to the publishing house. Not only did Gorky not remain "unseen" during his numerous forays into various places in search of "first-hand material"; his journey more closely resembled a triumphal tour by an official foreign celebrity than a casual journey by an unassuming observer of Russian life. Special meetings of the writer with the "representatives of local communities" were arranged, and they included the presence of numerous state officials, from Andrei Zhdanov to local bosses of the Communist Party and the Communist Youth Organization (Komsomol). Similar celebrations accompanied Gorky during his second journey, when, in 1929, he visited Leningrad, Murmansk, Stalingrad, Rostov, Astrakhan, Sukhumi, Tbilisi, Vladikavkaz, and, most importantly for present purposes, the concentration camp on the islands of Solovki.

Gorky's tour of Russia in 1928 and 1929 reveals striking similarities to the usual ways the authorities in Soviet Russia used to handle foreign visitors coming to "learn the truth about the Soviet Union" and to get "first-hand material." Long before the Soviet authorities mastered the art of deception, de Custine wrote in 1839: "As a foreigner, and especially as a foreign writer, I was overwhelmed with expressions of goodwill by the Russians. But their condescension was limited to promises and no one permitted me to penetrate to the depth of things. A host of mysteries remained beyond the reach of my intelligence."[27]

De Custine's reaction was atypical in its unwillingness to bow to the deceptive politeness surrounding him. Be that as it may, the deception he experienced was nothing compared to that practiced by the Soviet hosts who welcomed visitors a hundred years later. Most of the celebrities visiting Soviet Russia never questioned the frankness and sincerity of their official guides. H. G. Wells, after a conversation with Lenin, announced to the world: "I have never met a man more candid, fair, and honest."[28] Lion Feuchtwanger, who witnessed the show trials of 1937, described Soviet Russia as a "true democracy" and contrasted it with the hypocrisy of Western democracies.[29] George Bernard Shaw went perhaps even further in his admiration for the homeland of the world proletariat, which he visited several times. After a visit to a Soviet show prison, he praised the Soviet penitentiary system in which, according to his description, prisoners were so content in jail that the authorities had difficulty in convincing them to leave at the end of their sentences. Before leaving Russia, Shaw wrote in the book of the "Metropol" hotel in Moscow: "Tomorrow I will leave this land of hope and return to the West where hopelessness rules."[30] Sometimes the Soviet authorities did not hesitate to construct entire Potyomkin villages, as they did on the arrival of American Vice-President Henry Wallace and Professor Owen Lattimore to the Kolyma region in 1944. The American visitors were pleasantly surprised by the energetic gold-mining enterprise in the area (watchtowers were temporarily dismantled in the labor camps visited by Wallace and Lattimore, and the prisoners were kept out of sight). They were also charmed by their host, General Nikishov (the legendary master of life and death of Kolyma's prisoners). In his book *Soviet Asia Mission,* Wallace describes the Soviet gold-miners as "big husky young men who came out to the Far East from European Russia." The pleasant impression of the American visitors to Kolyma was greatly reinforced by local culinary delights served them by their Soviet hosts. "The delicious fresh Kolyma River fish served us near Berelyakh led me to inquire about the presiding chef of this mining camp," Wallace notes in his account. Only on one occasion was this deception in danger of discovery. While visiting a collective farm (in fact, a women's prison farm from which the prisoners were temporarily evacuated), Wallace, himself an agriculture specialist, asked one of the "collective woman-farmers" (impersonated by the wives of the NKVD officers) a question regarding farming about which she had naturally no idea. Reportedly, the interpreter saved the situation.[31]

Gorky's account of his journeys around Russia in 1928

and 1929 could be placed in the category of such views of Soviet life as those just cited. Gorky, however, was not an outsider in Russia, but someone who had always considered himself a supreme expert on Russian life. His literary reportage from Solovki, just like his entire cycle *In and About the Soviet Union,* totally dominated as it was by official views, was not a result of its author's naiveté but of his authorial intention established before he even set foot in Solovki. The relationship between what Gorky actually saw in Solovki and what he was going to tell about it can be elucidated by an anecdote Solzhenitsyn repeats about Gorky's visit to the camp. The irresistible irony, verging on the grotesque, that permeates this account justifies quotation at length:

> The rumor reached Solovki before Gorky himself— and the prisoners' hearts beat faster and the guards hustled and bustled. One has to know prisoners in order to imagine their anticipation! The falcon, the stormy petrel, was about to swoop down upon the nest of injustice, violence, and secrecy. The leading Russian writer! He will give them hell! He will show them! He, the father, will defend! They awaited Gorky almost like a universal amnesty. The chiefs were alarmed too: as best they could, they hid the monstrosities and polished things up for show. . . . They set up a "boulevard" of fir trees without roots, which were simply pushed down into the ground. (They only had to last a few days before withering.) It led to the Children's Colony, opened just three months previously and the pride of USLON, where everyone had clothes and where there were no socially hostile children, and where, of course, Gorky would be very interested in seeing how juveniles were being re-educated and saved for a future life under socialism.

Only in Kem was there an oversight. On Popov Island the ship *Gleb Boky* was being loaded by prisoners in underwear and sacks, when Gorky's retinue appeared out of nowhere to embark on that steamer! . . . Where can this disgraceful spectacle—these men dressed in sacks—be hidden? The entire journey of the great Humanist will have been for naught if he sees them now. Well, of course, he will try hard not to notice them, but help him! Drown them in the sea? They will wallow and flounder. Bury them in the earth? There's no time. No, only a worthy son of the Archipelago could find a way out of this one. The work assigner ordered: "Stop work! Close ranks! Still closer! Sit down on the ground! Sit still!" And a tarpaulin was thrown over them. "Anyone who moves will be shot!" And the former stevedore Maxim Gorky ascended the ship's ladder and admired the landscape from the steamer for a full hour till sailing time—and *he didn't notice!* . . .

The Chekists of USLON fearlessly took him to Sekirka. And what was there to see there? It turned out that there was no overcrowding in the punishment cells, and—the main point—no *poles*. None at all. Thieves sat on benches . . . and they were all . . . reading newspapers. None of them was so bold as to get up and complain, but they did think up one trick: they held the newspapers upside-down! And Gorky went up to one of them and in silence turned the newspaper right side up! He had noticed it! He had understood! He would not abandon them. He would defend them!

They went to the Children's Colony. How decent everything was there. Each was on a separate cot, with a mattress. They all crowded around in a group and all of them were happy. And all of a sudden a fourteen-year-old boy said: "Listen here, Gorky! Everything you see here is false. Do you want to know the truth?" Yes, nodded the writer. Yes, he wanted to know the truth. (Oh, you bad boy, why do you want to spoil the just recently arranged prosperity of the literary patriarch? A palace in Moscow, an estate outside Moscow . . .) And so everyone was ordered to leave, including the children and the gaypayooshniki—and the boy spent an hour and a half telling the whole story to the lanky old man. Gorky left the barracks, streaming tears. He was given a carriage to go to dinner at the villa of the camp chief. And the boys rushed back into the barracks. "Did you tell him about the *pole torture?*" "Yes." "Did you tell him about the *prisoners hitched up instead of horses?*" "Yes." "And how they threw them down the stairs? And about the sacks? And about being made to spend the night in the snow?" And it turned out that the truth-loving boy had told all . . . all . . . all!

But we don't even know his name.

On June 22, in other words after his chat with the boy, Gorky left the following inscription in the "Visitors' Book," which had been specially made for this visit: "I am not in a state of mind to express my impressions in just a few words. I wouldn't want, yes, and I would likewise be ashamed, to permit myself banal praise of the remarkable energy of people who, while remaining vigilant and tireless sentinels of the Revolution, are able, at the same time, to be remarkably bold creators of culture."

On June 23 Gorky left Solovki. Hardly had his steamer pulled away from the pier than they shot the boy.[32]

The Soviet handlers of Gorky's 1929 journey around the Soviet Union had, among other reasons, a practical goal for Gorky's visit to Solovki, as well as for his presentation of the camp in humanitarian terms. A memoir from Solovki by the fugitive Sergei Maslagov had been published in England in 1926.[33] The publication could potentially have created a "public relations" problem for the Soviet government at a time when the regime sought normalization of its relations with the West. The Soviet timber exported to the West was produced by, among others, the prisoners of the SLON camp system. Gorky was expected to use his international status to "disprove" the recent revelations of Maslagov's memoir. There were rumors, also among the Solovki prisoners, that Gorky had accepted this mission in return for the Soviet regime's promise to improve the notorious treatment of the prisoners in Solovki. There is no evidence, however, as to what could possibly have made Gorky so credulous about the Soviet regime in 1929. Nor is there any evidence of Gorky taking any action later to verify the fulfillment of this alleged promise.

It is entirely clear that the purpose of Gorky's "Solovki," along with *In and About the Soviet Union,* was not to give an account of the realia of life in Soviet Russia but to provide a literary illustration of a preconceived set of ideological visions. The grand mystification of the universe of Soviet mass oppression that "Solovki" epitomizes is the product of a literary design based on choice of genre, careful arrangement of viewpoints, and skillful orchestration of themes and motifs within the chosen structure. This work will be analyzed as the creation of an ideological model of an empirically nonexistent universe, rather than as a reflection, more or less accurate, of the actual reality of the camp. We will examine this complex literary structure within the context of its primary purpose—the mystification, not the mere presentation, of Soviet reality.

Gorky's 1927 letter to Gosizdat, besides stating his intention to write a book about the "new Russia," had already indirectly indicated the writer's attitude towards his subject matter, long before his first encounter with it. He had indicated his need for factual, first-hand material of contemporary life as a necessary basis for the book. The book was planned as non-fiction reportage, and factual research was a necessary requirement. However, in his suggestions of places to visit, Gorky's preconceived priorities are apparent. "Factories" and "construction sites" are among the topical locations of Soviet propaganda, where the main mystery of the Soviet rhetorical and ideological universe—the construction of the economic base for the future utopia—takes place. The "workers' clubs," "schools," and above all the "colonies for children" were places marked by the new Soviet life-style, the locations where Soviet propaganda saw the transition from the old to the new superstructure taking place in the form of ideological indoctrination of youth. Gorky reassures his Soviet addressees that it is the birth of the new Communist awareness that is his focal point when he presents his list of chosen interlocutors: "Komsomol members," "workers' correspondents," "rural correspondents," "women-deputies," and so on. All these categories are products of the new system: they are either authors ("workers' correspondents," "rural correspondents") or favorite personages ("Komsomol members," "women-deputies") of Soviet propaganda. Having been abroad since 1921, Gorky is surprisingly in tune with the Bolshevik discourse whereby Russian society is presented. For instance, journalists (*zhurnalisty*) are replaced in Gorky's verbal universe by their new Soviet equivalents: *sel'kory, rabkory*. Other social groups, numerous in pre-revolutionary Russia, such as, for instance, clergy and merchants, are entirely absent from these lengthy enumerations, just as they are becoming absent from Soviet-made reality. Gorky is interested in the "new Russia" and knows he is supposed to see it through the eyes of its new Bolshevik rulers, who are the only ones authorized to define the meaning of the opposition of "old" and "new." The image of the new Russia is imprinted on the new Soviet language, and Gorky demonstrates his intimate knowledge of this language long before he enters the reality described by it. By internalizing the Soviet language, Gorky internalizes the Soviet point of view and presents his readiness to describe Soviet reality according to it. Moreover, he is in love with his vision of the "new Russia" before he even confronts its material equivalent. He writes: "Whenever I think about it, I get extremely excited."

By indicating his need to get to know Soviet reality and, at the same time, expressing a strong attitude toward this reality before encountering it, Gorky adopts the appearance of a writer torn by the inner tension between cognitive and expressive intentions, between the task of reflecting experience and the task of illustrating a preconceived world view with selected, arranged elements of that experience. Travelogues tend to oscillate between two extremes: an unassuming account by an attentive observer and a "sentimental journey" from which readers may learn more about the traveler than about the places he visited.

What may appear as a potential tension between the cognitive and expressive functions of Gorky's cycle of travel sketches is, in fact, reconciled within his work and subjected to a larger literary strategy based on a preconceived point of view. This strategy consists of the presentation of a surface appearance of objective, honest, impartial observation of reality, beneath which an intricate pattern of themes and motifs is arranged in order to mystify this "honest" view and transform it into a representation of the author's ideological projection.

A Traveler's Impressions from the Land of the Bolsheviks

On the surface, "Solovki" and the whole cycle *In and About the Soviet Union* are supposed to appear as a series of travel sketches written by an inquisitive observer returning to Russia after seven years' absence. The choice of the documentary, non-fiction genre of travelogue reflects the abandonment of the previous convention, dominant in the 1920s, of portraying Soviet terror in terms of an intense partisan involvement of the author in the violent revolutionary conflict. The new approach, unlike the literary visions of Tarasov-Rodyonov, Ehrenburg, Knyazev, Bagritsky, and other authors of 1920s-era literary justifications of Bolshevik victimization, was to create an illusion of distanced, objective observation and avoid preconceived sweeping ideological declarations. The new vision was to justify violence not *a priori* but *a posteriori*—to demonstrate its own faithfulness to real experience and "objectively" to dismiss all possible arguments about Bolshevik terror as evil. The genre of the travelogue served this purpose much better than lyrical declarations and novelistic plots.

A principal condition for the successful creation of such an appearance of distanced objectivity was, for Gorky, the reduction or concealment of all textual indications that the reader was dealing with the product of a creative arrangement of language on the part of the author, and that the universe presented in the text was a reflection of the author's own subjective vision. Thus Gorky breaks away from a preexisting tradition employing highly "poetic" styles of writing, along with their preference for quasi-Romantic monologs, heroic poses, and lofty metaphors. What Gorky avoids is visible "literariness," which he replaces with a documentary mode. Fiction is abandoned altogether, and Gorky creates an impression of journalistic honesty with such attributes as factuality, an abundance of directly quoted sources, and a multitude of numbers and statistics. The genre of traveler's sketches suggests here a revealing distance between the visitor (traveler-outsider) and the object of his description. It is used in order to create an effect of refreshing objectivity and lack of prejudice on the part of the author.

Apart from the choice of genre, Gorky creates this effect of objectivity by skillfully playing on the identity of his narrator-traveler. The traveler is Maxim Gorky himself: a great Russian writer and an outsider in Russia, all at once. Within the documentary formula chosen by Gorky, both attributes can be employed in order to create the effect of honest objectivity. Gorky would use them in complementary ways. As a "great Russian writer," Gorky appeared as someone qualified for the traditional cultural position of a speaker for the Russian communal experience and, at the same time, a moral instructor of sorts. Both claims belonged to the nineteenth-century legacy of literature as a central medium in the process of effecting the nation's self-recognition. As an "outsider," on the other hand, Gorky could claim a certain distance from the noise of localized arguments among the politically biased participants in current Russian cultural life. Thus, if revolutionary literature of the 1920s tended to represent one side in the conflict dominating Russian life, Gorky—the author of *In and About the Soviet Union*—appears seemingly "above" Russia's inner conflicts. His own biography could be used as additional capital and could be invested in the creation of this effect. His public position towards the Bolshevik regime before 1928 was quite ambiguous. While widely known for his support of the Bolshevik Party before the revolution, he was also recognized for his criticism of the Bolshevik dictatorship during and immediately after the revolution. His seclusion in the 1920s, though not exactly political emigration, could still lend him the appearance of a somewhat independent cultural figure of worldwide reputation, not just a Bolshevik propagandist. Neither a politically declared emigré nor an engaged Bolshevik literary *aparatchik,* Gorky decided to use this ambiguity in playing the role of a supra-partisan sage, a keen observer and a judge of Russian life.

Toward the end of the 1920s, when the official vision of the revolutionary struggle for survival was giving way to a new vision of the birth of a harmonious world of a classless society, the "spirit of social hatred" was becoming more and more outdated as the dominant attitude towards contemporary Soviet reality. The regime needed an "objective" acknowledgment of its success in turning its promises into reality. Gorky, a "great Russian writer" and an outsider at the same time, seemed to be an author exceptionally well fitted to perform this task.

Designing a Perception

Beneath the surface of objective, unbiased observation of the new Soviet reality, Gorky's cycle *In and About the Soviet Union* proves to be a complex composition of themes and motifs that convey an ideologically motivated mystification of this reality. Through a vision of transition from the old chaos to the new Bolshevik cosmos—a vision that constitutes the main conceptual framework of the work—Gorky created a model rationalization and justification of Soviet totalitarianism at its worst: the terror of the concentration camps.

While aiming at the creation of a contrast between the old world of chaos and the new Soviet harmony, Gorky ventures to describe both realities and thus to mark the principal structural opposition of his work. Naturally, as in the case of virtually all literary panegyrists of the Soviet regime, the main demarcation point between the negative, dark past and the radiant present was the Bolshevik *coup* of October 1917. Traditionally, the theme of revolutionary struggle provided this essentially diachronic opposition with a synchronic representation as the forces of the dark past and the bright future faced each other in battle. At the end of the 1920s this synchronic opposition no longer dominated the official vision of Soviet life. The official claim that Soviet Russia was moving from a stage dominated by inner conflict towards a conflictless world of socialist utopia had literary consequences for those authors who attempted to describe the new reality in terms of narrative dynamics. The revolutionary struggle had been the central source of inner dynamics of Bolshevik literature, and the removal of this source was bound to leave this literature in need of some substitutes for the old conflicts. However, the problem remained purely theoretical, for, owing to the failure of the world revolution, the synchronic opposition between the old and the new could be freshly addressed, in a global context, as the struggle between the homeland of the proletariat and the living embodiment of the past—the bourgeois world outside the Soviet Union.

Within this framework of diachronic and synchronic opposition between the old (pre-Bolshevik) and the new (Bolshevik) worlds, authors whose minds were set on glorifying the Bolshevik regime were in possession of convenient points of reference for illustrating the superiority of the new order over the old. Images of pre-revolutionary Russia and the contemporary (pre-revolutionary) world abroad served this function particularly well when used to address a young Soviet audience that had no knowledge of either pre-revolutionary Russia or the contemporary world abroad. Current Soviet reality was presented as a process of moving away from the past and a struggle against contemporary embodiments of that past (world imperialists and their agents).

These two oppositions provide the key dynamics for Gorky's universe as projected in *In and About the Soviet Union*. In 1935, six years after the completion of the cycle, Gorky wrote a letter to I. A. Rybakova, in which he reflected upon his decision to return to Soviet Russia in 1928 in order to write his "traveler's sketches":

In 1928, I came to the Soviet Union after six years spent abroad where I saw how bourgeois culture was losing its peacock feathers and how the great and petty bourgeoisie was rotting after the World War. I saw learned professors who worked as streetcar conductors and intellectuals who begged on the streets. In Germany, I saw workers starving, and their daughters becoming prostitutes. I also saw thousands of children of the war who were scrofulous, paralyzed, rickety, half-blind, mentally ill. When you see all of this with your own eyes, it becomes clear that the power of the bourgeoisie over the working class is an unjustifiable crime. As to what was happening in the Soviet Union, I knew about it from newspapers and stories told by comrades and friends who were coming from the Soviet Union. When I returned to Moscow, I saw how much the dictator-proletariat had accomplished in six years in the former Russian Empire. Needless to say, it excited me and made me happy and proud of the strength and talent of my compatriots. . . . Later on, I went to the site of the dam construction on the Dneper, to the collective farm "The Giant," to Tbilisi, Erevan, Baku, Kazan, Nizhny Novgorod. I visited almost every place I knew from the past, and besides that I went to Murmansk and Solovki where I had never been before. I looked at the gigantic labor of the Soviet proletariat wisely led by its Party, and ever since then I have been living in joy, filled with this peculiar energy which enriches the Soviet Union and inspires the proletariat of all countries to do what is right and to transform life.[34]

Gorky wrote this shortly after the completion by the Bolshevik regime of the collectivization of land, which cost the lives of several million peasants.[35] Gorky does not even mention it. His attention is focused on illustrating the general opposition of the Bolshevik ideological credo—the contrast between the new and the old—and reality does not seem to confuse him any more. The comparison of the West and the Soviet Union is but an exercise in illustrating this opposition with verbal motifs. Motifs of physical decomposition, illness, and chaos are ascribed to the West ("the bourgeois culture was losing its peacock feathers," the "great and petty bourgeoisie was rotting," "children were scrofulous, paralyzed, rickety, half-blind, mentally ill"); they form a clear-cut opposition to the vigor, health, and energy of the Soviet Union (happiness, pride, "strength," "talent," "joy," "energy," "the gigantic labor of the Soviet proletariat wisely led by its Party," and so on).

These are the negative and positive poles of the contemporary world according to Gorky: they are past and future living side by side. The principal dynamics of this world consist in the transition from the negative to the positive pole—from past to future. Each phenomenon in the empirical reality, perceived at the current moment, can be either instrumental or harmful or simply irrelevant in the context of this transition. To accomplish it involves turning elements of life harmful or irrelevant in the context of the general transition into its very instruments.

While the positive image of contemporary Soviet reality presented in *In and About the Soviet Union* is based on synchronic opposition to the "rotting West," it is nevertheless founded upon direct opposition between pre-revolutionary and post-revolutionary Russia. In his 1928 and 1929 travels through Russia Gorky visited places known to him before the revolution. This fact provided him with the ideal motivation for introducing the direct opposition between the world before and after the revolution. This opposition, born out of ideological preconception, was to appear as naturally conditioned by the cognitive position of the author—a traveler revisiting old places and noticing changes. Needless to say, the results of these comparisons are highly predictable.

For example, Gorky's visits to Baku in 1897 and 1928 are described in direct juxtaposition. Gorky recollects his first visit to Baku long before the revolution:

All day, from morning till evening, I wandered around the oil fields in a state of befuddlement. It was incredibly stuffy. I was coughing, and I felt poisoned. While straying in the forest of the oil towers dripping with oil, I saw between them oily ponds full of greenish and black fluid. These ponds seemed bottomless. The earth and everything on it, including people, were splashed and saturated with dark oil. Everpresent greenish puddles reminded one of decay. . . . Workers hurried all around: Russians, Turks, Persians dug channels in moist sand with shovels; they dragged from place to place long pipes, bars and heavy plates of steel. Piles of broken metal parts and other junk were everywhere. Unwound wire ropes covered the ground, and pieces of broken pipes stucked out of the sand. It was all junk, as if a hurricane had broken it into pieces. Workers looked as if they were half drunk: they yelled at each other in a purposeless frenzy, and it seemed to me that they were staggering. (p. 115)

The key motifs of this description—gloom ("I wandered around the oil fields in a state of befuddlement"), illness ("I was coughing, and I felt poisoned"), physical decomposition ("everpresent greenish puddles reminded one of decay"), chaos ("Piles of broken metal parts and other junk were everywhere," "Unwound wire ropes covered the ground, and pieces of broken pipes stuck out of the sand"), ruin ("It was all junk, as if a hurricane had broken it into pieces"), and mad frenzy ("Workers looked as if they were half drunk: they yelled at each other in a purposeless frenzy, and it seemed to me that they were staggering")—are analogous to the principal motifs with which Gorky describes the West in his letter to Rybakova. Here too, the mad, sick, and chaotic world of the past is directly juxtaposed with the bright, healthy, and vigorous world of the Communist future already visible in the Soviet present. The description of Gorky's visit to the Baku oil fields in 1928 makes this opposition abundantly clear:

> We are driving through the oil fields. I look around and, of course, I cannot recognize anything. The oil fields had grown incredibly, and now they reach very far. But what astonishes me even more is the silence around. In places where I expected to see again hundreds of people all covered with oil and unnaturally frantic, people are seen only rarely, and even those whom I can see are for the most part builders, stonemasons, carpenters. Here and there they construct buildings similar to castle towers; they put in place iron columns, and mix cement. . . . I do not see anywhere workers covered with black oil. I do not see anywhere

pre-historic dwellings—those squat, dirty shacks with broken windows. There are no half naked children, and angry women. I do not hear the hysterical screams and howls of the foremen. . . . This work without people makes one trust that in the near future people will learn how to approach their own labor rationally in all kinds of efforts. (p. 119)

The opposition between the noisy, chaotic, multivocal world of a declining bourgeois civilization and the silent, focused, univocal world to come echoes the famous opposition presented by Blok in his 1908 essay "People and Intelligentsia." In this essay Blok contrasted the intelligentsia (the highest manifestation of the old civilization) with the masses, and projected this opposition onto the image of the fourteenth-century Tartar and Russian armies facing each other on the opposite banks of the Nepryadva River before the Battle of Kulikovo, in which the Tartar forces were defeated, and from which point the advent of the Muscovite political power followed. Blok wrote:

There are two realities: the common folk and the intelligentsia; one hundred and fifty million on the one side and a few hundred thousand on the other. These worlds do not understand each other. . . . Among the hundreds of thousands, there is some hasty mental ferment, ceaseless change of directions, moods, and banners. Above their cities a drone is heard out of which even an experienced ear cannot make sense. Such a drone as this one was heard, according to the stories, above the Tartar camp on the night before the battle of Kulikovo. Countless carts squeaked on the other side of the Nepryadva river, you heard human howling, and on the foggy river geese and swans splashed and cried. Today, among the tens of millions, it is as if sleep and silence ruled. But above the camp of Dmitry Donskoy, there, too, was silence.[36]

Gorky reintroduces this motif of noise versus silence in his 1929 "travelogue" as simply a reflection of his "objective" observation of reality before and after the revolution. Gorky's carefully orchestrated pattern of images, unlike Blok's admittedly synthetic, poetic vision, is supposed to give the impression of a simple observation of situation. This type of "observation" leads Gorky to irresistible conclusions: "Whatever the enemies of the Soviet Union say, the Soviet working class is boldly realizing 'the most necessary thing of our century,' as Romain Rolland called the ideas of V. I. Lenin which are implemented by his disciples. . . . Baku is indisputable and marvelous proof of the successful process of the construction of the workers' state and its new culture—such is my impression" (p. 124).

As a matter of fact, it is quite possible that the conditions in the Baku oil fields did improve between 1897 and 1928. The point is that Gorky's readiness to draw this and no other conclusion from his trip around Soviet Russia was admitted by him long before his first encounter with Soviet reality. The words *dokazatel'stvo* (proof) and *vpechatlenie* (impression) play a key role in Gorky's descriptions. Of course the image of Soviet Baku, selected and composed by Gorky, could be nothing but a "proof" of his general thesis about the ultimate superiority of the Soviet world. It was drawn precisely for this purpose. The literary strategy employed by Gorky aims at presenting this image as if it were the reflection of an "impression" of an impartial observer. Gorky's "impression" of the rapid transition of Russian life from pre-revolutionary chaos and decline (generated by the old socioeconomic system) towards the blossoming harmony of Soviet society (the gradual fulfillment of Marxist–Leninist prophecies) directly responds to the Bolsheviks' need for a new image of their attempts to construct a socialist utopia. According to this new image, these attempts must be presented as fully successful. "If the dictatorship of the proletariat should prove incapable, in the next few years, of organizing its economic life and securing at least a living minimum of material comforts for its population, then the proletarian regime will inevitably turn to dust," Trotsky wrote in 1924.[37] Four years later Trotsky's political career was over, but the inner logic of the ideology did not change. Fortunately, at this very moment, an "impartial observer" of Russian life, the "great writer" Maxim Gorky had an "impression": the Bolsheviks are succeeding; Soviet life looks more and more like the harmonious world of plenty promised in the Bolshevik scriptures. Such an image of current Soviet life makes the worries of Trotsky baseless: the Bolsheviks are already succeeding; their promises were apparently not empty.

Doctors and Patients in "Solovki"

In using the general strategy exemplified above, Gorky admits that the new Soviet reality is moving further and further away from both the dark, pre-revolutionary past and the sick Western world (the contemporary fossil of the past) towards the bright future defined by Lenin and Stalin. However, both the Soviet regime and Gorky agree that the transition, though dynamic and speedy, has not yet been entirely accomplished. An important function of Gorky's close look at Soviet reality is to show the transition in the making. If the juxtaposition of contrasting images of the alleged conditions of life and labor in pre-revolutionary and post-revolutionary Russia is the main topic of the cycle, through which the transition at the level of the economic base is presented, the principal topic by means of which Gorky shows the transition of human consciousness is that of the resocialization and reeducation of all "socially harmful elements"—criminal and political prisoners of Stalin's regime. The chief location where this transition takes place is the concentration camp, and the phenomenon of political oppression is peculiarly lumped together with the issue of the resocialization of criminals. This connection is crucial to Gorky's strategy for justifying the Soviet totalitarian coercion of society, which becomes the main focus of the last part of the cycle *In and About the Soviet Union*—a reportage from the camp on the Solovki islands.

The phenomenon of criminality has, in Gorky's view, a clear ideological explanation: it is an inevitable aspect of the old, bourgeois world dominated by inner conflicts among selfish interests of individuals. "In the Soviet Union, it is established that a 'criminal' is formed by the class-based society, and that 'criminality' is a social illness growing in the rotten soil of the system of private property. 'Criminality' will be easily eliminated if one eliminates the condition which created this illness, that is the old, rotten economic basis of the class-based society—private property" (p. 230).

Since criminality, according to Gorky and the Bolsheviks, is a "social illness" of capitalism, criminals constitute a category of unwitting victims of the old system. Thus it becomes the Bolsheviks' moral obligation to save these victims from their psychological yoke, just as the Bolsheviks saved other victims of capitalism in Russia from their economic yoke. And since it is the mind of the criminal that is infected by the old, degenerate values, the Bolsheviks must change the mind of the criminal even if this involves some initial coercion of his corrupted will. Since the actions of the "socially ill" are harmful and dangerous, these persons have to be locked up, just as they are locked up in any country. The Soviet penal system, unlike any other, is aimed at providing the criminal with the means to be cured of his psychological confusion, so that he will be able to see clearly the negative nature of his previous acts. We are dealing not with punishment but with treatment.

This approach to the phenomenon of crime as "social illness" was ideologically persuasive and appeared not to violate basic humanitarian values. On the contrary, it was built entirely on an acknowledgment of these values. Under Gorky's pen, this approach proved to be a very efficient instrument of ideological justification of Bolshevik totalitarianism in general and the Bolshevik system of slave labor in particular. "Criminals—victims of social injustice who challenged the bourgeois society—appeared to the Bolsheviks as ideal material that could be used to verify the most progressive ideas about the possibility of transforming human beings by reeducation. The most apparent victims of social illness, criminals, became guinea pigs of the new social medicine,"[38] Mikhail Heller wrote.

The entire literary strategy, designed by Gorky, of portraying Soviet totalitarian victimization as a positive phenomenon was based on the presentation of mass terror and concentration camps in the context of this "social medicine." The key element in this strategy consists of depicting all victims of concentration camps in terms applied to criminals. In "Solovki," the "humanitarian" image of the resocialization of criminals is simply stretched by Gorky so as to include the oppression and victimization of everyone whom the Soviet regime deems its enemy. The "socially ill," "confused" victims of the past, locked up in Bolshevik institutions for social treatment (concentration camps) are criminals and noncriminals and political opponents of the Bosheviks, as well as people who cannot comprehend why they are there.

The structural placement of the reportage entitled "Solovki," devoted entirely to the description of the concentration camp on the Solovki islands, within the cycle *In and About the Soviet Union,* serves as an authorial device for bringing the subject of Bolshevik terror under the topic of "social medicine." The description of Solovki appears as one of a series of descriptions of corrective colonies for under-age criminals. It should be noticed that, while addressing the topic of crime and "social medicine," Gorky pays most attention to under-age criminals, almost all of them orphans. In the case of young orphan-criminals, resocialization contains an element of patronage on behalf of the Bolshevik regime. The regime assumes a parental role in guiding the lives of these literally lost children. The inmates of the Solovki camp appear in a position analogous to that of orphans from the colonies described in previous parts of the cycle. The structural placement of the description of the Solovki camp associates the Soviet system of mass victimization with the resocialization of child-criminals.

This association is reinforced by the author when he begins presenting the prisoners of Solovki. Out of all the prisoners, he focuses on a group of young criminals. A long scene in which Gorky gets involved in a "spontaneous" conversation with a group of young criminals provides the first close image of Solovki prisoners. "These children's lives are similar to one another: war, hunger, escape, orphanhood, homelessness," he observes (p. 209). The terms of the description fit the concept of an orphanage rather than a concentration camp. But Gorky promptly explains that the boys are criminals and are undergoing resocializing treatment in the camp. Some of them seem still sunk in their old identities. For Gorky it seems to be enough to look at their faces in order to assess the extent of their social consciousness. "Of course, there are cunning and false smiles in their eyes, and there is toadying in their words, but the majority of these boys give the impression of cured people who are genuinely ready to forget their past. . . . One feels that many of them have definitively abandoned their past and do not like to talk about it any more. If they talk about themselves in the past they now refer to themselves in the past as to some strangers who were once deceived" (p. 210).

In general, the death of the old man and the birth of the new, resocialized and socially conscious, entails, for a former criminal, an overall revision of his self-perception. In order to achieve this new self-perception, the former "outcast of society" must look at himself through the eyes of the society to which he returns. If the old society made it impossible for him, the new society gives him a chance. If, within the old world, the young criminal was a lost orphan, in the new world he finds his father—the Bolshevik state represented by the camp regime. It may be a stern father, but the sooner the young prisoner starts identifying himself with the point of view of the new society, the sooner will he achieve the ability to see himself in a new light. During his conversation with the young criminals, Gorky notices: "Behind my back, I hear an argument in a low voice. 'They skin us alive here. . . .' 'Who is they? It's the hand of our own' " (p. 210).[39]

This "overheard" exchange between young prisoners leaves no doubt that Gorky's "impression" spelled out a few lines before was right: indeed, young criminals are already showing remarkable progress on their way to full citizenship in the new Soviet society. Some of them are already identifying themselves in the terms provided by this new society. Since the change of the criminal's self-perception from one antagonistic to society to one fully submissive to social expectations is the core of resocialization, the Bolshevik attempt to make Soviet people's self-perceptions fully subject to the political expectations of the regime could be described in terms applicable to some massive resocialization of criminals. Gorky presents Bolshevik efforts to change society's view of itself in these terms with one modification: the point of view of society (which is a norm to which the points of view of criminals must conform in the case of resocialization) is replaced here with the point of view of the Bolshevik leadership. Therefore, anyone whose point of view differs from that of the Bolsheviks is treated as a criminal in need of resocialization (Bolshevization).

As a matter of fact, non-criminal prisoners appear in "Solovki" only rarely. But whenever they are mentioned, they are automatically equated with criminals. And, among the criminals, it is those with "cunning and false smiles," rather than the reeducated ones, who stand close to the political prisoners. Gorky underlines the difference between the loyal criminals and the political prisoners of the camp: "The overwhelming majority of the inmates are criminals. The 'political prisoners' are counter-revolutionaries of the emotional type, 'monarchists,' people who before the revolution were called 'the black hundred.' Among them there are supporters of terror, 'economic spies,' 'wreckers,' 'bad grass' pulled from the field by the just hand of history" (p. 223).

The last metaphor—the just hand of history throwing away the weeds—recalls the atmosphere of revolutionary literature written in "the spirit of social hatred"[40] that proclaimed the great purge of the old world for the sake of the coming new world. This is the same biblical metaphor that Ilya Ehrenburg used in *The Life and Death of Nikolai Kurbov.*[41] In the traditional image of Christ weeding the garden (at the Last Judgment),[42] Ehrenburg replaced the figure of Christ with the Bolshevik henchman acting on behalf of history. He used the metaphor in presenting the theme of mass executions carried out by the Bolsheviks. This bloody association, however, is at odds with the "humanitarian" vision of Bolshevism created by Gorky. Moreover, Gorky does not give it the same meaning but uses it to create a contrast between the tough times of the revolution and the humane world of socialism-under-construction. The enemies who would have been physically eliminated not long ago are now treated as victims of the old world and, together with other victims (criminals), are undergoing resocialization. Like criminals, they must change their self-perceptions and begin to see themselves from the point of view of the very regime that has locked them up in the camps. The "weeds" are their old identities, not necessarily their bodies. The main condition of this transformation is the same as in the case of criminals: the "just hand of history" must be accepted as "the hand of our own."

Meanwhile, thanks to the humanitarianism of the Bolshevik regime, the "living vestiges of the past," the "enemies," are placed in the best possible situation—under the patronage of a new society that gives them a chance to be resocialized. If any reader is inclined to treat concentration camps as penitentiary institutions in the sense known to contemporary civilizations outside the Soviet Union, Gorky sets himself up to prove how wrong this is. Soviet concentration camps cannot be compared with Western prisons. In order to illustrate the point, Gorky gives us a "typical image" of the prisoners' living quarters in Solovki: "The woman-orderly shows us some of the rooms for women. In each room there are four or six beds, each decorated with personal things: private blankets, pillows; on the walls hang photographs and postcards; on window sills there are flowers. There is no impression of life being overregulated. No, there is no resemblance of a prison but instead it seems that these rooms are inhabited by passengers rescued from a drowned ship" (p. 223).[43] Indeed, Gorky's camp is a rescue ship, a place where confused and misled people of the past are rescued from the sinking craft of their old world and turned into passengers on the new, shiny steamship of the Soviet utopia.

In the course of convalescence, the inmates divide their time between rest in the seemingly cozy barracks and vigorous work in the woods and meadows of the Solovki islands. On his way, Gorky-the-traveler passes by a group of prisoners at work: "They are digging turf in a large glade: healthy lads in unbleached linen shirts and high boots shovel quickly huge pieces of moist dirt into the machine. . . . Everything goes perfectly smoothly. I am told: 'Look at the workers' boots!' I look. The boots are, of course, very dirty. But I am told that they are made of special waterproof leather. As proof, one of the workers takes off a boot. The inside is really dry" (p. 222).

This touching description exemplifies, in a way typical of this work, the fact that there are hardly any limits to Gorky's capacity for identifying and classifying people "at first glance." The working prisoners are "healthy lads," and the adjective is not just an example of casual verbiage on the part of the author. The impressive tempo of their labor is one "proof" of their splendid shape, and the waterproof boots provide a touching example of the care given to these lads by their masters. It seems that nothing can spoil Gorky's happy mood in the Solovki concentration camp. No observation or encounter raises any question about the positive character of this experience for the prisoners. The issue of the innocence of many among the "enemies of the people" imprisoned in Solovki never enters into Gorky's account.

Gorky, in fact, preempts the possibility of emergence of this potential issue by presenting several encounters with political prisoners who either claim their innocence or whose "crimes" may be questioned by a reader who happens not to share the political faith of the Bolsheviks. Each time, guilt is established beyond doubt. One such encounter brings together Gorky and a woman from Nizhny Novgorod, Gorky's hometown. The woman speaks: "They sent me here for ten years, oh well, God is joking! They said that I denounced workers and hid gendarmes in nineteen eighteen, but it is all lies, bad people made false accusations against me. Oh, well, I will suffer if I must" (p. 224).

Listening to the woman, Gorky can either believe her or not. To believe the story would mean to acknowledge the innocence of a Soviet victim and, indirectly, to allow the possibility of many more such cases. But this would not fit the general image of the humanitarian character of the Bolshevik camps. So Gorky dismisses it in a way typical of the work as a whole. He simply "sees through" what is given to him in experience. The woman must be lying. For the "keen observer" it is enough to look at her. For a skillful propagandist, it is enough to employ several clichés describing the outside appearance of a "typical liar." "When she speaks, she automatically starts examining me with her sharp, steely eyes: they touch me coldly all over, as if they searched for a spot to hit," Gorky comments (p. 224). The series of aesthetic impressions, verbalized in several metaphors ("she . . . starts examining me with her sharp, steely eyes"; "they touch me coldly all over, as if they searched for a spot to hit"), serves to indirectly dismiss the woman's claim and accuse her of lying. Gorky does not stop with this effect, but builds upon it. Once the sincerity of the woman is ruled out, Gorky continues along the path of negative associations, painting an extensive comparative context in which he places this encounter:

She makes me remember many other women just like her, with the same kind of looks, the same kind of eyes. I remember one of them sitting in the defendant's bench of the District Court in Nizhny Novgorod. The judge asked her:

"So, you are denying that you were sitting on the legs of your nephew when your lover was strangling him?"

"Your excellency! My lover falsely accused me, and that's why he is dead now. His conscience must have killed him! Except for him, nobody is guilty of this thing. At that time I was in church at the all-night service."

"It has been established that your nephew was strangled after the church service, he was seen alive at nine o'clock."

The woman crossed herself, sighed, and said:

"Don't insult a defenseless woman, your excellency! Is it possible to kill a human being straight after praying to God?"

But the defenseless woman did just that. She prayed to God, then went home and helped her lover, a salesman, to strangle her nephew, a schoolboy. His death made the "defenseless woman" the heir to a large estate. And when the salesman was arrested, she sent him poisoned patties in prison, the salesman ate them and died. But before that he confessed to the crime. His testimony was read in court. There was, among others, this statement: "I was strangling him and she was reading a prayer." (p. 225)

What does this story have to do with Gorky's encounter with the woman prisoner at Solovki? Nothing except that it is used by the author for an associative context within which the figure of the woman at Solovki is to be perceived by the reader. For it is the author's personal associations that provide a screen through which the "traveler's impressions" of the Solovki camp are filtered. The story of the woman murderer stands for the story of the woman at Solovki and provides the model through which the latter should be seen. If the author's knowledge about innocent victims of Soviet concentration camps (given to him in what the woman from Solovki said) seems problematic in the context of general praise of the concentration camps, the associations created by the author cancel out the validity of the source of his knowledge. The author's knowledge must be revised according to a preconceived ideological point. Thus the story of a murder and trial is evoked, and so the line between the woman met by the author at Solovki and the heroine of this story is blurred. The problem of guilt and innocence is not an open issue in the Bolshevik camp. Those who are there are there for good reasons.

In fact, there is no reason for the prisoners to complain about their fate in the camp. In Gorky's account the Solovki camp bursts with exciting, creative activities for its inmates. Regular concerts by prisoner-musicians are among Gorky's favorite forms of Solovki's cultural life. Immediately after the story of the woman murderer, Gorky describes a concert:

> We went to a concert in the theater. The theater is located in the monastery, in the old refectory, especially extended to serve the new purpose. Seven hundred people fit into it, and it was packed. A "socially dangerous" audience is hungry for spectacles just as any other audience is, and it applauds artists at least as warmly. The concert was very interesting and diverse. A small but very well coordinated "symphonic ensemble" played the overture to "The Barber of Seville," a violinist played Wieniawski's "Mazurka," and Rachmaninoff's "Torrents of Spring." . . . They sang Russian songs, danced "cowboy" and other exotic dances, somebody splendidly recited Zharov's "Accordion" to the accom-

paniment of accordion and piano. The group of acrobats was incredible: five men and one woman made such figures as one cannot see even in a good circus. During the intermission, in the "foyer," a great brass band played Rossini, Verdi, and Beethoven's overture to "Egmont." The conductor was by all means a big talent. The concert itself showed many talented artists. All of them are of course prisoners, and they seem to work a lot on stage. (pp. 225–226)

This is only one among many forms of cultural life flourishing in the camp. Gorky mentions also the camp theater, museum, library, and schools. All these institutions are run by professional people, who also happen to be "former class enemies" in need of resocialization. Moreover, "ethnographic research is conducted on the island; a journal is published as well as a daily newspaper which has been only temporarily suspended" (p. 226). Under Gorky's pen, life in the concentration camp could be the cause of envy on the part of inhabitants of the ordinary Soviet reality on the other side of the barbed wire. Solovki seems to have more musicians, actors, directors, and scholars than Nizhny Novgorod could ever hope for.

Eventually, however, Gorky reminds the reader (and, perhaps, himself) that, after all, Solovki is a concentration camp, not a resort. "Of course, the island is not a prison but it is certainly impossible to escape from it" (ibid.). Armed guards are an element of the Solovki camp as much as the enthusiastic laborers and talented musicians. The reader should not, however, confuse the presence of the guns in the guards' hands with any bad intentions towards the prisoners. Gorky describes a typical camp guard: "From frequent smiles the face of this man had become brighter, as if he had washed it.

Now it became clear that his face is good-natured and his dark eyes look at people softly and with trust" (p. 228).

In Gorky's account, the concentration camp—a highly humanitarian institution that transforms the confused victims of past society into full-fledged citizens of a better Soviet world—exemplifies two "truths." The first is that the Bolshevik regime represents an ethical ideal that is beyond comparison with the ethical ideals of the old world. The second is that the Bolshevik regime is succeeding in the implementation of its doctrine: the Bolshevik leadership and its methods actually change human beings and make them happier than before. "While observing the contemporary 'socially dangerous' people, I cannot fail to notice that in spite of the great difficulties which they encounter on their way upward, they understand the necessity of being socially useful. Certainly, this is caused by the circumstances in which they are placed now" (p. 215). In Solovki, as in other, similar institutions in the Soviet Union, "the psyche of people thrown into anarchy by their past is thoroughly transformed. Socially dangerous people are transformed into socially useful ones, professional criminals turn into highly qualified workers and conscious revolutionaries" (p. 231).

The goal of this psychological transformation of people is the unified, harmonious consciousness designed by the Bolshevik regime, and the day when this transformation will be accomplished seems to Gorky not very distant. It will be the day when the confusion of the old world disappears along with its last vestiges inside the human psyche, and when there is no more need for further reeducation. "Perhaps this process can be accelerated, perhaps Butyrki, Taganka, and other schools of this kind can be closed down earlier than we expect?" Gorky wonders in his concluding remarks (p. 231). For if the Bolshevik experiment of turning the confused, fragmented world of social struggle and injustice into the harmonious, rational, univocal world of justice and equality is really successful (and there is no doubt in Gorky's account that it will be), then the concentration camps will soon have accomplished their mission of resocialization. Therefore, they should soon vanish, along with prisons and other forms of resocialization.

The revolutionary struggle, by its Marxist definition, is a transitory stage, then, leading towards a harmonious reintegration of society. The resocialization and reeducation of the last Mohicans of the pre-revolutionary world also constitute a transition. When fulfilled successfully, they cancel themselves out. Disappearance of the last institutions of social reeducation is, therefore, an indirect measure of the regimen's success in creating the new, univocal, unanimous society. Before this can happen, Gorky admits, "It seems to me that the conclusion is clear. Camps such as Solovki are necessary" (p. 231).

Gorky's literary presentation of the Solovki concentration camp together with its general context of Soviet reality in the cycle *In and About the Soviet Union,* provides a vision of Bolshevik victimization in terms of high ethical ideals and with optimistic connotations. The image of Bolshevik terror, purified of all violent aspects, appears here (in contrast to 1920s visions of bloody "historic retribution" and "last judgment") as a bright part of Soviet reality. It is a transitory phenomenon, existing in Soviet reality only before it reaches the ultimate stage of total harmony in the Communist paradise. The concentration camp cleanses the old world, integrates it with the new, and makes the coming of the Bolshevik utopia more imminent. The mission of the concentration camps will be complete as soon as the last confused person from the old world finds his true identity within the new Bolshevik society. This will happen when he realizes that the hand of his Bolshevik oppressor is, indeed, "the hand of our own."

The World Reunited in the Camp

As we have already seen, the principal objective of Gorky's new literary strategy of reprogramming human perceptions of totalitarian evil consisted of presenting the Bolshevik terror as an element in the benevolent process of changing Soviet reality from the condition of revolutionary conflict to that of triumphant collective harmony. Consequently, in the literary reflection of this transition, the dramatic conflict between the dark past and the bright future (fundamental to literary visions of the 1920s) had to be reduced. All the same, even in a world of full social harmony and unanimity, the element of conflict, so crucial for narrative dynamics, did not have to be ruled out from Soviet literary works. What the reduction of the theme of social tensions required was a shift away from the theme of the struggle between old and new toward that of the struggle between the unified human collective and the as yet unconquered forces of nature. This struggle against nature was the central issue of the Communist world view. Revolution and the struggle of man against man are only a clearing ground for the ultimate struggle —the conquest of nature by man, leading toward the construction of the ultimate Communist utopia. From this perspective, forced labor appears as an especially effective and highly ethical form of resocializing the confused victims of the old world. They are, in fact, being included in the most praiseworthy activity of all—the creation of the material base for utopia. For those whose consciousness has been transformed, to work for such a goal is itself the highest reward for their efforts—hence the happy prisoners observed by Gorky, who work enthusiastically at processing turf in Solovki. The camp guards are no longer guards but comrades, since they are on the same side of the struggle of humanity against the unconquered wilderness. On this view, the forced labor of the concentration camps loses its characteristic of conflict between oppressors and oppressed. Both oppressors and oppressed stand side by side confronting the task of the construction of Communism. Among the prisoners are those who have not as yet discovered this liberating truth. It is for their protection from themselves that the guards bear weapons. Reducing the central conflict between victims and oppressors, Gorky breaks in a definitive way with the traditional view of Bolshevik victimization as a revolutionary struggle.

Besides this radical change in the overall ethical context of Bolshevik victimization, Gorky's new approach differs from the previous ones because of a new strategy aimed at persuading the reader to accept the image of reality projected by the author of "Solovki." The strategy, developed in literary works of the 1920s in order to present the theme of Soviet violence and oppression, is based on an ethical challenge. In works surrounding Bolshevik brutality with an aura of tragic necessity (by Tarasov-Rodyonov and Ehrenburg), the traditional moral priorities of the reader were indirectly challenged. The reader was presented with two supposedly equally valid moral codes: traditional Judeo-Christian "absolute morality" and Leninist "class morality." Literary heroes (Bolshevik henchmen) were presented as morally sensitive individuals involved in the Red Terror and thus entangled in the contradictions between these two moralities. Readers were expected to revise their traditional morality and to sympathize with the Bolsheviks who undertook such great moral tasks as the necessary elimination of social enemies. In works openly praising Bolshevik brutality, such as poems by Knyazev and Bagritsky, the reader's right to disagree was openly denied. In practical terms, the reader was presented with two alternatives: either to accept the author's view or to perish together with other

enemies of the revolution. The "class morality" was definitively acknowledged as superior to "eternal morality." To accept it, the reader had no option but to relinquish his former
ethical notions altogether and at once.

What is new about Gorky's approach to the phenomenon
of Bolshevik tyranny is that it appears not to challenge traditional ethical notions of the reader. On the contrary, Gorky
verbally reaffirms them over and over again. The reader is no
longer openly challenged and required to abandon the traditional "eternal morality" as a condition of assuming the only
correct ethical stand—the Bolshevik position. Instead, the
reader is swamped by evidence of Bolshevik benevolence.
The reader reads about orphans lost and found (in the camp)
and about people confused and enlightened again (in the
camp). What can be more humanitarian (in the traditional
sense) than bringing victims and outcasts of the abusive society of the past back to life in the new harmonious society of
today and tomorrow? It is this new context for traditional
moral values that provides the reader with an image of Soviet
reality within which mass victimization appears as a morally
noble and positive phenomenon.

Unlike in previous approaches, in Gorky's account the
ethical universe of the reader (who may still perceive the
world through traditional moral categories) is no longer as-
saulted by the author and the Bolshevik morality he represents. In fact, these two ethical positions seem to be no
longer two positions, but one. The author and the reader are
now presumed to speak the same language of values. The
conflict of values between author and reader assumed in the
works of the 1920s aimed at ethical challenge is now replaced by the presumption of harmony.

When seen in the general context of the Soviet post-
revolutionary ideology of the late 1920s and the early 1930s,

this change in the ethical assumptions underlying the communicative strategy for presenting the topic of Bolshevik terror reflects a more general change in the ideological perception of contemporary Soviet reality: Soviet reality is supposedly undergoing a transition from revolutionary struggle through a unified, harmonious effort to construct a better future. Inner conflict ceases to be the principal structural dominant of the Soviet world. It is now replaced by the principle of harmony among people. The abandonment of the presumption of ethical controversy between author and reader is an indirect literary indicator that this supposed transition is actually under way.

Consequently, the author does not have to challenge the reader, whose ethical views are essentially consistent with his own. Instead of the passionate expression of the point of view of someone deeply engaged in the battle between past and future, Gorky presents an account of an observer whose quite traditional moral views serve to underline his objectivity. Readers, tranquilized by this apparent moral accord between themselves and the author, are supposed to accept Gorky's view of Soviet reality as essentially objective and undeniable. Meanwhile, Gorky's claim to objectivity is based entirely upon a manipulative ideological assumption: namely, the general Bolshevik teleology, according to which only those elements of reality that contribute to the realization of the ultimate future goal are "objectively" important and positive. So Bolshevik violence as practiced in concentration camps becomes, in this teleological framework, a positive, constructive phenomenon, because it increases the control of the situation by the Communist Party—the leading force behind society's movement toward the future goal. Even if the reality of Bolshevik terror may seem drastic to an uninformed observer, brutality and destruction are only accidental complications accompanying an essentially positive activity. In a letter to Aleksandr Afinogenov, Gorky explained how to present Bolsheviks and their activities in literature: "What is important about the Bolsheviks is not their shortcomings but their merits. Their shortcomings are rooted in the past which the Bolsheviks themselves are destroying. But their merits are anchored in the present, that is, in the Bolsheviks' efforts to build the future."[44] True, brutality and terror may appear as indelible elements of the experience of life in the Soviet system of mass coercion, but the experience itself cannot be a measure of the truth. Gorky makes it clear that only those people who manage to avoid being "caught in the net of primitive empiricism" and do not "generalize upon their individual experiences" are capable of seeing the reality in its only true dimension—"from the height of our [that is the Bolsheviks'—that is, everyone's] future goals."[45]

It is this view from the top, "from the height of our future goals," that enabled Gorky to reach what was thus far the highest degree of literary mystification of the Soviet camp experience. Slave labor and victimization (live evidence of the increasingly obvious failure of the Bolsheviks' claim that they were creating a just, humane social order) were presented, in accordance with Gorky's new literary convention, as evidence of the Bolsheviks' success. "If any 'cultured' European society dared to conduct in its own country an experiment such as this colony," Gorky writes in the conclusion of his "Solovki," "and if this experiment yielded fruits such as ours, that country would blow all its trumpets and boast about its accomplishment. . . . Is it because of our modesty or for some other, perhaps less noble, reason that we do not know how to write about our accomplishments even when we see them and try to describe them?" (p. 231).

"Solovki" was written in order to "compensate" this alleged excess of Soviet modesty. Soon it became the model for transforming the horrors of the Soviet camp experience into images of glory.

The Choirs of Belomorkanal

Whereas Gorky's "Solovki" marked the firm establishment of the leading Stalinist literary strategy for reprogramming people's perceptions of Soviet totalitarian abuse, the model realization of this new convention was a truly unusual book known as *Belomorkanal* (*The Joseph Stalin White Sea–Baltic Sea Canal: History of Its Construction*).[46] This unique, 614-page book published in 1934 glorified the construction of the marine route between the White and Baltic Seas.

The White Sea–Baltic Sea Canal was the first in a series of major Soviet industrial projects officially contracted for the political police and accomplished by slave labor. The official literary glorification of the project was intended to provide an argument in favor of slave labor as an important element of the Soviet economy and as a highly effective method of reeducating the "socially ill" segments of Soviet society. Stalin set a stringent deadline of twenty months, from September 1931 to April 1933, for the completion of this 140-mile-long canal, and the project had to be completed at a very low cost. This meant doing it by means of the manual labor of hundreds of thousands of prisoners who were afforded neither contemporary technology nor adequate living conditions. The main source of slave labor employed in the project was peasants arrested during the collectivization. The realities of prisoners' lives in these massive slave works reflected their status as working livestock. The task given by Stalin to his police, to construct the marine route between the White and the Baltic Seas over difficult terraine and under extreme climatic conditions, without the necessary machinery and against an unrealistic deadline, could be accomplished only by means of terror and the extreme exploitation of prisoners. The exact number of deaths at the Belomorkanal construction site (measured in tens of thousands), just as in the case of the Kolyma (measured in millions) and most other massive slave-labor projects, is still difficult to establish.

The system of mixed incentives and punishments, developed in Solovki, was further perfected in the Belomorkanal camp. The prisoners themselves were expected to contribute to the general fiction of the successful transformation of "socially ill" elements into full-fledged citizens of the Soviet utopia. Solzhenitsyn writes:

> While taking away life, they even earlier crawled into the breast and searched for the soul. And this was the most difficult thing to bear on the canals: they demanded that in addition to everything else you *chirp*. You might be *on your last legs,* but you had to make a pretense of participation in public affairs. With a tongue growing numb from hunger you had to deliver speeches demanding overfulfillment of plan and exposure of wreckers! And punishment for hostile propaganda, for *kulak* rumors (and all camp rumors were *kulak* rumors). And to be on the lookout to make sure that the snakes of mistrust did not entwine a new prison term about you.[47]

The canal was completed on time, and Stalin himself was present at the official opening on 2 August 1933.[48] Just two weeks later, 120 Soviet writers, led by Gorky, visited the canal and sailed its length on a steamer. Their task was to learn about the canal and the process of its construction, to talk with the prisoners and guards, and to write a collective report about what they learned. Here is a prisoner's account of this visit as related by Solzhenitsyn (not surprisingly, it brings to mind Gorky's visit to Solovki):

> On August 17, 1933, an *outing* of 120 writers took place aboard a steamer on the just completed canal. D. P. Vitkovsky, a prisoner who was a construction superintendent on the canal, witnessed the way these people in white suits crowded on the deck during the steamer's passage through the locks, summoned prisoners from the area of the locks (where by this time they were more operational workers than construction workers), and, in the presence of the canal chiefs, asked a prisoner whether he loved his canal and his work, and did he think that he had managed to reform here, and did the chiefs take enough interest in the welfare of the prisoners? There were many questions, all in this general vein, and all asked from shipboard to shore in the presence of the chiefs and only while the steamer was passing through the locks.[49]

In fact, the presence of these writers at the canal was even less relevant to what they were about to write than Gorky's presence in Solovki was relevant to his reportage about that camp. But before the writers even said or wrote anything, the press that covered their trip printed stories and images of the famous literati "beaming" while listening to the prisoners at the Belomorkanal. The writers presented in the press appeared so excited that they could hardly "hold their notebooks," and "their fingers were shaking from astonishment."[50] After the return of the 120 writers, many of them gave enthusiastic interviews and talks about the construction of the canal, and thirty-six of them participated in the composition of the book.[51] The press informed its readers widely about the work in progress and created an atmosphere of anxious expectation.[52] Finally, the volume appeared in January 1934, exactly at the time of the Seventeenth Congress of the Communist Party, to which it was dedicated on behalf of the newly created Union of Soviet Writers, the organization that was to monopolize Soviet literature while adhering strictly to the party line.[53] The first printed copies were delivered directly to the Congress, where, according to *Literaturnaia gazeta,* they were seen "in the hands of nearly every delegate," and 2,500 copies were supposedly sold at the Congress's bookstands.[54]

Belomorkanal follows the basic descriptive strategy introduced by Gorky in 1929, but develops it on a scale unprecedented in Soviet literature. Among the crucial effects created by Gorky was that of objective, impartial, factual observation of Soviet reality. If Gorky's reportage from the Solovki camp was an account of a writer's visit to the site of what appeared to him to be an inspiring and successful social experiment, *Belomorkanal* is an account of a similar visit by 120 writers, each being supposedly an independent, inquisitive observer. The visit had a clear and openly acknowledged goal: the writers went to this special place in order to be able to illuminate in literary form something that had already been widely publicized by propaganda as a great triumph in the Soviet effort to achieve the long awaited socialist utopia.

A period of more than four years separates "Solovki" and *Belomorkanal.* It was the time of Stalin's first Five-Year Plan, when the official Soviet image of the country's success in the transition from the stage of revolutionary struggle to that of the harmonious universe of socialism was constantly advanced by propaganda and became an ideological axiom. The official image of Soviet reality was encapsulated in the normative formula pronounced by Stalin at the Seventeenth Congress of the Communist Party: "Life has become better, comrades, life has become gayer."[55]

Stalin's opinion was by no means his personal, subjective

impression. He could refer to numerous descriptions of Soviet life, made by numerous writers, filmmakers, and painters. They provided ample evidence that the joy and optimism of the Secretary-General was by all means well founded. If Stalin read the inside press of the growing camps of the early 1930s, he could find there daily reports, written by prisoners themselves, testifying to the alleged enthusiasm of camp inmates outdoing one another in their slave labor. *Belomorkanal,* favorite reading of the delegates at the Seventeenth Congress, was among the most convincing testimonies to this joy and optimism, this time coming from Soviet writers. The editorship of this collective work was provided by Maxim Gorky himself, assisted by Leopold Averbakh, leader of RAPP (the Russian Association of Proletarian Writers),[56] and the commander of the labor camp at Belomor Canal, Semen Firin. This joint editorship of writers and a camp commander is one of the most illuminating examples of the two complementary aspects of totalitarianism: its physical victimization of people, as a direct means towards utopian goals, and its organized attempts to reprogram human perceptions of this victimization. In its effort to create a positive image of the Soviet totalitarian horror exemplified by the Belomor Canal camp, the book employs the general literary strategy designed earlier by Gorky and pushes it to its furthest limits. The book represents the fullest implementation of this strategy in Soviet literature.[57]

In "Solovki," Gorky's mystification of Soviet violence was accomplished, as we have seen, by two means: the creation of a positive image of Soviet victimization within a specially designed ideological universe and the orchestration of a rhetorical situation between author and reader aimed at imposing this image successfully upon the audience. In his attempt to create a positive image of Soviet institutionalized terror, Gorky moved away from a formula of revolutionary violence toward one of humanitarian reeducation. In the overall structure of his universe, as presented in his work, this shift reflected a more general movement in the Soviet regime's ideological self-image from revolutionary strife to the harmony of the socialist utopia-in-the-making. By analogy to the universe described within the work, in the rhetorical situation between author and implied reader, the principle of conflict and challenge characteristic of literary predecessors of Gorky in the 1920s is replaced by a manipulative presumption of harmony and unanimity.

Belomorkanal surpasses "Solovki" on all these counts. It develops Gorky's notion of the world's transition from the conflict-driven past to the conflictless socialist future so as to construct a positive image of Soviet victimization and impose it on readers. The image of life in Soviet camps created in this 1934 official "masterpiece" is even more substanceless and contradictory to experience than the images projected by Gorky in 1929. At the same time this vision of the future is proclaimed in an incomparably louder, more pompous way. Even as the promise of the collective harmony and well-being that, according to Gorky's 1929 prediction, would eliminate prisons and concentration camps became ever more distant from Soviet reality, praise of the concentration camps became louder and more enthusiastic than ever before. In *Belomorkanal,* reality itself becomes a reservoir of themes and motifs supporting the general idea of the triumphs and achievements that occurred in the invisible world inside the minds of Soviet ideologues. The result is a mind-boggling presentation of an all-encompassing totalitarian experience that entirely denies reality, substituting for it a verbal universe of make-believe.

Following Gorky's model, the authors of *Belomorkanal,* in order to create an ideological image of Bolshevik reeducation in a labor camp, start by establishing a general opposition between the old, fragmented world of inner conflicts and the new, univocal utopia promised in the Communist scriptures. In the same fashion as in Gorky's *In and About the Soviet Union,* this opposition has its diachronic and synchronic aspects, represented by, respectively, the opposition between pre-revolutionary and post-revolutionary Russia and the opposition between Soviet Russia and the contemporary (still pre-revolutionary) West. The pre-revolutionary Russia presented here is a world of chaotically different concepts and viewpoints in which any human effort aimed at establishing a better social order is doomed, for the simple reason that it lacks the unifying, objective, true perception of reality that only Marxism–Leninism is able to provide. About pre-revolutionary Russia the authors say:

> 140 nationalities lived in Russia. A certain bishop complained in 1912 that Orthodox missionaries, having worked for 50 years, could not implant the concepts of "god" and "morality" in the mentality of the Siberian natives. "They are true savages," he wrote. . . . "In the language of the Chukchas, there are 23 words denoting various types of walrus, 40 words describing various kinds of ice and icebergs, 16 various terms defining different flukes of the harpoon, but the words 'wheel,' 'machine,' 'school' are untranslatable into the language of the Chukchas." (p. 34)

Of course, it is self-explanatory to the authors why the missionaries' efforts to turn this cacophony of languages, concepts, and values into an all-encompassing, universal language were not successful. The basis for the missionaries' own universal point of view was as mistaken as the concepts of the Siberian natives. But it took nothing more than introducing the right world of ideas to the lives of the Siberian natives to immediately turn this chaotic cacophony into a choral harmony. Where the Christian Church failed, the Communists succeeded instantly:

> In 1931 the Soviet Central Publishing House printed political brochures and textbooks in all languages of the Soviet minorities. Concepts such as "proletariat," "revolution," "collective" were introduced into the vocabulary of the Siberian tribesmen. This assimilation of the new universe of ideas is not obstructed by unsurmountable obstacles. The new social and economic structure inspires the vigorous development of languages. Among the Tungusians, where hunters' cooperatives have been around for two years, the word "collective" is entering the language faster than the word "god" was entering the language of the savages converted by the missionaries. (p. 34)

As the transition from the world of misconceptions, conflicts, hostilities, and overall discord of voices expressing various points of view takes place in post-revolutionary Russia, the West represents the developed and decaying (yet temporarily frozen) mode of existence of a world based on the cacophonous principle. The ultimate example of this principle as the foundation for social life is, for the authors of *Belomorkanal,* the United States:

> Many point to the example of contemporary America which was born in the last century. . . . A new breed of people conquered America: farmers, energetic salesmen with tanned faces, shrewd dealers, industrious businessmen. They were in a hurry to outdistance each other; their wagons rushed through the prairie westward—to the gold of California and the ore of the Salt Lake. Who will be the first to stick his sign in the ground? Who will conquer more land? Negroes from Africa were

kept together with the cattle—they were the working animals of the new factories and workshops. This was the fit of colonialism and competition; it was the fight of all against all, with gold in one pocket and a gun in the other. (pp. 24–25)

The authors from the very beginning clearly differentiate between the world of the West and the new world built in the Soviet Union:

It would be senseless to compare these two births: the birth of capitalism in the New World and the birth of socialism in the Soviet Union. The only thing they had in common was the element of birth. Their essence is profoundly different. The idea of socialism inspires masses greater than those in America. What inspires them is not the private pocket but universal bliss, not the destruction of nations conquered by the pioneers but the development of previously oppressed nationalities. (p. 25)

An accurate perception of this fundamental difference between the old (Western) and the new (Soviet) worlds—that is, between the world of the "fight of all against all" and the world of "universal bliss"—promotes an understanding of the two ways in which enemies, adversaries, or simply "others" are viewed within each of these universes: "Destroying the enemy" is the way the enemies are treated in the West (p. 25). In Soviet Russia, on the contrary, enemies are given a chance for a successful "transformation" (*peredelka*) or, in another formulation, "reforging" (*perekovka*) (p. 25). Furthermore, the authors specify: "We eliminate only the most stubborn and stiff-necked enemies. As for people of the old world caught opposing the new, we try to transform them. This book tells the story of one brave and successful attempt at this transformation" (p. 25).

In this way, at the very beginning of the book, the authors spell out their actual subject. We gather that this subject is not the reality of life in the Soviet concentration camp, but the historic completion of the task of transforming the world from chaos into order, of reeducating enemies seen as such from the point of view of the "pedagogues." That the task has been completed successfully is assumed from the very beginning of the book: one does not officially dedicate to rulers literary descriptions of their failures.

Because the concentration camp is the institution in which the successful transformation of enemies into well-integrated members of the happy collective takes place, the theme of camps and prisons becomes an additional platform on which the general opposition of the two worlds is represented. This representation is a highly peculiar one. In order to build his black-and-white opposition, Gorky exaggerated or simply emphasized the negative sides of life in Western countries as he knew them, juxtaposing that image with a beautified, ideologically conditioned image of Soviet reality. The borderline between the West and the Soviet Union remained the divide on either side of which the author exaggerated positive or negative aspects of local reality in order to illustrate a preconceived thesis. *Belomorkanal* goes even further. What is striking in its literary method of "comparative" description of the two worlds is that it crosses the divide. For, unlike Gorky, the authors of *Belomorkanal* do not evade negative aspects of the Soviet concentration camp reality; they merely project them across the firmly established border between the two worlds and use them as illustrations of the inherent inhumanity of the cacophonic universe in Western countries.

Thus, for instance, one of the most notorious characteristics of the Soviet system of slave labor was the direct dependence of food allowances and punishments on production quotas that forced prisoners to work beyond their physical capacity. The alternative between exhaustion from excessive labor in bad conditions and starvation became one of the constant perils of the Soviet camp experience.[58] The reader of *Belomorkanal* for whom the camp experience was not entirely a new subject may have been struck by familiar associations while reading in *Belomorkanal* almost sensational "information" about concentration camps in Finland.

Finland. The country of lakes and forests. One language is spoken on both sides of the Soviet–Finnish border. In the Ekanas prison, there are 500 political prisoners. The majority of them have life sentences. They die slowly. The damp dungeons of Ekanas are hotbeds of tuberculosis. Here, the food is rarely edible. On July 17, 1932, the majority of the prisoners were poisoned by spoiled food. Carpentry is the work of the prisoners. Here, beyond the border of Soviet Karelia, they do not know specialization. You may be a lawyer, a locksmith, a driver, or a shoemaker—it does not matter, you are supposed to saw wood. You have your work quota, and it does not matter if you are strong or weak. Just saw! If you don't make your work quota you end up in the cooler. Four days and nights on bread and water. If you don't make the quota again, you go to the cooler for two weeks. And if, in spite of all, you miss your quota for the third time, that means the cooler for an indefinite time. All of the coolers are overcrowded. The quotas are so high that nobody can make them in time. Hardly anyone leaves the Finnish prison other than straight to the cemetery. (p. 58)

This description, which could serve as a fairly accurate depiction of many Soviet concentration camps in the 1930s, is written in order to point up the contrast between the horrors of the West and the humanitarianism of the Soviet penitentiary system.

Another of the particular characteristics of the Soviet system of victimization was its totalitarian aim of reprogramming people's perceptions of the very system that oppressed them. This aspect as well did not go unnoticed in *Belomorkanal*. Here is a description of camps in Germany, dating from as early as 1933, written, again, in order to emphasize the contrast between the West and the Soviet Union, and to show that the horrors of Western reality would not be possible in the homeland of the world proletariat:

> In fascist Germany, there is everything that exists in all of the prisons of the bourgeois regimes: hunger, chains, religion, tortures. But here, all this exists on a scale much larger than anywhere else. Besides this, in Germany, there are concentration camps. Let us have a look at them. . . . Fascist Germany can be distinguished from other countries by the fact that torture and fanatic cruelty in Germany have a philosophical basis. In addition, they educate the prisoners: each morning there is an hour of national readiness when they chorally sing patriotic songs. Twice a week, they have noodles in the shape of the swastika—for the purpose of national education. There is not enough of these noodles to eat. (pp. 59, 63)

Again, the fact, presented as especially repulsive, of the existence of a philosophical basis for victimization and of the ideological indoctrination of the victims perfectly reflects the Soviet reality. And, just as in the case of labor quotas, it is used precisely as an example of a world the opposite of the Soviet world. Generally speaking, in the Western world "fetters clink everywhere," "in all bourgeois countries, they beat prisoners," and the guards habitually abuse political prisoners by calling them "old swine" and "red swine" (pp. 51, 64).

In such ways the initial chapter of *Belomorkanal* projects negative aspects of the Soviet camp experience outside the Soviet world. Now the authors can turn to the central subject of their work—the Belomor camp itself. They do so directly after these descriptions of Western horrors. "These are the camps and prisons built by the bourgeoisie," the authors assert in concluding their lengthy description of foreign horrors. "But what awaits people who have been arrested in the USSR, and sent to the Soviet camps? The following chapters will talk about it" (p. 64). The remaining chapters constitute a lengthy exhibition of positive examples of successful reeducation and redemption of the confused victims of the old regime.

Before turning to these positive examples, it is important to admit that the opposition between the old, cacophonic world (represented by the images of pre-revolutionary Russia and the West) and the new, harmonious world under construction (images of Soviet territory) is in fact an opposition between the realms of pure negativity and pure virtue. An element of reality identified as negative is automatically ascribed to the pre-revolutionary realm, and vice versa. The actual subject of *Belomorkanal* is the transition from the negative to the positive world. This ideal process must be illustrated by elements of Soviet reality so that it appears to take place in the real world. The Soviet concentration camp—as Gorky construed it in "Solovki"—is an institution designed specifically to facilitate this change. Thus it is by definition positive. All its negative aspects having been projected upon the opposite side of the general dichotomy of old and new worlds, what are left as characteristics of the camp are solely positive aspects existing mainly in the realm of ideological concepts associated with the camp. These theoretical concepts must now be presented in literary form as objectively existent facts.

The idea is supposed to be described as existing in reality: the Bolshevik way of thinking that Sinyavsky called "Marxism with its feet in the air"[59] will build one of its most radical literary monuments, in which the monstrous, devastating experience that cost the lives of thousands of people will be presented as a triumphant transformation of the chaotic lives of thousands of confused individuals into a harmonious, happy, collective existence, lived in eager expectation of still greater joys to come.

Because Gorky's strategy of turning the reality of Soviet victimization into a positive image of reeducation was based on the manipulative assumption of a basic ethical agreement between author and reader, the human subjects of reeducation had to be presented in literary accounts as both confused (victims of the old world's ideological chaos) and dangerous in simple ethical terms. Being an adversary or merely alien to the Bolshevik regime became almost synonymous with being guilty of some common crime violating the traditional sense of morality as well as a politicized, utilitarian ethics. Thus, for instance, Gorky's meeting in "Solovki" with a woman prisoner who claimed to be innocent turned immediately into a vague accusation of the woman, based on a hazy association that the woman's looks evoked in Gorky's mind.

Belomorkanal is more explicit than "Solovki" in this treatment of the issue of prisoners' guilt. It leaves no ambiguity in establishing the link, always present, between the notion of the "enemy of the people" and that of a transgressor of common moral values. The source of this double transgression on the part of the prisoner is, of course, the basic confusion characteristic of the old polyglot and cacophonic world that

entraps some people. For instance, the speed of collectivization of the land—while being proof of the successful transition to a harmonious Soviet utopia—found, according to the
Soviet writers, many people unprepared to fully appreciate
the change.

> Sixty million new collective farmers appeared in the
> country. Many have their old habits. They are used to
> thinking that the road to a happy life leads through the
> strengthening of their private property, their private
> homes. They are full of doubts. They are not accus-
> tomed to communal life. The *kulaks* take advantage of
> these people's doubts and lack of trust for the new
> forms of social life. Somebody must help the new col-
> lective farmers to understand the facts. Somebody must
> explain to them the future of the country. (p. 25)

Naturally, those among the collectivized peasants who reveal an acute lack of willingness to be helped by Bolshevik
educators are to be given special attention—they are to populate the concentration camps. Unwillingness to cooperate
with the regime seems insufficient in itself, however, in the
view of the authors of *Belomorkanal,* to justify imprisonment
in the camps. The fact (or accusation) itself of contesting the
regime's policy does not seem serious enough to fall within
the traditional ethical view of incarceration—even if benevolent and educational—as a way of dealing with people who
have committed unethical acts. Curiously enough, the "slow
learners" among the population of the Bolshevik state tend
to commit harmful deeds—usually against people in general—and so earn the semantic status of "enemies of the
people." The authors explain: "The new world is achieving its
victory but there are still many people hostile to it. Their opposition takes many forms" (p. 29). Examples of hostile acts
promptly follow:

Today one can easily expose the hidden mechanisms of the old customs and former morality. They became visible in the time of the changes. Here is what people report from some villages where collective farms had just been established. The village of Kubasovo: Collective farm "The Road to Communism" was organized. The collective farmers work in the fields from dawn. When they leave their houses for the fields, unknown people break into their barns and cages, and steal all their supplies. The chairman of the village council is drunk all the time. All day long he sits in the house of Antip Fedorov whose brother, a *kulak,* was exiled for counterrevolutionary propaganda. "You are in trouble," he told a female member of the collective farm, Nikitina, who wrote a report to the Party's District Committee, "you dig potatoes out of frozen soil for the collective farm, and all of it will be sent away anyway. I pity you. Leave the collective farm." One night, in November 1930, Antip Fedorov was arrested when he and the son of Nikolai Fedorov were stealing a blanket and bags of grain from the hut of the collective farmer Zharov. (pp. 30–31)

In this example, the "kulak," an "enemy of the people" and a target of state persecution, almost automatically becomes a notorious thief—a literal enemy of the people. In another place, a former Menshevik turns out to be an even more disgusting criminal:

Meat preserves were brought to a factory. Workers were buying them quickly. But in the evening women gathered near the factory. They screamed and started throwing opened cans at the salesman who hid himself under the counter. In the cans were foul preserves made of skin, teeth, hair, and bulls' sexual organs. An investigation was ordered. It was discovered that the preserves were prepared by the enemies of the people, who were in charge of meat processing plants. "No problem, the comrades will eat it," one of them used to say. "We decided that the time for action had come," said another one—a Menshevik from Moscow. (p. 29)

If the Moscow Menshevik is strikingly reminiscent of an incarnation of Fedor Sologub's literary figure of the "petty demon," from his novel of the same title, the authors of *Belomorkanal* go even further into Russian literary history and find, in Rostov, a villain strikingly similar to Petr Verkhovensky, a negative character in Dostoevsky's *The Possessed:*

A proclamation printed in Rostov and prepared for distribution in the Cossack collective farms began with the words: "Cossacks of the quiet Don, rise against the parasite Communists!" It went further: "Kuban is our mother and Don is our father. . . . The Bolsheviks are ruining our villages in order to destroy the Cossacks." The author started by distributing a thousand of these pamphlets in mailboxes. He was arrested and disclosed the existence of a small underground organization. He had recruited new members using deception: "I am a member of the organization 'Sun' which has many thousands of people. Do you want to join us?" Thus far, they had met in an apartment, drank vodka, and ate stuffed peppers. (pp. 32–33)

The crimes "against the people" vary from polluting canned meat to ruining harvests in the collective farms (and thus starving the population):

In a journal of agriculture, a theoretical article was published in which the author argued that the government policy of early ploughing and sowing in the Urals district was wrong because the harsh climate of the Urals kills the seeds which are sewn early. Later on, the argument presented in the article was proven wrong but meanwhile the early sowing was suspended in some areas. A sad mistake, isn't it? But the author of the article, who was arrested a few months later for his involvement in a counterrevolutionary organization, confessed: "As a matter of fact, I wrote an article about the harm of the early sowing because the early sowing would make the crops in the collective farms more abundant." (p. 32)

In these examples, besides exposing odious crimes against the whole population, the authors, in a typical Soviet way, explain the reason for what many readers might have perceived as failures of the Soviet economy.

Yet it is these villains who become the heroes of *Belomorkanal,* thanks to the internal transformation accomplished in the camp. Though identified as enemies of the new world, they have, in fact, no positive basis for such identification, as if the only reason for their existence was to "be against." Like the devil (*diabolos* means "slanderer"), they represent pure negation and no positive, unifying principle. In short, they are live incarnations of the world of cacophonic chaos—the world of the "140 nations of pre-revolutionary Russia" and of the "fight of all against all." Their apprehension and resocialization in the concentration camps constitute their only chance to regain harmony with the rest of humanity.

When finally brought to the realm of unifying harmony, they do not turn into full-fledged participants in the new collective overnight, but drag their former identities along with them for a while. Here is an illustration of the beginning of the long process of reeducation. The new life begins:

They put up tents hastily by the sides of huge bon-
fires, they build huts, because there are not enough
tents; detachments of prisoners are continually arriv-
ing. The most unexpected encounters take place
at Tunguda. Some were thieves together, some met
in counterrevolutionary white detachments, others in
murder affairs or conspiracies. Half-baked students,
police sergeants, commercial travelers and their
clients, esperantists, antiquarians. . . . They are dressed
in every kind of garment: some in tatters, some in bast
shoes, others in leather jackets, but their trousers lacked
seats. It is a motley crowd: Kulaks who have run away
from factories, merchants, profiteers, sharpers, pick-
pockets and along with them, crying and laughing on
their way to the camp, prostitutes, and those jolly
thieves, the underworld women, always dancing and
singing. . . . The different nationalities here keep to
themselves, and apart from one another. The Jews behave quietly, the Tyurks very quietly and apathetically.
(p. 141)[60]

This is still the world of the "140 nations," of many conflicting points of view, many identities, languages, individual am-
bitions, enmities, group loyalties, and peculiarities. It is the
unruly human material out of which the Bolshevik genius is
about to construct the most homogeneous, harmonious, just,
and happy society on earth.

The principle of conflict and cacophony still prevails
among the newcomers to the camp. The cacophony and heteroglossia[61] are represented directly in the description of the
first night spent by a group of female prisoners in the camp:

In a new barrack there is no electricity yet. There are
two oil lamps. An iron stove gives warmth. . . . On the

stove, there is an iron, a tea kettle, and a pot. On the table—a newspaper, some scattered tobacco, and curling irons. . . . A radio speaker in a corner patiently explains work quotas and regulations. It announces names of those who distinguished themselves at labor, and those who drag behind. But the women don't want to listen. "Man'ka, gag his mouth!"—someone yells. The radio, choked with a rag, mumbles and gurgles, and becomes almost silent. Singing begins:
"In our sleigh
the yellow suitcase stood
Everyone put his hand
on the gun in his pocket. . . ."
The song tells how "the heavy door opened", and the piles of money "looked at us."
"Hail Mary full of grace . . ."—nuns sing in a corner.
"Modestly dressed in a gray English overcoat.
with a flower in his lapel . . ."
"The Lord is with you . . ."
"At seven thirty sharp, he left the capital
and didn't even glance at my window . . ."
"Blessed art thou among women, and blessed is the . . ."
Two songs interlace in the air until both of them fall silent. (p. 137)

What is presented here is a literal example of the principle of cacophony that rules in the old world. The two songs sung by women collide and blend with each other, thus giving the effect of disharmony, while the "patient" voice of the radio is not listened to. Both songs—the underworld romance and the religious prayer—represent the old world which the women drag along with themselves into the camp but will ultimately discard, thus proving their transition into the new realm represented here by the voice from the radio. For the time being, however, they and other new prisoners live in darkness—unaware of the true dimensions of the reality in which they live. What all of them—prostitutes, nuns, thieves, and the rest—have in common is that they are deprived of the true image of the world and of themselves within this world. Misplaced expectations, confusion, abuse—all attributes of the old world—are the sources of the prisoners' transgressions. Just like Gorky's orphan-criminals, they must find a sense of paternal guidance in the camp. Under this guidance, provided by the Soviet regime, they will undergo the transformation that will unite nuns and prostitutes, thieves and old-fashioned farmers, uncautious agronomists and common criminals. The 140 unruly nationalities will speak the same Soviet language. What will ultimately transform and unite them will be the canal built by their common effort.

It seems appropriate to pause here and quote another literary account from another concentration camp where a prisoner's function was that of a disposable working tool. The motto above the gate to this camp was very similar to the famous slogan of the Belomorkanal—"Nature we will teach—freedom we will reach." The new German version read: "Arbeit macht frei" (Labor makes one free); the gate was that of the Auschwitz main concentration camp. Primo Levi, who spent about a year in one of the Auschwitz subcamps called Buna, wrote:

> The Carbide Tower, which rises in the middle of Buna and whose top is rarely visible in the fog, was built by us. Its bricks were called *Ziegel, briques, tegula, cegli, kamenny, matoni, teglak,* and they were cemented by hate;

hate and discord, like the Tower of Babel, and it is this that we called it:—*Babelturm, Bobelturm;* and in it we hate the insane dream of grandeur of our masters, their contempt for God and men, for us men. And today just as in the old fable, we all feel, and the Germans themselves feel, that a curse—not transcendent and divine, but inherent and historical—hangs over the insolent building based on the confusion of languages and erected in defiance of heaven like a stone oath.[62]

The fiction of *Belomorkanal* may be seen as seeking an effect diametrically opposed to the one just quoted. *Belomorkanal* is the myth of the Tower of Babel *à rebours.* The motifs of transformation and unification represent the more general concept of salvation. Here, for instance, is the story of a woman prisoner's life, as quoted from *Belomorkanal:*

Motya Podgorskaya tells her neighbor the story of her life. "When I was three I became an orphan. My parents died from charcoal poisoning. I was taken to an orphanage. I lived there until I was fourteen. Once I went to the garden and got acquainted with a man named Kolya. He was an officer, and he started asking me who I was, and then he began courting me and inviting me to his apartment. I wanted to eat and I went. He gave me food, and on the same evening he raped me. At the beginning he was very charming but then he started looking down at me. He started beating me. I had nowhere to go, they threw me out of the orphanage, but there was such a storm in my soul that I decided to leave him. Later there was someone else just like Kolya. I left him too. It happened a few times. Finally, I reached the stage where I was called a prostitute. My soul longed for love but that was only a sweet dream."—Motya speaks more and more quietly, and she falls asleep. The whole barrack is sleeping now. (P. 138)

Those who come to the camp are confused victims of their own past. Even educated engineers are in the same situation as the petty thieves, prostitutes, and (supposedly very ignorant) nuns. For a while, before the prisoners can reach higher levels of self-awareness, it is only the guards who are capable of perceiving them for what they really are: "The engineers are anxious for some reason. The Chekists of Medgora watch these learned folks respectfully, and though they know their souls, they cannot help being puzzled: why these educated men who can understand the science of life written in many languages cannot understand the most important thing—that socialism alone can transform life and create the new world, the new Earth . . . damn it! But let's not rush too much, comrades. Life sometimes delays the explanation of many strange things" (p. 137).

The story of the world's transformation from a realm of chaos, crime, and confusion to a realm of harmony is the story of prisoners gradually turning their own self-perceptions into those projected by their guards. The actual transformation, as in Gorky's "Solovki," takes place thanks to forced labor: "The trees in the forest are gray, straight, tall, and hard. Just try to cut them, and you will see how hard they are. Here are the big, tough hands of a peasant, and the slim hands of a pickpocket, and the pale hands of an intellectual. It is equally hard for all of them to take an axe and to chop this forest" (p. 140).

The collective task—clearing the woods—and the common tool—the axe—together constitute the new common denominator for various individuals gathered in the camp. The transition is under way. The psychological orphans find their new father—the Bolshevik regime. Stories of villains turned positive heroes constitute much of *Belomorkanal*.

Listen to Volkov. He is a stocky fellow with very quick, dexterous movements. He is a second-storey man "with a great past." He has twice been at the Solovki Islands and escaped both times, he was in a labor commune, from which he also ran away. A hard-labor prisoner and a drunkard, he was brought to Belomorkanal from a Siberian camp. "I was imprisoned at Taganka in 1926," he relates. "Professors came there to study criminology. . . . They tried to find out how one person could be so criminal. They wanted to help me. When my term expired they put me to work in a candy factory, rolling candies. But the candy did not make me any sweeter, and again I went my old way, for the 'criminality' had not been rooted out." Now listen further to Volkov. His sentences become short, soldier-like, he has pulled himself together, he is all action. "We came as a brigade. The brigade had been got together from different train loads. We did not know one another. Well, they looked. They listened. They thought. Volkov had been everywhere. They elected me chairman. Of what? Of the labor collective. Thinks I—what's that—a labor collective? First time I've heard of it. I worked for about a month and a half. It's all right." (p. 146)[63]

The criminal Volkov, a typical confused victim of the old world, accepts his punishment and finally shows promise as a future citizen of the Soviet utopia. He has already discarded his criminal past and reached the stage when his own self-perception does not collide with that of his guards. This is the stage when the initial heteroglossia (*raznorechie*) and conflict between the prisoners and the guards, as well as among the prisoners themselves, is overcome by the new, unifying consciousness. If the cacophony of two different prisoner songs competing with each other and with the voice of authority was an acoustic representation of this old chaotic world, the camp experience leads toward the world in which one song unites everyone: the intellectuals, the kulaks, the prostitutes, the nuns, and all others. The subject matter of this song is neither romance nor religious faith but something much more graspable by everyone—the camp wheel barrow.

> Masha, Masha, Mashechka,
> She is a very hard-working little wheelbarrow
> We put together wings for her
> So she can be faster than others. (p. 139)

This song—the expression of enthusiasm for forced labor on the part of the camp population—unites the guards and the prisoners in one joyful collective, where some among its members draw up plans, others dig the ground and clear woods, and still others watch them with guns.

As the internal transition of people's minds from the confusion and fragmentation of the old world towards the harmonious unity of the new world takes place in *Belomorkanal,* so does the external transition of the "objective world." A slave labor project like the Belomor Canal unites the process of constructing the material foundations of the future utopia (base) with the process of creating the consciousness (superstructure) of the new man who will populate it. The principal narrative structure of *Belomorkanal* consists in the story of the construction of the huge marine route; it follows the idea, the plan, and all of the technological stages up to the triumphant completion of the project. Human stories of internal psychological transformation are interwoven into this overall structure. Transitions within human minds (superstructure) and the material transition of the socialist industrialization (base) are inseparable and fully complementary within the universe presented in the book. The slave-labor camp becomes the emblem of this dual transition. The story told in *Belomorkanal* is the story of man's victory over the chaotic elements of nature—represented both in the construction of a gigantic canal in the midst of the hostile country of the north and in people's victory over their own elemental individualism and anarchism. The ultimate symbol, as well as the ultimate result of this process of transformation of nature and man, is the canal itself.

Such is the universe that the authors of *Belomorkanal* constructed in order to turn the traumatic experience of Stalinist slave labor and mass victimization into a verbal representation of something opposite to what it was. The communicative strategy designed to impose this new view of the universe upon the reader was based on an extension of the principle introduced by Gorky in 1929: the universe presented here should not challenge the reader's own traditional cognitive and ethical categories but should appear as unquestionable, entirely natural, and totally objective.

The documentary genre and style, with its non-literariness and manifest matter-of-factness, were used by Gorky to create an impression of the unquestionable objectivity of his account. *Belomorkanal* develops and transcends this strategy of Gorky. The difference is that in implying the objectivity of his account of Soviet reality in *In and About the Soviet Union* Gorky reduced all direct indications of the author's creative involvement in constructing the image presented in his work. The only limitation that Gorky failed to overcome in his effort to create an impression of full objectivity was the inevitable textual indication that his account of Soviet reality was, after all, an account of Gorky's individual, personal experience. As such, Gorky's image of Soviet triumphs in building the future utopia, no matter how convincingly presented, was open to question by any other account or, simply, any other experience of Soviet reality, including the reader's own. Though Gorky made efforts to avoid such a confrontation, the implied harmony and univocality between author and reader (the crux of Gorky's strategy) remained vulnerable as long as the author could not conceal his individual, subjective point of view.

Belomorkanal overcomes this shortcoming by simply admitting the collective authorship of the entire 614–page-long "documentary" account of the "reality" of the Soviet concentration camp. On the title page of the book, next to the alphabetical list of its thirty-six authors and opposite the portrait of Stalin, an introductory note states: "All of the authors take full responsibility for the text. They helped one another, corrected one another. On this account it is difficult to indicate just who wrote the various sections. But the fact must be stressed that the real author of the entire book is the whole collective of those who worked on the history of the White Sea–Baltic Canal, dedicated to Stalin" (p. 1).

Thus, the universe presented in the book is no longer the product of an individual vision; it is a supra-individual, collective, common truth. If a contradiction between the image of reality presented in the book and the reader's experience arises, the reader is simply outnumbered in this confrontation. The individual, subjective experience of the universe of the reader is confronted here by the collective, universal experience. Because universality, in addition to verifiability and communicability, is an essential standard for objectivity, the collective authors' superiority over the reader in this respect becomes unquestionable. Furthermore, outnumbered in this rhetorical situation, the reader cannot turn to other sources for support of his view against the view championed by the book, for the simple reason that any other sources representing points of view that undermine the dominant one have been suppressed. Polyphony, challenge, and dialog have been eliminated not only from the universe presented in the book, but also from the rhetorical situation projected by the text and determining the dynamic between the collective author and the reader. Polyphony, challenge, and dialog have been eradicated from the entire cultural and communicative universe in which the book is to function—just as they have been eliminated from Soviet public discourse as a whole. Thus the positive image of Bolshevik abuse of power presented in *Belomorkanal* not only mystifies the reality of this historical experience, but also appears as an unquestionable, unchallenged, fully normative, and exclusively true view of this experience. This claim to exclusivity is supported by the apparent testimony of many, which cannot be contradicted merely by the testimony of one. Needless to say, no objective test of truth favors the perception of one against the perception of many. Besides, the reader whose perception of Soviet reality is contradictory to the "true image" presented in the book becomes associated with the confused characters in *Belomorkanal* who found themselves in urgent need of reeducation. In other words, the reader who has difficulties in accepting the only correct vision may well become the next candidate for treatment in the camp.

Besides imposing the ideologically motivated view of Soviet victimization upon the reader, the collective authorship of *Belomorkanal* performs a crucial poetic function in creating the overall notion of the world's transition from the stage of chaotic cacophony toward harmonious univocality. This transition is presented by means of the topic of Soviet forced labor, anchored in a network of oppositions, themes, and motifs generated by ideological dogma. At the same time, the book itself serves as an example of the world's transition from heteroglot chaos to univocal harmony. The collective authorship of the book appears as the victorious outcome of the individual authors' struggles against their own individualism, in search of a supra-individual, universal point of view. Immediately following the note about the collective responsibility of all authors for the work is another note—a series of dates indicating the stages in the process of creating the book:

August 13th, 1933—The chief editorial board of the *History of Factories and Industrial Enterprises* declared its intention of including in its plan of work a book describing the construction of the White Sea–Baltic Canal.

August 17th, 1933—A delegation consisting of 120 writers from the R.S.F.S.R., Ukraine, White Russia, Tadzhikistan and Uzbekistan undertook a trip through the Canal.

September 10th, 1933—The plan of the book was drawn up and the work was divided up among the various authors.

October 20th, 1933—The Collegium of authors began their conferences to discuss and criticize the manuscript.

November 28th, 1933—The assembly of the book began.

December 12th, 1933—The manuscript was handed over to the printers.

January 20th, 1934—The book was published.(p. 4)[64]

The story of the book's creation is itself a story of turning many individual views, perceptions, and voices into one supra-individual, univocal expression of a universal view. Just as the crowd of unruly, confused, heterogeneous prisoners changes in the concentration camp into a harmonious, homogenized collective, so do the writers who take on the common task of presenting this transformation. It is not only the number of the writers but also their apparent heterogeneity that makes this effect all the more impressive. Among the authors, one finds previously politically uncommitted "fellow-travelers" of the Bolshevik regime (Mikhail Zoshchenko), former emigrés (Alexei Tolstoy), a Polish Communist (Bruno Jasienski), literary experimenters (Viktor Shklovsky), and more traditional realists (Maxim Gorky), and so on. Writers of different Soviet nationalities participated in the original project (Russians, Ukrainians, Belorussians, Tadzhiks, and Uzbeks are mentioned in the preface). Like the 140 nationalities of the Russian Empire, which could not find a common language for God or traditional morality but which immediately joined together in their appreciation of the new ideology, writers of very different backgrounds, literary schools, and styles became similarly capable of speaking the new common language and of seeing reality according to the categories implied in that language. The story of transcending the polyphony of the literary life of the past and moving toward the univocality of the future—along with the story of massive reeducation of the confused people of the past in the spirit of Soviet utopia (built with their own hands)—is a sign of the times.[65] These stories testify to, and praise, the new stage that reality was supposed to be entering under the Bolshevik regime. Soviet reality in its "constant progress" should have been near the stage when "all class antagonisms are being abolished" and "solidarity," "love," and "friendship" form the "basis of society."[66] These writers made it look as though it did.

The year of the book's publication, 1934, was to remain fixed in Russian literary history as the date of the First Congress of Soviet Writers, at which all existing literary styles and orientations were once and for all officially dismissed in order to make way for the Union of Soviet Writers to codify the one and only literary doctrine for all literature: socialist realism. *Belomorkanal* was intended as one of the models of this newly proclaimed literary style.

Silence

Belomorkanal was the most radical example of literary praise of the Soviet system of mass victimization in the camps. In it, the convention of ideological mystification of the painful experience of life under Bolshevik terror achieved its maximally complete realization. Written in 1933–1934, the book functioned as an exemplary panegyric to Stalinism, only to be banned by Stalin in 1937, the year of the unprecedented escalation of Bolshevik terror. In contrast to the terror at the time of the creation of *Belomorkanal,* the terror was now directed against numerous Bolshevik activists, along with "traditional" targets—the "kulaks," "wreckers," and other "enemies of the people." From 1937 on, the theme of the Soviet concentration camp (up until then a topical setting for descriptions of the triumphs of the regime) vanished altogether from Soviet literature.

The sudden removal of the topic of the Soviet camps from public and literary discourse to the domain of taboo meant that the strategy of ideological mystification of the camp experience, designed by Gorky in "Solovki" and mastered in *Belomorkanal,* lost its functionality in the eyes of the designers of Soviet totalitarianism. What undermined the convention was the same factor that had undermined the conventions presenting Bolshevik terror in the 1920s. In both cases, the positive vision of Bolshevik oppression projected in literature failed to fulfill the condition of teleological verification implied in the ideological basis of Bolshevism. Confronted with the historic reality of the dramatically increasing terror of the 1930s, the internal logic of Gorky's convention of "humanitarian reeducation through labor" was bound to collapse. What this confrontation destroyed was the very basis of this convention's "optimistic" and "humanist" pretense. According to the logic represented in "Solovki" and *Belomorkanal,* the camps were a temporary means of reeducating class enemies and overcoming the last obstacles of the past on the road to a brighter future. If this reeducation was as successful as "Solovki" and *Belomorkanal* presented it, the "enemies of the people" should have been a disappearing species, and the camps should have been about to be transformed into voluntary labor colonies, thereby losing their coercive aspects.[67] But the further escalation of mass terror and the obsession with enemies directly contradicted this assumption.

Moreover, the subsequent targeting of Bolsheviks themselves by the Stalinist terror of the late 1930s undermined another vital aspect of the literary convention of "constructive violence"—its political criteria of defining positive versus negative characters and right versus wrong points of view. If the Chekists are presented in *Belomorkanal* as figures endowed with an unerring sense of the correct perception and evaluation of reality, in the context of the Stalinist purges in the late 1930s within the Bolshevik apparatus itself, those same Chekists must be included among the list of potential enemies. To follow this logic, one would have to admit that twenty years after the victorious revolution, the class-consciousness of its warriors, instead of improving, had become even more vulnerable to the influences of the decaying world of the past. In Stalin's Russia everyone, including the Bolsheviks themselves, became potentially suspect: today's dogmas could become tomorrow's heresies; today's heroes could turn out to be tomorrow's villains. So the main reason for banning *Belomorkanal* in 1937 was that it glorified the chief of the OGPU, Genrikh Yagoda, under whose patronage the Belomor Canal was built. Yagoda was purged by Stalin as a traitor to the Soviet Union, and his former actions had now to be seen as hostile to the homeland of the proletariat.[68]

Under the new conditions of the late 1930s the "documentary" pretense of "humanist" camp literature could not be maintained. One could no longer correctly identify real-life heroes and villains, for they could easily exchange places from day to day in the official view of reality. This situation is best summarized in a famous Soviet anecdote. In the Lubyanka prison, three prisoners occupy bunks next to one another. "Why are you here?" the first prisoner asks the second prisoner. "I was against Karl Radek in the 1920s," he responds, and returns the question. "Oh, how strange," the first prisoner says, "I was a supporter of Karl Radek in the 1930s and that's why I am here." The third prisoner who has not said anything yet chimes in: "This is really funny; I am Karl Radek." In short, the political principle of identity—the cornerstone of the Bolshevik univocal, integral universe—was, in fact, shaken by Stalin. To continue writing about the Soviet camps within the convention designed by Gorky required continuously "updating" fundamental notions of "right" and "wrong" and continually discovering who was a hero and who a villain—quite an Orwellian prospect. In this light, Stalin's imposition of a taboo as the dominant strategy for addressing (or, rather, not addressing) the Soviet camp experience after 1937 seems to have been the most functional option. In 1937 the *Great Soviet Encyclopedia* explained the meaning of the phrase "concentration camp":

Concentration camps—special places of imprisonment established by fascist regimes in Germany, Poland, Austria and other countries. Fascism, a regime which represents barbarity and oppression of peoples, causes constant expansion of the numbers of prisoners. Regular prisons are incapable of housing them. The system of concentration camps was established to complement the system of prisons. The concentration camps where revolutionary and anti-fascist activists are held are places of unlimited tyranny and cruelty towards the inmates (torture, abuse, murder). Political prisoners of concentration camps are kept in conditions far worse than criminals. Fascist regimes send people to concentration camps for indefinite periods of time, without any concrete evidence of guilt, and without due process.[69]

The topic of the Soviet camp, celebrated officially by Soviet propaganda just months earlier, disappeared from public discourse at the moment when fear of the camps was becoming more prevalent than ever in the Soviet state. Perhaps this taboo, imposed and maintained for nearly two decades precisely at the time of the most overwhelming presence of state terrorism and camps in Soviet life, was the most complete form in which, as Aleksander Wat put it, the "grandiloquent terms and the opposing monstrous reality were kept side by side [in the Soviet state], ostentatiously and with diabolical perseverance."[70] There was, however, one modification. Short of specific "grandiloquent terms" applicable to the "monstrous reality" of the camps, the regime designed a new fiction—the fiction of absence—and resolved to coerce the entire population to contribute to this fiction by silence.

4

HOPE BEYOND HOPE

Communist Martyrology and the Post-Stalinist Thaw

Father, father, what have you done to us? We are
your children . . .

    —Georgy Shelest, *The Kolyma Notes* (1964)
   (From a prisoner's monolog addressed to Stalin)

n the fall of 1962, an unusual competition took place between Aleksandr Tvardovsky, editor of a leading Soviet literary journal, *Novyi mir*, and Aleksei Adjubei, editor of the
daily *Izvestia* and son-in-law of Nikita Khrushchev. Each
of the two editors had in hand and was determined to be
the first to publish a newly acquired literary work whose
topic and point of view were previously unpublishable
and dangerous even to discuss in the Soviet Union. Both
works focused on the presentation of life in Soviet labor
camps.

The topic, banned from Soviet public discourse since the
late 1930s, began surfacing unofficially in numerous spoken
accounts of thousands of prisoners released from camps and
allowed to return to major Russian cities in 1954 and 1955.
The official breakthrough came in 1956, three years after
Stalin's death, when Nikita Khrushchev, speaking to the
Twentieth Party Congress, accused Stalin of serious abuses of
power. Four months later, on 30 June 1956, the Central
Committee of the Soviet Communist Party issued a decree
"On Overcoming the Cult of Personality and Its Consequences," thereby adopting Khrushchev's revisionist position
as the official position of the party. The media became filled
with the officially accepted criticism of Stalinism. From the
very beginning, however, the parameters of this critical debate were determined by Khrushchev's position that Stalin's
crimes constituted an aberration in the otherwise positive
Bolshevik system. The debate focused almost entirely on the
victimization of numerous Communists during the purges,
and left virtually unexamined such campaigns of mass terror
as, for instance, collectivization. The main cause of Stalin's
crimes was linked to personal flaws in the character of the
former dictator, not to the nature of the Soviet system. Stalin
was viewed as a traitor to the Communist Party, and the new
motto of the Soviet regime was that of the "return to the

Leninist norms of life." In fact, the regime was now dissociating Stalin from Lenin and the Communist Party and was focusing all the blame for the ills of the past on the person of Stalin. This official line of criticism found its ultimate ritual expression at the Twenty-Second Party Congress, in October 1961, in the following announcement: "Owing to a serious violation of Lenin's last will by Stalin, as well as Stalin's mass repressions against honest Soviet people and other acts performed during the period of the cult of personality, the further presence of the casket with Stalin's body in Lenin's mausoleum is impossible."[1] Soon Stalin's body was removed from the public display it had enjoyed in Red Square along with the corpse of Lenin and was buried next to lesser Bolshevik leaders. Thus the Soviet regime under Khrushchev exorcised its demon. At the Twenty-Second Congress Khrushchev once again denounced Stalin and called for further public debate about his crimes. The limits of this debate were already clear, but nevertheless many people in the Soviet Union felt encouraged by Khrushchev's appeal.

Despite this quite lengthy period of changes in the official Soviet attitudes toward the issue of Soviet abuses of power, there was still, by the fall of 1961, no officially published Soviet literary work in which the experience of life and death in Soviet camps appeared directly as the central theme. This was the moment when Aleksandr Tvardovsky and Aleksei Adjubei, encouraged by the official line of the Twenty-Second Party Congress, became determined to break this taboo, each of them rushing to publish a literary work written by a camp survivor. It was not only the topic of the two literary pieces being promoted by the two editors that determined their highly unusual status within the context of Soviet literature. It was also the point of view expressed in these works. Both of them presented the Soviet camp experience from a point of view never before admitted into Soviet literature—the point of view of the victim. This time the victim was not the former class enemy transformed into the new Soviet man, but precisely and literally a victim—an innocent human being oppressed and crushed by the unbearable reality of the Bolshevik concentration camps. The authors of these competing works shared a number of characteristics: both were survivors of Stalin's concentration camps; as writers, both were as yet unknown to the literary audience; both of them lived and worked in provincial towns, far from Russian cultural centers: Aleksandr Solzhenitsyn, author of *One Day in the Life of Ivan Denisovich,* was a schoolteacher in Ryazan; Georgy Shelest, the author of the short story "A Nugget" and the cycle *The Kolyma Notes,* lived in Chita.

The story of the publication of *One Day in the Life of Ivan Denisovich* is among the most widely publicized episodes in the history of Soviet literature. Solzhenitsyn completed the novella in 1959 but did not seek publication until November 1961. Meanwhile, the manuscript was circulated among Solzhenitsyn's friends and, through them, other readers of the *samizdat.* It was the public disclosure and criticism of Stalin's terror offered by the Soviet leadership under Khrushchev at the Twenty-Second Congress of the party which prompted Solzhenitsyn to reveal his literary account of the Soviet camp experience. Among the critical statements voiced during the Congress about Stalinist terror, one of the most important for Solzhenitsyn was that of Aleksandr Tvardovsky, himself a member of the Communist Party's Central Committee. Tvardovsky called upon writers to courageously address the traumas of the recent Soviet past through the literary medium, and thus to revive the century-old Russian tradition of literature's moral commitment to social causes. Solzhenitsyn chose to respond to this call, and in November 1961 *One Day in the Life of Ivan Denisovich* found its way on to Tvardovsky's editorial desk at *Novyi mir.* Despite the climate created by Khrushchev's leadership of official criticism of the Stalinist terror, it took Tvardovsky a year of behind-the-scenes efforts to secure the publication of Solzhenitsyn's debut work. Tvardovsky managed to present Solzhenitsyn's work to Vladimir Lebedev, Khrushchev's aide, and through him to Khrushchev himself, who expressed his support for Tvardovsky at the Plenary Session of the Central Committee and managed to ensure the Central Committee's approval of the publication.[2]

That was the moment when Aleksei Adjubei, having learned about the imminent publication in *Novyi mir* of Solzhenitsyn's literary revelation of the camp experience, rushed in with his own version of the literary rediscovery of the Soviet camps—*The Kolyma Notes* by Georgy Shelest. Unlike the case of Solzhenitsyn, little is known about Shelest's literary beginnings except that he completed his cycle of short stories about the Kolyma camps in 1961 and shortly after presented it for publication in Tvardovsky's journal, only to be rejected on the grounds that "the writing was poor and the stories did not ring true."[3] The year 1962 proved more advantageous for Shelest: in the fall, Adjubei reached him in his hometown of Chita and not only offered immediate publication but, in order to save time, asked Shelest to dictate his short story "A Nugget" (from the cycle *The Kolyma Notes*) over the phone from Chita (more than 3,000 miles east of Moscow) directly to the *Izvestia* office.

Finally, on 6 November 1962, in the holiday issue celebrating the forty-fifth anniversary of the Bolshevik revolution, *Izvestia* printed "A Nugget," a short story by Georgy Shelest based on his experiences in the Kolyma camps.[4] On this date, for the first time since the Soviet regime's decision in 1937 to withdraw *Belomorkanal* from public circulation and to place a taboo on the topic of the Soviet concentration camps, the camp experience reentered the thematic scope of

Soviet literature. The taboo was broken. Within several days, the eleventh volume of *Novyi mir* containing *One Day in the Life of Ivan Denisovich* appeared.

As a matter of chronological fact, and contrary to popular perception, it is not Solzhenitsyn but his now forgotten rival, Georgy Shelest, who deserves credit for breaking, during the late post–Stalinist thaw, the literary taboo on the topic of the Soviet Gehenna of the concentration camps. Moreover, while not the first to reintroduce the camp experience into Soviet late-thaw literature, Solzhenitsyn's work was not unique in addressing this topic at the time. It was, in fact, accompanied by more literary revelations of the Soviet camp experience than are commonly acknowledged or remembered. Just as Shelest's cycle of the Kolyma stories passed with little notice and left virtually no mark in Russian literary and cultural history, so did a whole series of literary works reexamining the camp experience and written by former prisoners of Soviet camps. The years 1963 and 1964 brought, besides the complete version of Shelest's *The Kolyma Notes,* the publication of Yuri Pilyar's novel *People Remain People,* Boris Dyakov's *The Story of What I Lived Through,* and Andrei Aldan-Semenov's short novel *Bas-Relief in the Rock.*[5] All these works dealt with the horrors of the Soviet concentration camps in startling detail and presented them from the point of view of the victims. They all also shared the fate of Shelest's Kolyma cycle and passed into oblivion, leaving space in the cultural memory for virtually undivided attention to Solzhenitsyn and making his revelation of the totalitarian camp experience the only one in Soviet literature to be kept alive within the larger cultural context.

The historical status of *One Day in the Life of Ivan Denisovich,* overshadowing the other works of the late-thaw camp literature, is fairly easily explained by the quite obvious disparity between the literary merit of Solzhenitsyn and the remaining works. Clearly, Solzhenitsyn's novella stands apart and well above the other works in question when judged by literary criteria. Yet this disparity represents something more than mere superiority of artistic talent of Solzhenitsyn over Shelest or Dyakov. There seems to be a close interdependence between the literary shortcomings of the works by Dyakov, Shelest, Pilyar, and Aldan-Semenov and their ideological commitment. The evaluation of Shelest's stories by the editors of *Novyi mir,* that "the writing was poor and they did not ring true" can be seen as valid, to a greater or lesser degree, in the works of each of the forgotten pioneers of late-thaw camp literature. But while the "poor writing" may be attributed to limitations of individual talent, these works do not "ring true" because, unlike Solzhenitsyn, none of the authors attempts or manages to present the camp experience other than through a filter of an explicitly formulated set of preconceived values and ideological frameworks. These ready-made ideological filters are imposed on the images of the camp experience so rigorously that the experience itself becomes the subject of a particular selective approach: elements of the camp experience are chosen and combined according to their usefulness in supporting the preconceived ideological point of view. As a result, literature whose potential power lies in the unprecedented character of the experience presented reduces the unprecedented and the shocking to the familiar and the anecdotal. Dyakov, Shelest, Aldan-Semenov, and Pilyar approach the experience of dehumanization and annihilation in the totalitarian universe of the camps from the point of view of insiders—the victims. At the same time, these are insiders who rarely seem confused or morally challenged by the trials of the camps. They seem never to run out of verbal means of quick and always unmistaken evaluation of the reality they are a part of. The experience itself neither changes them nor reveals to the reader the sources of human motivations that would remain unexamined were it not for this traumatic test of the limits of humanity.

The Camp Experience and the Problem of
Its Literary Representation

These charges need a broader explanation. Is literature written from the point of view of the victims of concentration camps capable of rendering the unprecedented, unique character of this experience in a manner free from the impact of the cognitive, evaluative, and communicative filters external to the experience in question? Can the unprecedented and the unique be reflected upon and communicated except by referring to the familiar and the habitual? This issue should be addressed in comparative and relative, rather than absolute, terms, in order to avoid the pitfalls attendant on the irresolvable problem of the relationships between the human cognitive and communicative apparatus, on the one hand, and reality, on the other.

This problem is crucial to totalitarian camp literature of the twentieth century, regardless of its historical, cultural, and ideological coloration. Through presentation of a great variety of experiences of human beings under totalitarian pressures, camp literature not only uncovers rarely scrutinized aspects of human nature but also reveals contingencies and limitations in writer's capacity to respond to, and verbally render, the humanity under conditions of extreme adversity. Andrzej Werner, who analyzed many of the literary works written by survivors of the Nazi camps, concluded:

[R]eality in the camp is seen in these works through the filter of the consciousness with which the authors entered the camps. Regarding the unique, unprece-

dented character of the [camp] experience, it is astonishing how powerful and decisive is the impact of previous world views brought in from outside the camp.
[Usually], it is not the camp experience that changes
this world view but the opposite that is true: the reality
of the camp, defined within the framework of this *a priori* vision, cannot overcome the limitations of this world
view. Even if these cognitive dynamics are reciprocal,
the process of challenging and reshaping consciousness
is usually minimal; it concerns matters of secondary importance and rarely overcomes the limitations of a potential inner evolution assumed within the *a priori* basis
of this world view.[6]

This assessment of what Werner believes to be the most
common tendency found in works of Nazi camp literature
enables him to formulate his notion of the interrelationship
between *a priori* ideological belief and the artistic value of
camp literature: "I am not discussing the purely theoretical
problem, whose resolution is impossible; I approach this issue
on a relative, comparative scale. . . . It is possible to assume
that the original world views brought by the victims into the
camp from outside are unchangeable. Then, the scale of comparisons among them would refer to the inner margin of
freedom possible within various world views, and distinguish
between world views more open and inclusive and those
closed and dogmatic."[7] Under such conditions, close commitment of a literary work to the latter type of world view is
likely to limit this work's capacity to respond to the challenge
implicit in the unprecedented nature of camp experience.

In order to plumb the depths of the camp experience,
writers must respond to the challenge of presenting the
moral impact of this experience—often devastating—on the
human being subjected to it. This impact may be reflected in

the challenge posed by the camp experience to the value systems brought by victims from their familiar realities outside the camp into the special reality of the camp. Elie Wiesel's *Night,* an autobiographical literary account of his experiences in the place emblematic of the twentieth century's most extreme assault on humanity, Auschwitz, serves as a singular example of a response to this challenge. In it, Wiesel reveals his discovery of aspects of humanity so disturbing that they unsettle the entire deep-rooted world view that organized his life experience outside the camp. When Wiesel's autobiographical protagonist, a Jewish boy, Eliezer, enters Auschwitz, he immediately experiences a profound collision between the reality inside the camp and his world view (shaped in the world outside the camp), which fails to provide him with terms whereby even the existence of this new reality can be acknowledged. Here is the description of this experience:

> Not far from us, flames were leaping up from a ditch, gigantic flames. They were burning something. A lorry drew up at the pit and delivered its load—little children. Babies! Yes, I saw it—saw it with my own eyes . . . those children in the flames. . . .
>
> So this was where we were going. A little farther on was another and larger ditch for adults.
>
> I pinched my face. Was I still alive? Was I awake? I could not believe it. How could it be possible for them to burn people, children, and for the world to keep silent? No, none of this could be true. It was a nightmare. . . . Soon I should wake with a start, my heart pounding, and find myself back in the bedroom of my childhood, among my books.[8]

In this description of his initiation into the camp, the experience of the reality of the camp can be identified by

Eliezer only in terms of a bad dream. But only a few months later, his concept of reality has already significantly altered. Some time after his imprisonment, he is forced, along with other prisoners, to watch a public execution. Under the impact of everyday routine horrors, Eliezer's moral sensitivities have become progressively numbed. Yet the execution described here occupies a moment in which Eliezer finds still existing in himself the capacity to be morally shocked: the single victim of this execution, unlike the thousands who perish every day in the gas chambers and at work, is not depersonalized enough to fail to awaken the sense of horror in a boy. But suddenly a crude comment by a fellow prisoner clashes with the solemn mood of the author-narrator. " 'Do you think this ceremony'll be over soon? I'm hungry . . .' whispered Juliek." [9] Juliek is an older, more experienced prisoner; watching the execution does not strike a note of horror in him. His mind is focused on food. This realization could serve as a conclusion to the scene, but it is not the end of it. Only a few moments after the execution, soup is being dished out for the prisoners. And no trace of horror is left in the mind of Eliezer. "I remember that I found the soup excellent that evening," he notes. [10]

Within the new framework of reality, developed by the prisoner after a relatively short period in the camp, watching an execution and enjoying a meal are no longer two incompatible activities. In an environment where horrors and deprivations are routine, human responses to them often evolve in ways much more complex than the traditional expectations shaped outside the camp would allow. This process may (though by no means must) lead to a gradual numbing of moral sensitivities of the camp victim. This aspect of the camp experience was explored with singular power by Tadeusz Borowski in his Auschwitz stories. Borowski, himself a survivor of Auschwitz, fictionalized his autobiographical ego to the point of questioning, but not entirely severing, the connection between Tadeusz Borowski (the author-survivor) and Tadek (the narrator). In stories whose titles alone provoke the ethical sensitivities of the reader, such as "This Way for the Gas, Ladies and Gentlemen," "Auschwitz Our Home," and others, the narrator—an Auschwitz insider—tends to talk about horrors of the camp as other people talk about their daily routine.

Tadek, a prisoner with the life-saving function of an orderly in the Auschwitz hospital, describes his activities:

> Just when the flowers were about to bloom, we finished the soccer field. . . . One day I was a goalkeeper. As always on Sundays, a sizeable crowd of hospital orderlies and convalescent patients had gathered to watch the game. Keeping goal, I had my back to the ramp. The ball went out and rolled all the way to the fence. I ran after it, and as I reached to pick it up, I happened to glance at the ramp. A train had arrived. People were emerging from the cattle cars and walking in the direction of the little wood. All I could see from where I stood were bright splashes of color. The women, it seemed, were already wearing summer dresses: it was the first time this season. The men had taken off their coats, and their white shirts stood out sharply against the green of the trees. . . . The people sat down on the grass and gazed in our direction. I returned with the ball and kicked it back inside the field. It traveled from one foot to another and, in a wide arc, returned to the goal. Once more I ran to retrieve it. But as I reached down, I stopped in amazement—the ramp was empty. . . . Between two throw-ins in a soccer game, right behind my back, three thousand had been put to death. . . . In the following months, each day, as I got up in the

morning to scrub the hospital floors, the people were walking. Women, men, children. When I sat down to dinner—and not a bad one either—the people were walking. On warm evenings I sat at the barracks door reading "Mon Frère Yves" by Pierre Loti—while the procession continued on and on.[11]

The power of Borowski's deliberately provocative camp prose lies in his masterful use of a literary strategy whose stylistic dominant is not hyperbole, typically expected in addressing such grave topics, but understatement. Borowski's narrator, Tadek, a non-Jewish prisoner who witnesses endless processions of Jews transported to the gas chambers, is not an ethically retarded monster; nor are his sensitivities blinded by some anti-Semitic folly (he identifies the victims as "people," "men," "women," not even as "Jews"). On the contrary, he is presented as "normal" to a frightening degree. Mass murder conducted continuously around him becomes an element of his daily routine, to which he reacts the way "normal" people react to things that just happen every day. He adjusts. As a result of the highly visual first-person narrative technique, the reader is conditioned to perceive reality through Tadek's eyes. These are the eyes that follow the ball on the grass and are not distracted by the horrors happening just behind his back. The mind behind these eyes is capable of perceiving the colors of the women's dresses and relating them to the idyllic scenery of nature, but it is no longer capable of being morally shocked by the reason behind these women's presence—not even when Tadek is gazed upon by people minutes before their death. His mind focuses on his game, daily activities, meals, readings. The continuous presence of horror numbs his moral sensitivity and indeed evokes his silent acceptance of this reality, just as one accepts natural phenomena beyond one's control. By this passive, almost involuntary acceptance, his innocence and his right to the moral superiority of victim over oppressor become less and less apparent. Tadek, a temporary inhabitant of the higher circles of this hell, whose death in the camp was deferred but nevertheless remains the only fate predictable, belongs to the category of victims who are presented with the opportunity to struggle in the camp in order to delay this fate further and further or simply to stay alive against all odds. In Borowski's world it happens that victims become victimizers and executioners before their own executions. The reason for this is usually as simple as an additional bowl of soup, but sometimes also a silk shirt or fancy shoes.[12]

Both Wiesel and Borowski, each in his own way, subject their autobiographical (or, in Borowski's case, semi-autobiographical) personae to the devastating dynamics of life in the camp, expose their moral vulnerabilities, and let the literary renditions of these vulnerabilities become testimonies to the profound nature of the threat of dehumanization inherent in the world of the camps. At this point, it must be made clear that there are aspects of the experience of the Nazi camps (especially those directly related to the Holocaust) that are unique and find no equivalent in the Soviet camps. The blatant, naked evil committed by the Nazis without even a pretense of justification, which culminated in the systematic hunting down and cold-blooded murder of Jews, was a phenomenon of unparalleled character. In the Soviet camps, the annihilation of prisoners was never an admitted goal of the regime, though in many locations over many years under Stalin the conditions of life and labor reduced prisoners' chances for survival to a bare minimum, often to zero. It is the experiences of those prisoners of Nazi and Soviet camps who were presented with the elusive chance to struggle in order to delay their fate that present many characteristics in common. Hunger, exhaustion, violence practiced by both camp guards and deranged fellow prisoners, with no possibility of restoring justice, were among those common aspects of the daily experience of victims of both Nazi and Stalin's camps. The everyday assault on positive human values and emotions, such as dignity and compassion, was a key common experience. If, as Wiesel and Borowski show, camp prisoners routinely exposed to such unmatched horrors as the mass murder conducted in Auschwitz might become vulnerable to a gradual numbing of their moral sensitivities, this vulnerability is presented as even more pervasive in testimonies to the Soviet camps, whose evil did not assume the blatant nakedness of the Holocaust but was usually accompanied by elusive declarations of the regime's ultimately "good intentions." The explorations of the moral vulnerabilities of camp victims by Wiesel and Borowski are echoed by Varlam Shalamov, a survivor of the Soviet camps of Kolyma. Shalamov's literary technique of understatement can be compared only to that of Borowski. In one of his semi-autobiographical stories, "Dominoes," his narrator reminisces:

> I ended up in a small sector of a transfer camp . . .
> Huge barracks held five or six hundred prisoners each.
> . . . Next to me slept a lieutenant in the armored forces, Svechnikov, a polite, rosy-cheeked youth, convicted by court martial for some crime or other while in military service. Here he was under investigation too: while working in the gold mine, he was caught eating the flesh of human corpses from the morgue. He carved out morsels of human meat, "of course not fatty morsels," as he quietly explained. One does not choose neighbors in the transfer camp, and there are obviously things worse than dining on a human corpse.[13]

Before we explore specifically Soviet variants of the more general issue of the moral impact of the camp on its victims, let us go back again to Wiesel. One of the most prominent themes in his *Night* is the bond between Eliezer and his father, both of whom suffer together in Auschwitz. Staying together, not allowing themselves to be separated—these are the goals of their daily efforts. The presence of his father links Eliezer more strongly than anything to the world of humane values and feelings that he was forced to leave behind. It protects his sense of dignity from the dehumanizing pressures of the camp and provides him with a most tangible object for such humane feelings as love, compassion, and readiness for sacrifice. But the camp is a universe created in order to break the bonds established by the victims in the world outside. It is precisely the feeling of compassion and solidarity with the weak that are being targeted and destroyed in the camp. For the camp population can be controlled all the more efficiently if the prisoner's worst enemy is not the guard but another prisoner. In the camp, fear and deprivation are meant to be accompanied by a sense of loneliness and helplessness in each individual lost in a mass of slaves. "In the world of driving necessity and physical disabilities many social habits and instincts are reduced to silence," Primo Levi wrote in his autobiographical *Survival in Auschwitz*.[14] Levi came to the conclusion that life in the camp, dominated by the relentless competition for physical survival, divides people into two categories: those who have a chance of surviving and those too weak to make it—the saved and the drowned. Levi wrote:

> This division is much less evident in ordinary life, for there it rarely happens that a man loses himself. A man is normally not alone, and in his rise or fall is tied to the destinies of his neighbours; so that it is exceptional for anyone to acquire unlimited power, or to fall by a succession of defeats into utter ruin. Moreover, everyone is

normally in possession of such spiritual, physical and even financial resources that the probabilities of a shipwreck, of total inadequacy in the face of life, are relatively small. And one must take into account a definite cushioning effect exercised both by the law, and by the moral sense which constitutes a self-imposed law; for a country is considered the more civilized the more the wisdom and efficiency of its laws hinder a weak man from becoming too weak or a powerful one too powerful. But in the Lager things are different: here the struggle to survive is without respite, because everyone is desperately and ferociously alone. . . . In history and in life one sometimes seems to glimpse a ferocious law which states: "To him that has, will be given; to him that has not, will be taken away." In the Lager, where man is alone and where the struggle for life is reduced to its primordial mechanism, this unjust law is openly in force, is recognized by all. With the adaptable, the strong and astute individuals, even the leaders willingly keep contact, sometimes even friendly contact, because they hope later to perhaps derive some benefit. But with the mussulmans, the men in decay, it is not even worth speaking, because one knows already that they will complain and speak about what they used to eat at home. . . . And in any case, one knows that they are only here on a visit, that in a few weeks nothing will remain of them but a handful of ashes in some near-by field and a crossed-out number in a register. Although engulfed and swept along without rest by the innumerable crowd of those similar to them, they suffer and drag themselves along in an opaque intimate solitude, and in solitude they die or disappear, without leaving a trace in anyone's memory.[15]

Primo Levi, along with numerous other witnesses, states that the dynamics of physical survival in the camp pressured the victim to dissociate himself or herself socially and psychologically from those who were perishing.

> To survive in the camp, one has to fight against the current; to battle every day and every hour against exhaustion, hunger, cold and the resulting inertia; to resist enemies and have no pity for rivals; to sharpen one's wits, build up one's patience, strengthen one's willpower. Or else, to throttle all dignity and kill all conscience, to climb down into the arena as a beast against other beasts, to let oneself be guided by those unsuspected subterranean forces which sustain families and individuals in cruel times. Many were the ways devised and put into effect by us in order not to die: as many as there are different human characters. All implied a weakening struggle of one against all, and a by no means small sum of aberrations and compromises. Survival without renunciation of any part of one's own moral world—apart from powerful and direct interventions by fortune—was conceded only to very few superior individuals, made of the stuff of martyrs and saints.[16]

These words of Levi, based on his experience in Auschwitz, are echoed by survivors of Soviet camps. Dmitry Likhachev, a survivor of the Solovki camp, described Solovki as a perfect totalitarian system in which prisoners given even the most limited power over other prisoners would almost automatically abuse this power and victimize their subjects. Varlam Shalamov, a survivor of Kolyma, writes: "The camp was a great test of man's ethical strength, of simple human morality. And ninety-nine percent of the people did not pass the test." [17]

Let us now return to Wiesel's story of Eliezer and his father. How long can their bond survive in the world of "the drowned and the saved"? For Wiesel, the importance of this story is central in terms of the test of human values presented in his book. Wiesel's constant preoccupation with this bond turns it into a principal thread of the narrative. The theme of Eliezer and his father is reflected in other stories of fathers and sons in the camp, related by the protagonist-narrator throughout the book. The pattern whereby the narrator refers to these stories signals the growing anxiety in Eliezer as to whether he will be able to remain compassionate towards his father, and thus connected to the world of humane values, if (or when) the ultimate challenge of survival comes.

This anxiety grows with time as Eliezer becomes immersed more and more deeply in the camp experience. It reaches a prolonged crescendo as the end of the narrative comes nearer. This final phase starts with the beginning of the evacuation of the Auschwitz camp by the SS in January 1945, when Soviet troops approach the area. In the midst of the horrific winter march, when thousands were constantly dying of cold, hunger, exhaustion, and bullets, Eliezer meets an old man, Rabbi Eliahou, searching for his son. When asked by the rabbi, Eliezer tells him that he has not seen the young man, and then immediately recalls seeing him, in fact, secretly abandoning his staggering father. Eliezer realizes that the rabbi's son, expecting his father's imminent death from exhaustion, left him behind to free himself from the burden of caring for the old man. "I had done well to forget that," Eliezer admits, "and I was glad that Rabbi Eliahou should continue to look for his beloved son. And, in spite of myself, a prayer rose in my heart, to that God in whom I no longer believed. 'My God, Lord of the Universe, give me strength never to do what Rabbi Eliahou's son has done.' "[18]

Wiesel's protagonist is capable of distinguishing right from wrong according to the value system that he brought with him to the camp. What he is no longer capable of is predicting his own behavior regardless of this value system. And the fear of succumbing to the animalistic dynamics of survival at any cost is reinforced in him more and more as the deprivation deepens. As the story of the evacuation continues (now the prisoners are packed in open cattle cars on a train), Wiesel describes the following situation:

One day when we had stopped, a workman took a piece of bread out of his bag and threw it into a wagon. There was a stampede. Dozens of starving men fought each other to death for a few crumbs. The German workmen took a lively interest in this spectacle. . . .

In the wagon where the bread had fallen, a real battle had broken out. Men threw themselves on top of each other, stamping on each other, tearing at each other, biting each other. Wild beasts of prey, with animal hatred in their eyes; an extraordinary vitality had seized them, sharpening their teeth and nails. . . .

Not far away I noticed an old man dragging himself along on all fours. He was trying to disengage himself from the struggle. He held one hand to his heart. I thought at first he had received a blow in the chest. Then I understood; he had a bit of bread under his shirt. With remarkable speed he drew it out and put it in his mouth. His eyes gleamed; a smile, like a grimace, lit up his dead face. And was immediately extinguished. A shadow had just loomed up near him. The shadow threw itself upon him. Felled to the ground, stunned with blows, the old man cried: "Meir, Meir, my boy! Don't you recognize me? I'm your father . . . you're hurting me . . . you're killing your father! I've got some bread . . . for you too . . . for you too. . . ."

He collapsed. His fist was still clenched around a small piece. He tried to carry it to his mouth. But the other one threw himself upon him and snatched it. The old man again whispered something, let out a rattle, and died amid the general indifference. His son searched him, took the bread, and began to devour it. He was not able to get very far. Two men had seen and hurled themselves upon him. Others joined in. When they withdrew, next to me were two corpses, side by side, the father and the son.[19]

A few days later, having arrived at Buchenwald, Eliezer discovers in himself instincts he did not suspect. When his father is exhausted to the point almost of dying, Eliezer suddenly becomes separated from him: "I went to look for him. But at the same moment this thought came into my mind: 'Don't let me find him! If only I could get rid of this dead weight, so that I could use all my strength to struggle for my own survival, and only worry about myself.'" And, overwhelmed by shame, he admits: "No better than Rabbi Eliahou's son had I withstood the test."[20]

This dark premonition of ethical disability becomes the central focus of the narrative. The inner voice in Eliezer's mind, which suggests abandoning his father, is now echoed by a voice from outside. A doctor-prisoner reveals to Eliezer something that he has already heard in himself: the logic of the survival in the camp. It sounds like a verdict:

Listen to me boy. Don't forget that you are in a concentration camp. Here, every man has to fight for himself and not think of anyone else. Even of his father. Here, there are no fathers, no brothers, no friends. Everyone lives and dies for himself alone. I'll give you a sound piece of advice—don't give your ration of bread and soup to your old father. There's nothing you can do for him. And you're killing yourself. Instead, you ought to be having his ration.[21]

This pronouncement constitutes the prologue to the scene of the death of Eliezer's father. Eliezer's father, ill and exhausted, is beaten unconscious by an SS man. Eliezer watches this scene but does not respond to his father's cries for help. "My body was afraid of also receiving a blow," he notes. With his father still alive but already unconscious, Eliezer goes to sleep, and when he awakes at dawn, there is a new prisoner on his father's bunk. "His last word was my name," Wiesel writes about his father. "A summons, to which I did not respond. I did not weep, and it pained me that I could not weep. But I had no more tears. And, in the depths of my being, in the recesses of my weakened conscience, could I have searched it, I might perhaps have found something like—free at last!"[22]

Wiesel takes the reader closer to the ultimate abyss of the camp experience than most other authors: it is the point of annihilation both physical and moral. The tragedy of the experience portrayed by Wiesel lies not only in the physical suffering and death but in the irresistible guilt and shame that overwhelm the survivor. This experience, as described by Wiesel, Borowski, Levi, Shalamov, and other authors, not only robs its numerous victims of their lives and feelings, but also seems to deprive them, in a cruel way, of the sense of moral victory of the victim over the oppressor.

The discovery and literary rendition of this experience of humanity under extreme totalitarian pressure, along with its philosophical, theological, and aesthetic consequences, is a lasting achievement of twentieth-century camp literature. But this is not to say that it should be treated as the discovery of the ultimate truth of the camps. There are only individual truths and individual experiences of this reality, and they belong to the persons who experienced it. What makes these literary works important is that they found words capable of bringing to our consciousness those particular aspects of the camp experience that we were not well equipped, morally, emotionally, or intellectually, to deal with. What we are much better equipped to deal with are those aspects of the camp experience which can be (to use Andrzej Werner's words) "immediately adapted to traditional expectations, so that they do not exceed the fixed limits of one's own world view and do not require the necessary revision of one's own value-system." [23] Literary presentations of these aspects of the camp experience tend to generate images constructed according to the implicit priority of upholding the value systems of the authors. If these value systems happen to follow society's expectations, this type of approach may create a cultural convention that provides society with the reassurance that its positive values have passed the most demanding test.

For instance, many works of Polish camp literature of the 1940s through 1960s follow a noticeable pattern in which one of the basic organizing principles of the image of the camp experience is that of heroic human resistance against dehumanizing pressures. Among Polish writers who strove to implement this principle were some who spoke directly about the evaluative filters they used while describing the world inside the Nazi camps. "I purposely avoided showing the bottom to which man fell, for I did not want to shift the weight of my work towards the macabre. I did not want to evoke unhealthy sensations in the audience," Wanda Jakubowska, a film director, said of her highly publicized film about Auschwitz, *The Last Stage*. "It would have been very difficult to explain to the viewers who did not share these experiences that moral defeat and symptoms of degeneration were caused by the camp system itself and not by the fact that people whom Germans kept in the camps were all morally deranged to begin with. . . . I wanted *The Last Stage* to show the truth about Auschwitz and to evoke a feeling of contempt towards Nazism." [24]

In this and many other statements by author-survivors of the concentration camps, the didactic, evaluative function of showing the triumph of humane values over dehumanization takes priority over the need to communicate the unprecedented challenge that the camps posed to these values. In *Smoke Over Birkenau,* Seweryna Szmaglewska described her fellow prisoners in the Auschwitz–Birkenau camp for women: "Some of them have on their faces complete silence and the mysterious sign of peace. . . . One cannot forget them. The faces of others are twisted by passion, fury, hatred. Those one wants to forget." [25] Again, the commitment to humane values is so primary in this vision that it creates a selective framework for the memory: only those who pass the moral test of the camp are to be immortalized through literature. This tendency to link memory with ethical purpose was also reflected by Levi and Wiesel. While describing the departure of prisoners from Italy to Auschwitz, Levi notes: "Many things were then said and done among us; but of these it is better that there remain no memory." [26] And for Wiesel, after the death of his father, his further experience becomes hollow, pointless; thus, he finally admits, he has "nothing to say" about it. [27] In the case of Szmaglewska, however, this ethically oriented selective framework of memory plays a structural role in her artistic design. The main purpose of her literary account seems to be didactic: she interprets her writer's obligation as first and foremost an obligation to positive ethical values. Hence she aims at reinforcing the positive values in her readers' minds by focusing on those instances from her camp experience in which these values proved themselves stronger than the dehumanizing pressures of the camp. In emphasizing the positive examples, she downplays the moral ambiguities and vulnerabilities. As a result of this strategy, she leans towards the martyrological discourse that, as Erich Auerbach put it, "knows only clearly outlined men who act from few and simple motives and the continuity of whose feelings and actions remains uninterrupted. In the legends of martyrs, the stiff-necked and fanatical persecutor stands over against an equally stiff-necked victim." [28]

There are various reasons why this martyrological formula assumed its prominent position in the majority of works of camp literature written by survivors. A reason not to be overlooked stems from the fact that philosophical and narrative preoccupations typical of the martyrological convention were instrumental not only in forming the actual narratives but also in shaping the very ways in which these authors experienced their fate in the camps. The point at which these accounts differ radically from the accounts of Wiesel, Levi, and Borowski is that the martyrologically oriented camp literature puts its principal emphasis on the unchangeability of the identity of its author-protagonists in the camp. That identity, formed outside the camp, is the chief semantic position generating terms whereby the reality of the camp is experienced and presented. At the same time, the preservation of this identity as fixed and intact is the most common way in which these authors describe their efforts to overcome the threat of dehumanization. For dehumanization means here, first and foremost, the disintegration of this identity. Survivors usually write from the point of view of those who have passed the test of their own humanity under the extreme conditions of the camp. It is the moral outlook brought by them into the camp from outside, and projected upon their subsequent experience, that helped them save their human dignity. The chief artistic challenge to literary testimonies of these moral victories is to avoid the inadvertent trivializing of the whole issue by showing the moral victors so completely protected by their values that the very experience loses much of its actual weight and ceases to be perceived as a profound moral shock. Writer-survivors focusing on presenting their visions of moral victory in the camp face a difficult task: they must find means of presentation powerful enough to alter the parameters of our reception of literature. These are the parameters according to which experiences that fail to change their human subjects profoundly tend to lose much of their dramatic significance. And society, preoccupied with the daily business of living, tends to welcome verbal and psychological techniques of forgetting and neutralizing the moral challenges of the past, no matter how recent.

In 1946, at the moment of his literary debut, Tadeusz Borowski anticipated that readers' responses to testimonies of the horrors of Auschwitz would immediately become dominated by techniques of avoiding the moral challenge. His literary strategy was, in fact, based on evoking, then frustrating this assumed response. The first two of his Auschwitz stories, "This Way for the Gas, Ladies and Gentlemen" and "A Day at Harmenz," published in 1946 in a collective volume co-authored by two other Auschwitz survivors, are preceded by these words written by Borowski himself:

> We are united by daily death without solemnity. The cause of this death was not the fatherland and honor but the exhausted body, ulcers, typhus, swollen feet. Years of continuous efforts to avoid this death, to outsmart it, to outlie it, bind us together as strongly as years

in the trenches, although these were not heroic years. . . . This struggle was devoid of ideological elements. It was a primitive struggle waged by the lonely, degraded prisoner against the equally degraded SS man and the horrible violence of the camp. We emphasize this strongly because many myths and legends will be born regarding this subject. We did not struggle in the camp for the idea of the nation or for the inner transformation of man. We struggled for a bowl of soup, a place to sleep, women, gold, and watches from the transports.[29]

This statement was intended by Borowski as a polemical provocation. Borowski feared that the depth of the human experience revealed in the camps would be covered over by martyrological designs imposed by both writers and readers on the subject. He believed that, although appropriate in many cases, these martyrological conventions could not be applied automatically without turning into clichés. While paying the price of making his vision of the camps dramatically one-sided, Borowski created a literary testimony that, long after the reality of the camps is gone, still does not allow the reader to face this topic without being morally disturbed. Testimonies like this highlight a dimension of the camp experience without which the extraordinary character of the moral victory of the countless victims who managed to save their human dignity in the camps could perhaps not be sufficiently acknowledged.

A Soviet "Discovery"

Given the tendency, common among works of camp literature, to approach the camp experience through the filter of value systems brought to the camp from outside, the Soviet works of the late thaw—those written by Shelest, Dyakov,

Pilyar, and Aldan-Semenov—seem to follow a larger, supra-cultural pattern. However, what is peculiar about the literary images of the Soviet camp experience created by these authors is the very content of the value system they affirm and project in their works. In the most common literary testimonies to the Nazi horrors, fundamentally positive human values and actions are usually attributed to the victims, who are set in direct opposition to the oppressors and their values. This presumption is sometimes tested and challenged but is always implicit. The people who created and ran the concentration camps are presented as the ultimate destroyers of positive human values—the agents of evil. But it is not so in the Soviet works in question. While their presentations of the Soviet camp experience are constructed to affirm a certain value system common to all of them, there is no longer a presumption of an uncompromised opposition between victims and oppressors. And the values that allow innocent victims to preserve their human dignity in the camp are identified as essentially the same values that inspired the creation of the concentration camps in the first place. These are the fundamental values of the Communist creed. For the protagonists of Dyakov, Shelest, Pilyar, and Aldan-Semenov are different from Solzhenitsyn's Ivan Denisovich in this important respect: unlike Ivan Denisovich, but quite like the architects of the Soviet camp system, they are outspoken, fervent believers in Soviet Communism. It is this ethical paradox underlying these literary visions of the camp experience that determines their unique status among the most striking accounts of the twentieth-century totalitarian experience: they may be seen as inspired by a peculiar need of the victims to justify their oppressors' right to oppress.

Approached from this angle, the camp prose by Shelest, Dyakov, Pilyar, and Aldan-Semenov—a forgotten episode in the history of second-rate Soviet literature—becomes a subject worthy of special critical attention for reasons other than literary value. It becomes a unique historic example of the degree to which the persuasive power of ideologically motivated categories of perception overshadows reality in forming a cultural reflection of this critical experience of the twentieth century. It also sheds light on literature's potential as a medium for both revealing and obscuring traumatic historical experiences, depending on the content and limitations of the ideological preconceptions involved.

In order to address these issues, one needs to examine the works of forgotten camp prose of the Soviet late thaw in the analytical context of preexisting Soviet literature that focused on the troubling issues of the Bolshevik terror and concentration camps. Although the very existence of Soviet literature of the 1920s and 1930s devoted to the topics of the Red Terror and concentration camps was largely overlooked by the late-thaw literary criticism accompanying Dyakov, Shelest, and others, the literary works in question show close dependence upon the earlier Soviet literary and ideological conventions applied to this subject. They seem particularly dependent on the convention introduced by Gorky in his literary sketch of the Solovki camp and developed in the collective reportage on the Belomor Canal. The nature of this dependence is complex: while quite openly polemical regarding these conventions on the surface, Shelest, Dyakov, Pilyar, and Aldan-Semenov are, at their core, set on promoting the ideology represented by the vision of the camp experience in "Solovki" and *Belomorkanal*.

Gorky's formula of presenting the Soviet camp as a benevolent institution of "social medicine," aimed at the harmonious reeducation and resocialization of ill-adjusted individuals, in order to be convincing had to fulfill a series of literary requirements (examined at length in the previous chapter). One of them was that the camp experience, harsh as it may have been, be envisioned as essentially constructive. The "factual," intentionally non-fictional presentations of life in the camps at Solovki and the Belomor Canal were supposed to provide proof of the constructive character of this experience. They show and quote hundreds of prisoners who may not have been aware of their crimes at the moment of imprisonment but who, thanks to the camp experience, abandon their old selves and begin seeing themselves through the eyes of the Soviet regime—that is, from the only correct point of view. In the universe presented in "Solovki" and *Belomorkanal,* the experience of the camp is an experience of rebirth.

To an inexperienced reader, it might have looked as if the wave of late-thaw literary revelations of Soviet camp experience had dealt the final blow to the old vision of Bolshevik violence as "social medicine." Now there were no happy prisoners smiling at work, no miraculous conversions of old enemies to the Communist faith, no concerts and theater performances in the camp. Compared to the reality presented by Shelest, Pilyar, Dyakov, and Aldan-Semenov—the actual survivors—Gorky's notes of the enthusiastic visitor to Soviet camps could not seem further from the truth. It is food, warmth, sleep, and the chance of staying alive for one more day that defines the horizon of the prisoner's immediate concerns in the camp as presented in these new accounts. Physical deprivation and slow destruction, the motifs excluded from the earlier Soviet convention, are the undeniable, constitutive elements of the victim's perception of the camp. If the essence of life in the Belomor Canal camp was defined by Gorky and his followers with rhetorical slogans about socialism under construction and man's transformation into a member of the happy collective of the future, the authors of the new Soviet camp prose formulated it frequently in much simpler words. In Pilyar's novel *People Remain People,* an old, experienced prisoner introduces a novice to the camp: "Here, my friend, you have to understand one thing: if you fulfill your work quota you will get a bowl of soup; if you don't—the bowl will be smaller. And the smaller bowl means you will be able to work less. And if you work less the bowl will be still smaller. And you will go down like this very fast, until they start dragging you out to work. That's how people get finished off. Here, in the camp, the work quota is everything. It's your god. It's your life." [30]

A vicious circle of physical destruction represented in the "option" between starvation and exhaustion provides the basic framework of the prisoner's daily preoccupations in the camp. This mode of existence in the camp had been described and loudly condemned in Soviet literature before—in *Belomorkanal*. There, this constant "choice" between starvation and exhaustion was presented as a key example of bourgeois inhumanity and was frequently used as a motif in images of concentration camps in countries such as Finland, Poland, and Japan.[31] In the works by Pilyar, Shelest, Dyakov, and Aldan-Semenov, in contrast to Gorky's image of the camp, it is physical destruction, not reeducation, that constitutes the essence of the camp experience. Descriptions of physical violence and abuse are more radical in these works than in Solzhenitsyn's literary debut of 1962. Direct accounts of the death of starved, exhausted prisoners appear frequently. One of Shelest's protagonists, Admiral Dushenov, dies in the camp of overexhaustion.

Unlike in "Solovki" and *Belomorkanal,* here prisoners do not change from socially ill-adjusted into full-fledged Soviet citizens: the change that takes place is from naive, surprised novice to a "goner"—that is, gradual annihilation. Even the most unusual physical stamina and strong will to survive, characteristic of literary types of Russian peasant-soldiers tested by the wars and calamities of the twentieth century, are broken in the camp. A character named Vinyatin in Yuri Pilyar's *People Remain People* is such an indestructible Russian peasant-soldier, victim of numerous assaults by history, always capable of rising from destruction. In his first encounter with a Stalinist camp, where he is taken directly from a Nazi camp, he says: "I am not scared of work. As far back as I can remember I have always been doing hard work: in our village, on the frontline, most of all in the POW camp. My whole life. And as to food . . . well you know how it was. Under siege we used to dig dead horses out of the snow and eat them. On the frontline I carried pieces of a cannon on my back. They were heavy as hell. And I didn't perish. And I am still alive. And I will live." A few paragraphs later, the narrator adds: "He died on an early December morning."[32]

These and many other indications of the finality of the camp experience leave no room for arguments about the pedagogical functions supposedly realized in the camps. Even if it were the authors' assumptions that Shelest's Dushenov (a Bolshevik veteran sentenced in the 1937 purge) and Pilyar's Vinyatin (a former prisoner of a Nazi camp during World War II) had been sent to the camps for valid reasons, neither of them would ever have a chance of reeducation. For them, as for many other characters shown in the new Soviet camp literature, the camp means irreversible annihilation—death. Even those who do survive the camps are not approaching any Soviet-style transformation into happy participants in a bright future. If for Gorky and his followers the essence of the camp experience was the transformation of "socially unaware" people (criminals or enemies of the Soviet order) into declared Communists, in these new works there are no villains-turned-heroes of Communist labor. On the contrary, the very art of survival practiced by these "socially unaware" types—criminals and enemies of the Soviet state—excludes all forms of identification with the regime. In the opening section of Shelest's *The Kolyma Notes* we encounter a prisoner—a former criminal and veteran of the Belomorkanal camp. About ten years after the completion of the Belomor Canal, the event described in 1934 as a glorious example of the resocialization of social enemies, this prisoner-veteran is still in the camp, now more educated by it than ever. The nature of this camp education becomes clear as soon as he speaks. As he learns about the new massive labor project to be accomplished by forced labor—a railroad to Vorkuta—he comments: "They are looking for specialists. They need foremen, engineers, and other fools to make the road to Vorkuta. But here the most important thing is the kitchen, storage, bread-cutting ward, or at least the disinfection chamber. Let Yezhov and Stalin build the road by themselves. I built the Belomorkanal. Enough!"[33]

Thus, without directly mentioning the 1930s literary vision of the camps, the camp literature of the late thaw seems to categorically reject it. In this new literary view, the camp destroys and degrades people, and if it teaches them something, it is nothing new: a cynical criminal learns his lesson of survival at all cost, which only deepens his cynicism. In fact, no single character is transformed in the way projected by Gorky and his "school" in the early 1930s. This abandonment by the late-thaw literature of the ideological formula of the transformation of human minds was nothing new either. Even the authors of Soviet law during Stalin's reign had abandoned the rhetoric of reeducation and resocialization. A Soviet law textbook from the early 1950s defines the notion of legal punishment in terms strikingly distant from the "pedagogical" phraseology of the 1930s: "The purpose of punishment is to inflict upon a convict suffering and deprivation."[34] Thus, even in the official interpretation of Soviet law, suffering and deprivation, not reeducation and resocialization, appear as the essence of the camp experience.

The pattern of inner dynamics of the camp experience presented in the new Soviet camp literature is, in fact, the exact reversal of the previous pattern. Instead of framing the transformation of the prisoner's identity from an enemy of the people into an enthusiastic builder of the new order, the new pattern is that of the absolute immobility of the prisoner's fixed identity even under the impact of the camp. The world views and value systems that prisoners bring into the camp do not change under the conditions of the camp. Characters defined as positive or negative remain such throughout their camp experience. It is precisely the luggage of the views and convictions brought by the prisoners from the "free world" that determines their moral status and the way they behave in the camp. Thus, for instance, criminals shown by Pilyar, Dyakov, Aldan-Semenov, and Shelest do not turn into heroes of socialist labor thanks to the camp but only become more what they were before—that is, vicious, totally immoral egoists. Far from changing people's identities, the camp merely makes them more clear-cut.

The Posthumous Triumph of Maxim Gorky

The new pattern of characters' psychological and ideological immobility, while determining the polemical character of the new camp literature in relation to the tradition of Gorky, also provided it with a new kind of limitation. Because of this pattern of the character's inner immobility, the works of Soviet camp literature published at the time of Solzhenitsyn's debut may be viewed as just a few more instances of a substantial trend in twentieth-century camp literature in which the camp experience does not reshape identities and value systems brought by people from "normal life" but only serves as an illustration of the validity of these already fixed identities and values. The main weakness of this literature derives from the fact that the outcome of the alleged test of human values tends to be determined before the actual experience takes place. If a literary work of this kind is preoccupied with promoting a given set of values, then the characters who represent these values are defined as positive and remain such throughout the camp experience, and the camp experience becomes merely a reservoir of situations, themes, and motifs illustrating the triumph of these values.

In second-rate literary works, the task of identifying characters as representatives of preconceived value systems requires simplification of their psychology. With very little awareness of characters' psychological dimension, Shelest, Dyakov, Pilyar, and Aldan-Semenov are preoccupied with defining positive and negative value systems through the medium of characters' direct speech plus narrators' comments. However, what is peculiar about these literary works, and at the same time quite characteristic of Soviet literary tradition, is the equation between the characters' status as representatives of positive versus negative values and these characters' political partisanship. For if the camp experience is presented in these works from the point of view of the victim, it is not the point of view of "any" victim. The only point of view expressed here is that of either a Communist (usually a member of the old Bolshevik elite) arrested in Stalin's purges or, at least, a Soviet patriot supportive of the system. Thus, all the main characters in Shelest's *Kolyma Notes* are high-ranking Bolsheviks: the narrator is a *kombryg* of OGPU (the Soviet security police); Admiral Dushenov is the former commander of a Red Fleet and an old seaman from the battleship *Aurora*;[35] Major Karpov is a civil war hero twice decorated with the Order of the Red Flag; General Zaborsky fought in the civil war as a Bolshevik commander. Dyakov talks about distinguished Soviet scientists who, though imprisoned in the camp, never abandon their Communist beliefs. Petrakov—a positive hero of Aldan-Semenov—takes his prisoner's cap off while passing by the monument of Lenin, on his way to slave work.[36]

Since characters are judged according to the values (easily definable) that they bring into the camp from outside, the authors leave no doubt that what they seek to promote in their works are Communist values. It is Communist values that preserve the human dignity of these characters under the degrading impact of the camp experience. They remain faithful to these values, choosing death rather than doubt. After the death of Shelest's Admiral Dushenov, one of his fellow prisoners, a Communist, delivers a eulogy at the grave site: "Comrade Communists! Today, we are burying our friend, an old Bolshevik, a sailor from 'Aurora,' and the commander of a Red Fleet. He died at his post and did not let the banner of Lenin fall from his hand. He considered his incarceration a test, and he used to say, 'Time is working to our advantage and nobody will defeat Leninism.' He lived with faith, and with faith he died."[37]

The character of Dushenov, created by Shelest, is clearly a positive hero, a martyr who never compromises his values under the dehumanizing impact of the Soviet camp horror. He is but one in a long series of Communist martyrs in Soviet camp prose of this period. They are the key figures in this literature, human models who represent its main message—the triumph of Bolshevik values over the degrading circumstances created, ironically, by the Bolshevik power itself. This paradox and irony usually goes unadmitted by Soviet authors and critics. A Soviet critic commented on Dyakov's *The Story of What I Lived Through*: "The power of Dyakov's novel stems from the fact that it speaks about real Soviet people, true Communists. In difficult circumstances, they did not lose their human dignity; they were faithful to Party ideals and to their Motherland. They rejoiced at each accomplishment of their nation, at each step forward. They painfully experienced violations of the law, but they nevertheless preserved faith in the inevitable victory of Lenin's truth and Lenin's ways of life. Their faith triumphed, thanks to the efforts of the Party." [38]

It is precisely here that the unique character of this literature originates. For the purpose of this literature is paradoxically twofold: simultaneously to discover the Soviet camp experience and to provide it with an ideological cover-up. It simultaneously accuses and excuses Soviet totalitarianism at its worst. This paradox stems from the fact that the set of values promoted in this literature as the sole source of human dignity and moral survival under the impact of the camp is, in fact, the very same set of values that provided the ideological basis for creating and operating the camps in the first place. Thus, the cast of positive heroes of this literature, by protecting this Communist set of values in the camp, provide an ideological and ethical basis for their own victimization as well as the victimization of others. Within the universe presented here, there is only one fully acknowledged value system—the Bolshevik ideological credo. This is the value system which brings about human suffering and degradation and, at the same time, provides the only basis for moral resistance against this degradation.

The point of view of the victims, expressed here, is what is most peculiar: they seem incapable of admitting, let alone examining, the connection between the totalitarian value system they preach and live by and the very fact of totalitarian victimization to which they, along with thousands of others, are subjected. The experience presented in these works shows a peculiar incongruity between two basic components of human experience as such: pure empirical reflection (physical, sensual data) and inevitable evaluation (intellectual, moral). The victims can describe the horrors of their experience and are deeply aware of the wrongdoing to which they are subjected. Yet, at the same time, they have no other set of values by which to evaluate their experience than the value system of their oppressors. Thus, without abandoning their feelings of innocence, the victims tend to internalize the point of view of their oppressors, to the extent of ultimately confusing the categories of innocence and guilt.

Analyzed in this context, Soviet camp literature of the late thaw shows a new, unexpected connection with the 1930s literary strategy aimed at reprogramming human perceptions of the Soviet camp experience. True, at the level of phenomenal description these first-hand accounts of the dehumanizing brutality of the camps refute Gorky's image of benevolent reeducation through labor. At the level of philosophical messages, however, the works of the new Soviet camp prose exemplify a major triumph of the 1930s strategies. For if the final measure of success of Gorky's literary strategy is represented by the image of victims internalizing the only correct, all-embracing, fully objective point of view of their oppressors, the accounts of thirty years later indeed show Gorky's model put into practice. While bitterly protesting against pain, hunger, and injustice, the protagonists of Shelest, Dyakov, and others are incapable of rejecting the basic notion that the hand that punishes them so brutally for uncommitted sins is, just as it was supposed to be in "Solovki," "the hand of our own" (*svoia ruka*). Vladlen, a teenager in Shelest's stories, is imprisoned for reading Lenin's testament, where unfavorable opinion about Stalin was expressed. "After all the camp is Soviet and not fascist!" he says with relief as he enters his barracks for the first time.[39] This attitude is shared by the narrator of Pilyar's *People Remain People*. "In spite of all, the mood is cheerful," he thinks on his way to a logging site. "Work is a good thing after all! The woods, the snow, the sun. . . . The real axe. Real pines trans-

formed into logs, and then into planks, paper, mine casing.
. . . Everything would be all right, just give us a little more
bread and thicker soup, and take away the armed guards, and
get rid of the bedbugs in the barracks. No problem!" [40]

For Pilyar's narrator, the conditions in the camp could
stand some improvement, but he does not question the fact
of being imprisoned and punished for no crime. This kind of
attitude on the part of a prisoner was presented, though with
a much different purpose, by Eugenia Ginzburg in her *Into
the Whirlwind*, a book originally intended for publication in
the Soviet Union in the 1960s, which was rejected by the
Soviet censorship. Ginzburg cites a conversation among
women prisoners transported in a cattle train to Kolyma.
One of them objects to the custom of shaving prisoners'
heads. Another woman, a Communist, responds: "Well, simply to crop someone's hair is hardly an insult. It was very different in the Tsarist prisons, where they shaved only one half
of your head!" [41] The difference between Ginzburg's account
of this attitude of a victim towards the regime and the accounts of Shelest and Pilyar is fundamental. While Pilyar puts
the words about the joy of camp work into the mouth of his
narrator and thus gives them finalizing significance, Ginzburg
uses dialog in order to create a sarcastic counterpoint. Someone on the train says: "That's the spirit, girls! Let's compose a
letter to Comrade Stalin. 'Life's better and gayer now.' One's
no longer shaved on only one side but on both. Thanks, father, leader, creator of our happiness!" [42] Apart from being rejected by the Soviet censorship, the book by Eugenia
Ginzburg differs from the literary material presented here by
the fact that the camp experience described in *Into the Whirlwind* has a dynamic character and brings about an inner evolution of the authorial protagonist. For Eugenia Ginzburg,
the camp represented a major challenge, and the fact that,
unlike Shelest, Pilyar, Dyakov, and Aldan-Semenov, she chose

to face this challenge in her literary account excluded her book from Soviet public view at the time.[43]

"Us" and "Them," or Who Is Who in the Camp

The issue of crime and innocence, though frequently avoided, does not remain totally unexamined in the late-thaw camp prose. On the contrary, it is the peculiar way in which this fundamental ethical issue is addressed that determines the unique status of this literature. The innocence of the Communists and Soviet patriots imprisoned in the camps is emphasized here almost constantly. The protagonists perceive themselves as victims, not penitents. The status of the main characters is indicated more or less directly in the very openings of these works. Shelest begins from the scene where his narrator-protagonist is admitted to the camp:

> "Your party affiliation?"—the commander asked.
> "I am a member of the Communist Party," I answered.
> "What kind of a Party member are you?! What were you tried for?"
> "I didn't have a trial. They just read my sentence to me. . . ."
> "Oh, look at him, what a special fellow! He doesn't know what he was convicted of!"—the commander said. The typist giggled. Somebody pointed a finger at me, laughed, and yelled, "Just look, what innocence!"
> "Rebellion, terror, sabotage! And you are telling us, you don't know why they sentenced you? Where did you work? Your profession?"
> "Commander of a Red Army brigade. In the army since 1917."

The commander looked at me with his unyielding
eyes.

"Forget about it. Now you are a *zek,* a prisoner. You
don't consider yourself guilty? It means, you
refuse to surrender! You are and will remain an
enemy of the people." [44]

Dyakov begins *The Story of What I Lived Through* with a similar scene of a dialog between an officer and the protagonist:

"Your case was examined by the Special Tribunal of
the Ministry of the State Security. . . . Ten years
of special camp."
"Ten years?! Why?!"
"You should know better than I. Sign here."
"But this is a mistake! Who can I complain to?"
The man in the leather jacket smiled and pulled on
his cigarette:
"To the prosecutor at the Ministry of State
Security." [45]

Condemned without crime, victimized and brutalized in
Soviet camps, the protagonists of these literary works find
themselves among thousands of other prisoners; they realize
they are part of a historic experience on a massive scale.
Strangely enough, however, none of them allows himself to
admit his status as essentially equal or analogical to that of
other political victims. The human instinct to seek solidarity
in suffering is oddly limited in these accounts, and this is all
the more striking when compared to the very common motifs of victims' solidarity in the literature of the Nazi camps.
There, solidarity is emphasized as a source of victims' resistance to totalitarian degradation aimed at creating conditions

for mutual hatred among the prisoners. In numerous literary works on the Nazi camps, the individual victim's experience of being innocently oppressed projects an inclusive generalization to other victims. The individual experience of totalitarian victimization becomes a universal, supra-individual problem.

By contrast, in official Soviet literature on the Bolshevik camp experience no efforts are made by the protagonists to reach out to other prisoners or to acknowledge their common fate. The only exception to this rule is other prisoner-Communists. The status of innocent victims is reserved for the protagonists themselves along with other prisoner-Communists. Communists are the only prisoners granted the authors' full attention. Their voices and points of view, which dominate the universe presented here, are separated from those of the rest of the victims, whose presence is reflected indirectly and who always remain in the background. This structural separation of the Communist prisoners from the others is not the only means of systematically dividing these two categories of people. The crucial division is frequently defined in direct generalizations. Shelest, for instance, describes the camp population: "There were Ukrainian nationalists from Bandera units, White Guards from Manchuria, Gestapo men, Vlasov's soldiers, former policemen who collaborated with the Nazis. There were also criminals, and thirty of our men—Communists. The year was 1950 and they brought to the camp many Bandera people, policemen, and all kinds of half-fascist sewage." [46]

The borderline between innocent victims (Communists) and those who seem to be in the camp for good reason (everyone else) is as clear-cut and categorical as the difference between "our men—Communists" and "half-fascist sewage." This line is never to be crossed: it constitutes the principal opposition that divides the universe of the camp into the spheres of positive versus negative, innocent versus guilty-by-definition. This opposition overshadows and replaces the opposition characteristic of the literature on the Nazi camps—that of victim versus oppressor. Because this line between Communist and non-Communist worlds is fixed once and forever, neither reeducation of the enemies nor moral defeat of Communist heroes is possible. Just as immorality is a fixed characteristic of criminals, heroic faith in Communist values is a stable, constitutive feature of a Communist prisoner. Nothing seems to undermine this faith, least of all his experience of victimization in the camp. For instance, one of Dyakov's protagonists believes that he is the victim of an unfortunate mistake. His sojourn in the camp is a time of awaiting the annulment of the sentence and the triumph of justice that—the prisoner believes—is imminent. He says: "Take me, for instance. I believe that the truth will be revealed. But it's not easy here. There are not only victims of mistakes in this camp. There are also our real enemies. Watch out!" [47]

"Our enemies" means, here, the enemies of the Bolshevik regime and its camps. In these terms, "us" in the camp means the prisoner-Communists and the camp guards taken together. The rest of the prisoners are "them." The message is: Watch out for "them." Once again, Eugenia Ginzburg recalls a similar attitude on the part of a prisoner. One of the personages presented in *Into the Whirlwind*, Julia Annenkova, a publisher of a Communist journal, imprisoned in 1937, advised Ginzburg not to associate with non-Communist prisoners: "Who knows which of them is a real enemy and which are victims of a mistake, like you and me? Do go on being careful, to make sure you don't commit a real crime against the party after all. The best thing is to say nothing." [48]

Right and Wrong, or the Ethics of the Grand Guignol

This totally politicized approach to the question of "who is who in the camp" results in a unique case of moral confusion. It is this politicization of the moral issue of guilt and innocence that renders this literature incapable of addressing the ethical challenge of twentieth-century totalitarianism in more universal terms. As a result, instead of asking why did "people prepare this fate for other people,"[49] this literature goes no further than asking, "Why us, good Communists?" An obvious source of this philosophical and artistic handicap lies in this literature's faith in Leninist ethics, which turned political partisanship into a fundamental category replacing other, non-utilitarian moral notions. By directly admitting that "our morality is entirely subordinate to the interests of the class struggle of the proletariat,"[50] Lenin divided people into two categories—people instrumental to the cause and people who were seen as obstacles to it. This division legitimized the victimization and elimination of all those defined as standing in the way of the revolution. It is not personal intentions nor even deeds that determine one's status as a partisan or an enemy of the revolution. What determines it is one's belonging to the right category, the right group. Bolsheviks placed themselves at the positive pole of this key opposition between right and wrong (good and evil) and defined others in a politically flexible way, according to their usefulness at a given moment. Thus, notions of guilt and innocence have little importance and are of a fluid nature within Leninist ethics. According to these ethics, one's status as an enemy (the basis for being punished or eliminated) does not necessarily depend on the subjective intentions of an individual but, rather, is treated as an objective fact, fully comprehensible only to the party leadership. It is so because only the party leadership, being the source of all good (the avant-garde of the revolution), represents a point of view that encompasses the future consequences of each current fact.

Arthur Koestler gives a telling dramatization of these Leninist ethics in *Darkness at Noon,* a novel written in 1941 that presents the ideological dilemmas of a Bolshevik sentenced to death in one of Stalin's public trials. Koestler's protagonist, Rubashov, reasons while in his prison cell:

> We were the first to replace the nineteenth century's liberal ethics of "fair play" by the revolutionary ethics of the twentieth century. In that also we were right: a revolution conducted according to the rules of cricket is an absurdity. Politics can be relatively fair in the breathing spaces of history; at its critical turning points there is no other rule possible than the old one, that the end justifies the means. . . . That is why we will *in the end* be absolved by history. . . . Yet for the moment we are thinking and acting on credit. As we have thrown overboard all conventions and rules of cricket-morality, our sole guiding principle is that of consequent logic. We are under the terrible compulsion to follow our thought down to its final consequence and to act in accordance to it. We are sailing without ballast; therefore each touch on the helm is a matter of life and death. . . . For us the question of subjective good faith is of no interest. He who is in the wrong must pay; he who is in the right will be absolved. That is the law of historical credit; it was our law.[51]

The Leninist ethics of "historical credit" are the same ethics that Tarasov-Rodyonov put in an allegorical monolog of his protagonist, the Chekist Zudin. Let us recall it here: "What is guilt? Is a bourg[e]ois guilty of being a bourg[e]ois? Is a crocodile guilty of being a crocodile?"[52]

This is the ethical world of the protagonists of Shelest, Pilyar, Dyakov, and Aldan-Semenov. To understand the moral paradox of this literature requires an acknowledgment of the deterministic and fatalistic character of these Leninist ethics, which constitute the key to this world. The category of belonging to the right or the wrong ("class consciousness," political partisanship, and so on) is a form of moral predestination that essentially divorces the domain of one's responsibilities from the realm of one's choices. Guilt and innocence do not apply in this universe. We are dealing here with condemnation and redemption determined by historical forces out of the reach of most people. Within the totalitarian universe, Andrzej Werner wrote, "a person who asks 'what am I guilty of' will never find an answer. Here, the category of guilt is irrelevant; this universe denies the admissibility of such questions."[53]

Within the Bolshevik totalitarian universe, people are, in fact, divided into two categories: those who are "in the right," and thus are entitled to commit crimes against others, and the others—that is, those who are "in the wrong" and thus may be subjected to crimes committed by those "in the right." The particular ideological basis upon which the division between "right" and "wrong" is formulated is called "the class interest of the proletariat." Regardless of ideological formulas, in practical terms, the Communist's desire to "be in the right" means to be among those who persecute and punish, not among those who are punished and persecuted.

This moral (or rather, immoral) determinism underlies the universe presented in the official Soviet camp literature in question. The central drama portrayed in this literature is the drama of the sudden, unexpected change of fortune—the personal fall from glory to destruction. None among the authors presented here is remotely concerned with the camp experiences of those who were never included among the "right." Having removed them, structurally and ethically, to the margins as "half-fascist sewage," all authors focus on characters who formerly belonged to the category of the "right" only to find themselves (without a valid explanation) among the condemned. It is this fact of being once among the "right" that distinguishes them from everyone else in the camp. Their point of view differs significantly from that of other victims: what concerns them is not the very existence of the system of total control and degradation, but their own sudden, unpredictable reversal of fortune. This reversal, in addition to physical punishment, involves an unexpected change of identity from judge to judged. As the rules by which people are judged under totalitarianism are grotesquely arbitrary, the central question of this literature, "Why us?," leads only to more and more confusion. In her book of camp reminiscences, Eugenia Ginzburg realized the grotesque character of the Soviet totalitarian universe. The world created upon the basis of Lenin's ethical categories reveals itself to her as a nightmarish theater of horrors, where personal fates and identities possess little stability and change according to the uncontrollable whims of some powerful stage manager who puts this world in motion. "Some actors in the Grand Guignol had been cast as victims, others as persecutors." [54]

As the world of the grotesque, through its negation of any rules of predictability, evokes horror and laughter at the same time, so does the totalitarian world of completely arbitrary victimization. Whereas Eugenia Ginzburg compares Stalin's Russia to the theater of horror, Andrei Sinyavsky finds the rules of comedy applicable to this world. "Stalin was apparently a great humorist," Sinyavsky wrote. "Stalin, with his irrational, artistic nature, reveled in his humor—black humor mostly, but humor nevertheless. It was one more tool he used to control people's lives and fates, to bring them good and evil. As if he were above good and evil. Stalin played deliberately on this ambivalence: turning evil into good and good into evil. . . . The endless possibilities for substituting evil for good and vice versa were the stuff of Stalin's unfathomable mystery, of his black secret." [55]

A Matter of Faith

Among the authors of Soviet camp literature of the late thaw, written from the point of view of Communist victims, there is no single author capable of the distance achieved by Ginzburg and Sinyavsky. From the moment of their arrest, all the way through their camp experience, the protagonists of this literature never stop expressing their surprise and demanding explanations from the regime. Their horizon never broadens but remains limited by their former identities. Thus, for instance, Shelest's main protagonist is a *kombryg* of OGPU—that is, somebody who in the "normal" course of events should send others to camps. The world is obviously off of its normal track for him, since instead of sending others, he himself ends up as a prisoner: from a hunter he suddenly becomes prey. His disappointment is as obvious as it is unrevealing. These "revelations" by a protagonist of Dyakov's *The Story of What I Lived Through* are very characteristic of the philosophical range of this literature: "Do you remember how restlessly we tried to understand what was the root of this evil, and who was to be judged by whom? Now we understand. Stalin, intoxicated by his power, treated his own people as enemies, and punished them!" [56]

These characters, though deeply wounded by unjust sentences, remain "Stalin's own people," even in the camp. It is not Stalin's terror against the Soviet population that concerns Dyakov's hero and his likes in other literary works, but Stalin's decision to "punish his own people" (instead of keeping them in their positions of power). The existence of mass terror, never questioned, assumes the status of something quite natural: it seems to be a normal element of reality that needs no special explanation and justification. In this respect, Soviet camp literature of the late thaw seems more dependent on the totalitarian mind-set than were the creators of literary strategies of presenting Bolshevik victimization in the 1920s and 1930s. Tarasov-Rodyonov and Gorky asked general ethical questions and projected ideological answers—provocative, offensive, or manipulative. Shelest, Dyakov, Pilyar, and Aldan-Semenov no longer even ask questions beyond "Why us?" The fate of "others" is of no significance to them: "their" guilt is as clear as "our" innocence. Dyakov's protagonist confesses: "The most horrible thing is not the camp itself. Camps should be harsh for offenders. What is horrible here is something else: it is the punishment without crime. There are hundreds of people like us in these camps, and . . . it is frightening to think about it . . . maybe there are thousands and thousands! Who put us in here? Who announced that we are 'enemies'? Was this done by fascists or other enemies of the Soviet system? Oh, no! These barbaric acts are being committed by people who carry the Party cards just as we used to. . . . Together, we built the new life and defended it! This can drive a man out of his mind!" [57]

Blind and limited as they may appear from a distance, these attitudes can perhaps be treated as examples of deep moral confusion experienced by people whose bodies and minds are controlled by the totalitarian regime. What makes these works second-rate literature is the fact that the authors themselves seem to share the confusion and limitations of their characters' minds. Nevertheless, in order to examine the nature of the experience presented by this second-rate writing, one must respond to it by assuming for a moment the point of view it represents. What constitutes the core of the drama presented in this literature is the fact that, in the Leninist ethical world, there is no one to blame for historic injuries. Dialectically speaking, a victim is simply a person who appeared in the wrong place at the wrong time in history. A consequential Leninist has no grounds to protest his own destruction in the process of the revolution. Again, few authors presented this crucial point of the Communist world view as clearly as Arthur Koestler. His protagonist, Rubashov, writes in his prison diary:

> The ultimate truth is penultimately always a falsehood. He who will be proved right in the end appears to be wrong and harmful before it. But *who* will be proved right? It will only be known later. Meanwhile he is bound to act on credit and to sell his soul to the devil, in the hope of history's absolution. . . . We know that virtue does not matter to history, and that crimes remain unpunished, but that every error has its consequences and venges itself unto the seventh generation. Therefore we concentrated all our efforts on preventing error and destroying the very seeds of it. Never in history has so much power over the future of humanity been concentrated in so few hands as in our case. Each wrong idea we follow is a crime committed against future generations. Therefore we have to punish wrong ideas as others punish crimes—with death. . . . I was one of those. I have thought and acted as I had to; I destroyed people whom I was fond of, and gave power to others I did not like. History put me where I stood; I have exhausted the credit which she accorded me; if I was right I have nothing to repent of; if wrong, I will pay. But how can the present decide what will be judged truth in the future? We are doing the work of prophets without their gift. We replaced vision by logi-

cal deduction; but although we all started from the same point of departure, we came to divergent results. Proof disproved proof, and finally we had to recur to faith—to axiomatic faith in the rightness of one's own reasoning. That is the crucial point. We have thrown all ballast overboard; only one anchor holds us: faith in one's self. Geometry is the purest realization of human reason; but Euclid's axioms cannot be proved. He who does not believe in them sees the whole building crash.[58]

Koestler's protagonist, Rubashov, follows the internal logic of his Bolshevik world view to its ultimate conclusion. And this ultimate point is the choice between pure faith and skepticism. The true believer is one who does not question the Communist dogma of the infallibility of the party personified by its leaders. The true believer accepts his own destruction in the process of the revolution, for he believes that history will prove him right in the future (and the future is all that matters). At the other end of the spectrum are doubt and skepticism. To choose skepticism at the moment of ultimate crisis—in the camp—means to witness the disintegration of one's own monolithic, monological world of Communist dogmas into the chaotic realm of vague choices and eternal self-doubts—the dialogical world of uncertainty. While it is difficult for a Communist true believer to accept his own destruction, caused by an apparent mistake in the process of the revolution, it seems to be more difficult for him to renounce his belief in the revolution in the face of imminent destruction. To save the belief in spite of the facts—this seems to be the inner logic of the attitude presented here. Eugenia Ginzburg recalls a woman prisoner who wrote a short poem in her prison cell in Yaroslavl. The poem reads:

Stalin, my golden sun,
If death should be my fate,
I will die, a petal on the road
Of our great country.[59]

This poem, recited in the confines of Stalin's prison, is a desperate attempt to translate the realization of personal destruction into language that, for this person, defined the goal of her life. The need for positive faith is stronger here than any sense of paradox.

This misplaced need for positive faith is shown in Vassily Grossman's novel *Forever Flowing,* in a confrontation between a Communist true believer and a non-Communist, which takes place in a Vorkuta camp:

> People in camp were like dry grains of sand. Each for himself, to himself. Some, for example, believed there had been a mistake only in their own case, that as a rule "they did not arrest a person for no reason at all." Others had things figured out this way: "When we were free, we used to assume that they did not arrest anyone without a reason, and now we know that they do!" But they drew no broader conclusions from this and sighed submissively. An emaciated, twitchy former official of the Youth Comintern, a hair-splitter and dialectitian, explained to Ivan Grigorevich that he had committed no crimes against the Party, but that the security organs were right in arresting him as a spy and a double-dealer. For even though he had committed no crimes he nonetheless belonged to a stratum hostile to the Party, a stratum which had given rise to double-dealers, Trotskyites, opportunists, whiners, complainers, and skeptics. On one occasion in camp an intelligent inmate who used to be a Party official on the province

level got into a conversation with Ivan Grigorevich: "When they chop the forest, the chips fly, but the Party truth remains the truth and it is superior to my misfortune. And," he went on, pointing to himself, "I myself was one of those chips that flew when the forest was cut down." And he was nonplussed when Ivan Grigorevich said to him: "That's where the whole misfortune lies—in the fact that they're cutting down the forest. Why cut it down?"[60]

The first prisoner in Grossman's novel is a Communist true believer who accepts his fate with good faith and without blame. The latter is a representative of the "others," whose point of view is never presented in the works by Shelest, Pilyar, Dyakov, and Aldan-Semenov: he questions the foundation of Bolshevik ethics—the Bolshevik revolution itself. This is the greatest sacrilege imaginable for the true believer. To renounce the revolution means to renounce the legitimacy of the Soviet regime as such. This was to be the last thing permitted in Soviet public discourse, shortly before the collapse of the Soviet state itself.

A Matter of Hope

Shelest, Dyakov, Pilyar, and Aldan-Semenov never allow such ideological confrontations in their camp prose. Nor do they allow their protagonists to doubt. The approach presented in these works results from a paradoxical compromise between the simple human perception of the camps as wrongdoing and the ethical system that refutes this perception. However, even as the ideological sources of this peculiar attitude seem undeniable, there appears to be another, psychological factor at play.

As ideologically preoccupied as it tries to be, this literature presents a peculiar, yet not atypical, mode of human behavior in the face of extreme oppression. Within this mode, the ideological generalizations, wordy and ever-present as they are, play only a subservient role to other, much more elementary motivations. And the deeper motivation underlying such a peculiar attitude of victim towards oppressor seems to be the victim's basic hope for survival.

In the camp experience presented in this literature, the Communist "true belief" is continuously associated with survival. This fact has its pragmatic explanation: out of all possible approaches to the camp experience available to the victim, sticking to the Bolshevik ideology was, clearly, the only path potentially leading to the next reversal of fortune—now in the "right" direction—back to the "right side" of the dualistic world of "right" and "wrong." For in the Bolshevik Grand Guignol one never knows when the next change of costume is going to take place. In Shelest's *Kolyma Notes,* an old, experienced camp guard advises a young one:

> You know, all kinds of things happen. Sometimes you are a prisoner and, suddenly, the next day, you are a minister or even better than that. The commander of the nineteenth column told me: In September 1941, a general was put in a camp. And the commander of that camp was a terribly smart fellow, and he sent this general to hard labor. The general went quickly down the drain and became so skinny that he was almost transparent. But at that time Stalin suddenly recalled the general. "Where is such and such?" "He is in a camp," they told him. Well, they released the general, and gave him a division or an army. And the camp commander got transferred to the front as well. And there, one day, he ran into the general. Do you understand what can happen?[61]

Unlike in the Nazi system, with its categorical "racial" condemnation, in the Bolshevik Grand Guignol, as in the world of Kafka's *The Trial,* the victim—especially a Communist believer—is never certain as to the real state of his affairs. One simply does not know when to stop hoping for a reversal of one's fortune. The only thing that is certain is that salvation—if it comes—will come from the same source as the victimization. To detach oneself from the world of Communist values by making them responsible for one's unjust suffering means to detach oneself from the sole remaining source of hope. For what will happen when "Stalin recalls" a person? The only chance of helping along the reversal of fortune is to win back the lost trust of the Bolshevik masters and judges. And one who hopes for mercy does not try to prove his master wrong.

This mirage of hope—presented as an inextricable element of the camp experience as seen from the point of view of the Soviet late-thaw camp literature—enables a victim-Communist to avoid the dramatic choice between saving his faith by justifying his own destruction and admitting the terrible truth and seeing the "building of his beliefs crash." The formula for avoiding this choice was simple and psychologically effective: it was encapsulated in one persistent notion—a "mistake." "But this is a mistake!" [62] Dyakov's protagonist reacts to his conviction. In fact, all the protagonists of the late-thaw camp literature share this attitude. The formula of "mistake," or "exception," proves to be a highly functional mental technique for those who feel victimized but at the same time avoid identifying the source of their victimization in hopes of a reversal of fortune. Dyakov's protagonist wonders, two months after his imprisonment: "Tomorrow is a state holiday. And what if they release me tomorrow? It has been two months since my sentence. A lot of things must have changed meanwhile. The prosecutor has probably figured it out and noticed that the investigation was illegal, and that I am not guilty."[63]

The "mistake" is described by independent authors of camp literature as a mental technique characteristic of Communist "true believers" or, at least, of prisoners who identify themselves with the Soviet regime. "But the surprising thing was," Vassily Grossman wrote in *Forever Flowing*, "that the people who had been imprisoned and sentenced for due cause, for active and genuine opposition to the Soviet state, thought that all the political *zeks* were innocent, that all of them, without exception, should be freed. But those who had been framed and imprisoned on the basis of cooked-up, fake charges—and there were millions of them—were disposed to propose an amnesty only for themselves, and made every effort to confirm the authentic guilt of all the other falsely accused 'spies,' 'kulaks,' and 'wreckers'; they were quite willing to excuse the cruelty of the state."[64] The fundamental difference between these two perceptions reflects the opposition between people who hope for a change in the minds of their oppressors and those who renounce such hope.

Hope has been identified again and again, in numerous testimonies of twentieth-century camp experiences, as a force for survival and a source of dignity—even misplaced hope, as shown by Eugenia Ginzburg in a poem composed in prison after the news of the downfall of Yezhov and the rise of Beria reached her:

Tell us, O Beria,
Will life be merrier,
Lighter and airier,
Or even scarier?
Answer us, Beria.[65]

However, there is the other side of hope in the images of the totalitarian camp presented in literary testimonies. Having spent a large portion of his life in Soviet camps, Varlam Shalamov wrote in "The Life of Engineer Kipreev": "Hope always shackles the convict. Hope is slavery. A man who hopes for something alters his conduct and is more frequently dishonest than a man who has ceased to hope."[66] Shalamov's laconic statement, in connection with his literary image of the camp experience, constitutes a clarification of Grossman's puzzlement over the perception that the condition of innocence tended to be approached in Soviet camps in an exclusive way.

Tadeusz Borowski was even more blunt in his story "Auschwitz Our Home:"

> Despite the madness of war, we lived for a world that would be different. For a better world to come when all this is over. And perhaps even our being [in the camp] is a step towards that world. Do you really think that, without the hope that such a world is possible, that the rights of man will be restored again, we could stand the concentration camp even for one day? It is that very hope that makes people go without a murmur to the gas chambers, keeps them from risking a revolt, paralyses them into numb inactivity. It is hope that breaks down family ties, makes mothers renounce their children, or wives sell their bodies for bread, or husbands kill. It is hope that compels man to hold on to one more day of life, because that may be the day of liberation. Ah, and not even the hope for a different, better world, but simply for life, a life of peace and rest. Never before in the history of mankind has hope been stronger, but never also has it done so much harm as it has in this war, in this concentration camp.[67]

For both Shalamov and Borowski, the price of human dignity in the camp involves the abandonment of hope and, thus, the ultimate assertion of one's freedom, for which one is ready to pay with one's life. But even a discovery of a possibility of saving human dignity in the camp, as grim as the discovery of Shalamov and Borowski, is immediately followed by another doubt. Shalamov writes:

I believed a person could consider himself a human being as long as he felt totally prepared to kill himself, to interfere in his own biography. It was this awareness that gave me the will to live. I checked myself—frequently—and felt I had the strength to die, and thus remained alive. Much later I realized that I had simply built myself a refuge, avoided the problem, for when at the critical moment the decision between life and death became an exercise of the will, I would not be the same man as before. I would inevitably weaken, become a traitor, betray myself.[68]

What Shalamov—a prisoner of Kolyma—discovers is the same ultimate dynamics of survival that Elie Wiesel discovered in Auschwitz: it may be possible to erase the hope of survival at any cost from one's mind, but at the time of the ultimate test it is the physical body, not the mind, that may start determining human behavior. The sphere of ethical choices may become disconnected from the hungry, dying body driven by its instinctive hopes of self-preservation. Under these conditions, it becomes uncertain whether a human being can still be defined as an ethical entity.

Needless to say, for official Soviet camp literature this tragic, provocative dimension of the camp experience is far out of reach. The issue of the moral cost of such a basic human need as hope does not appear here. In these literary testimonies mothers do not give away their children in hope of survival. The price of hope is "merely" loyalty to the system and staying away from the truly condemned—those who hope no more.

Thus, as presented by Soviet late-thaw literature, the camp experience, while appearing as a test of values, is in reality a test of the victim's unconditional loyalty to the totalitarian system in hope of a reversal of fortune. In order to win back the favors of the masters, Communist victims are shown to be capable of great sacrifices. In Shelest's *Kolyma Notes,* a group of Bolshevik prisoners, while working in a gold mine, find a gold nugget that could be sold illegally without risk, thus sparing them from labor and providing food for long weeks. The official regulations of the camp, however, require the prisoners to turn the gold in to the management. The prisoners are caught between the temptation of food and loyalty to their masters. Their hesitations do not take long. Admiral Dushenov (who would die shortly afterwards) resolves the dilemma:

> Maybe my opinion is different than yours, but I think that we should turn the nugget in. Yes, we have to turn it in! And here's why: I am a Communist and you consider yourselves Communists too. Lenin used to say: Marxists should take into account the concrete situation and real life experience. Do you understand what it means? There is a war going on out there. Out of someone's ill will we have been falsely accused and put in this camp to dig gold. But still, there is a war out there! We have to help. Whatever happens to us, we are Communists! This is the meaning of our lives![69]

Dushenov's speech is a ritual rejection of temptation. For if a few weeks of a full stomach could not be overestimated in a Kolyma camp, the prospect of proving one's ultimate loyalty to the system by (hopefully, temporary) self-sacrifice associates itself with the prisoner's most cherished dream—

winning back the trust and favor of his oppressors. The response to Dushenov's advice to turn in the gold, by one of Dushenov's fellow prisoners (and fellow Communists), Golubev, is very characteristic: " 'Let's hope, this is happening in a lucky hour . . .' Golubev said. 'Maybe the time will come when they will thank us.' "[70]

The prisoners turn in the gold nugget to the authorities. Their frustration is barely describable when General Nikishov, the supervisor of the Kolyma camps, comes to accept their sacrifice:

> "Only this? Are you sure you haven't hidden anything? Did you search them?"
> "Yes, we searched them," the commander lied. "They are all fifty-eighters."
> "Don't trust them," said Nikishov, and pointed his finger at Dushenov. "What was your occupation?"
> "The commander of a Red Fleet."
> Nikishov gave him a guarded look. Dushenov stood in front of him in ragged padded pants with tufts of reddish padding sticking out of holes. His unshaven face was covered with stiff gray hair and wrinkles. His eyes were like the eyes of Jesus Christ on ancient icons. I saw his hands trembling.
> "One should shave more often, comrade Fleet commander. It's time to get cultured," Nikishov said, and pointed his finger at me. "And who are you?"
> "Brigadier of OGPU."
> Nikishov turned to Garanin, "Look, they haven't forgotten yet."[71]

The only reward Dushenov and his comrade-prisoners win is an additional bowl of soup. The sacrifice is rejected. Nevertheless, they take the disappointment without protest.

They will go on hoping. What could be the alternative to hope anyway? Either voluntary acceptance of one's destruction or making "the whole building of their beliefs crash" and the only chance of a reversal of fortune vanish.

However, as the finality of the camp victimization becomes more and more apparent in a never-ending series of frustrated expectations (Dushenov, as mentioned, dies of overexhaustion shortly after making his unaccepted sacrifice), the human need to blame someone becomes more and more urgent. To blame the system and its fundamental dogmas, which provide ideological grounds for massive victimization, would mean destroying the "building of one's beliefs." How to blame someone, yet not to see "the building crash," if the only logical object to blame is also the sole source of whatever is left of hope? This psychological paradox torments the heroes of Dyakov, Shelest, Pilyar, and Aldan-Semenov.

Dyakov's narrator-protagonist recollects a half-dreamlike vision: "The inner prison at Lubyanka: a wooden shield over the cell's window. One can see only a narrow strip of sky. And suddenly, on the sixth of November, in the morning, the red flag appeared right in this strip of sky. The red flag on top of the Ministry of State Security. . . . On that day, everybody in the cell was silent, speechless."[72]

The vision of the MGB (the Soviet Ministry of State Security) building with the red flag on top assumes a symbolic dimension—it stirs up feelings of confusing ambivalence that dominate the psyche of a Bolshevik believer punished by his own regime for nonexistent crimes. If Gorky, in his "Solovki," presented the ideal relationship between the Soviet individual and the regime as that of child and parent, thus assuming the regime's right to shape the life of the individual and to punish the individual when needed, Dyakov presents this relationship as ambivalent but natural. The Soviet phenomenon of a victim's loyalty towards his oppressor is summarized in the desperate words of one of Shelest's characters addressed to Stalin: "Father, father, what have you done to us? We are your children."[73]

This attitude arguably represents the greatest triumph of totalitarian attempts to reprogram people's basic ethical categories. Indeed, we are dealing here with individuals who fully and unconditionally subject their fates and their self-perceptions to the will of their master. The attitude presented here is one of "the religious worship of an omnipotent power that enjoys the right to resort to any means of violence, covert or overt."[74] The will of this powerful deity is mysterious and unpredictable to its subjects. In fact, the Communist political leadership—appointed by Lenin as the sole judge of right and wrong—is recognized here as the master of good and evil, itself beyond good and evil.

The Stolen Succession, or the Eschatology of the Grand Guignol

Are we dealing here, in this second-rate literature, with a peculiarly misplaced religious search for an object of worship beyond the categories of common reason and morality? In *Dostoevsky and Nietzsche: A Philosophy of Tragedy,* Lev Shestov argued that abandoning the categories of morality and reason is the only way to get closer to God. And one can get there only in the moments of terrible crisis, in the ultimate tragedy that makes man a living corpse.[75] Does the Communist regime appear in this literature in a position somewhat reminiscent of Shestov's supra-ethical God?

Though such a possibility appears in these works, it must be admitted that the authors, as if paralyzed by it, try to find a compromise between the immorality of the system and traditional moral values that they want to emphasize. Having faced the totalitarian reality of the unlimited power of a regime beyond good and evil, the writers immediately rush back toward the familiar distinctions between good and evil. While, in fact, recognizing one and the same source of both good and evil, victimization and hope, these authors search for a way to satisfy the psychological need to separate the object of loyal admiration from the object of bitter blame. Owing to this psychological requirement, a strange ontological operation takes place within the world presented in this literature: the figure of authority becomes subject to a peculiar dichotomy. This dichotomy divides the figure of Communist authority into two aspects: the actual, material, historically existing Communist regime (represented by the actual functionaries headed by Stalin) and the "pure essence" of the Communist regime—projected by the Bolshevik dogmas and represented by such immaterial, nominal (perhaps metaphysical?) entities as "the party," the "true legacy of Lenin," the "spirit of Lenin," and so on.

The two aspects of the Communist regime, its material, phenomenal aspect and its ideal, "metaphysical" aspect, are presented in mutual opposition. Within the world presented here, the phenomenal reality of the Communist regime seems to be in a state of rebellion against its own metaphysical foundations. It is this rebellion of reality against its ideological "essence" that is to blame for the temporary confusion in which even "good Communists" end up in Soviet concentration camps.

This ontological opposition becomes more accessible and concrete when projected upon the syntagmatic axis of the myth and described in terms of a narrative. The names of the two principal heroes of this myth are familiar to all: Lenin and Stalin. These two personages embody the two contradictory aspects of the Communist regime: its noble "essence" and its contaminated historical incarnation. The process of separating these aspects of Communist power is realized in a peculiar myth of stolen succession. The legitimacy of Stalin's rule is being questioned. Dyakov's narrator wonders:

> Is it possible that Stalin doesn't know what is going on? In 1937 they slandered and killed so many military commanders, Party secretaries, members of the Central Committee. They still keep behind barbed wires Todorsky and other totally innocent Communists, old Bolsheviks for whom the Party of Lenin constitutes the essence of their whole lives! And Stalin believes that these are his enemies? But if Stalin could be fooled, it means he is not the great and wise Stalin whom we loved and trusted, and called the "Lenin of today." And what if all of this comes from him? It was impossible to face these thoughts. My head was all burning, and there was a lump in my throat. I went up to the window. There were no bars. Snowy stars were shining through the window panes. In the dark of the speechless night I saw the vast expanse of the outside world: it was so close and yet so distant. What is happening to this world?[76]

From the point of view of Dyakov's protagonist-narrator, a Communist true believer, the problem of the legitimacy of Stalin's succession is not a mere political issue but a question of cosmic significance. The integrity of his entire world view is at stake, along with the explanation for his fate. What he examines here are the roots of evil in the Communist universe. Interestingly enough, Stalin's chief deficiency, which makes Dyakov's narrator question Stalin's status as the "Lenin of today," is not Stalin's unrestrained brutality and moral retardation, but his apparent lack of omniscience and omnipotence. Because of this lack Stalin made the mistake of persecuting "his own people"—the central issue of this literature.

The motif of Lenin's testament, in which he questions Stalin's abilities as the new Soviet dictator, assumes a principal position in this literature. Arthur Koestler, who wrote from a distance, presented this motif as an element of the Bolsheviks' quasi-religious mentality: "He was revered as God-the-Father," Koestler's narrator muses about Lenin, "and No. 1 [Stalin, D.T.] as the Son; but it was whispered everywhere that he had forged the old man's will in order to come into the heritage." [77]

Georgy Shelest, who should not be assumed to have read Koestler, introduces the motif of the stolen legacy of Lenin in the concluding part of his *Kolyma Notes.* An innocent child-victim, a young Communist, Vladlen (the name is a conflation of "Vladimir Lenin"), explains the causes of his and his friends' imprisonment in a Kolyma camp:

> It all started with me. At my home, there was a large library. It was my father's. He had been killed at the front. There was a lot of interesting stuff, and I always liked to browse. Once, before a test in school, I wanted to find some passage from Lenin, and I found in our library an old edition. And suddenly, I found an envelope in the last volume, and in this envelope were three sheets of paper typed and entitled, "Lenin's Will." And I started reading it. Yuri came, then Nikita, and I gave it to them to read. We talked about Lenin and Stalin, and Nikita said, "Give this to me, and I will show it to an old man I know." I gave it to him. On the next day Nikita came and said, "I went to the old man." This old man had been in the Party since 1916, he was retired, and he knew everything about the Party. He read this, and said: "Yes there was such a thing. It was announced at the Thirteenth Party Congress." And he advised us that we had better be careful with these papers because

otherwise we could get into trouble. But we couldn't help it, and we showed it to other boys and girls. . . . And in a week, the Ministry of State Security people came at night and arrested us.[78]

This story, woven around the motif of stolen succession, appears in the concluding part of Shelest's cycle and thus assumes a higher significance: it bears the appearance of some general explanation of the drama presented in his cycle of camp prose. Dyakov's question, "What is happening to this world?," finds an answer: the Communist world (good in its essence) seems to be in a state of confusion, in which the "right" are being punished along with the "wrong." The Communist world may not return to its right shape until the true power of its creator, Lenin (treated here as a metaphysical entity), is wrestled away from the pretender Stalin. Meanwhile, a handful of "true believers," the old Bolsheviks, "Lenin's old guard," are being subjected to the ultimate trial of their faith under the rule of the pretender. The apocalyptic pattern of associations emerges through this view. How else to explain overt religious motifs repeated throughout this literature, such as those dominating the eulogy over the grave of Admiral Dushenov in Shelest's *Kolyma Notes:* "He died at his post, holding the banner of Lenin firm in his hand. He considered his imprisonment a test, and he used to say: 'Time is working to our advantage. Nothing will ever defeat Leninism.' He lived with faith and with faith he died."[79]

Admiral Dushenov is presented as a martyr who withstood the trials of historical evil embodied in Stalin. What made him protect his dignity in the camp to the very end was his faith in the metaphysical Lenin and the future kingdom of Lenin on Earth. This sacred aura surrounded Dushenov before his death. When, after his heroic and sacrificial act of turning over the gold nugget to the authorities, he encounters the painful scorn and indifference of General Nikishov, his face is compared to the face of Christ on the icons: ("His eyes were like the eyes of Jesus Christ on ancient icons"). Here, according to the hagiographic tradition, a martyr is compared and juxtaposed with the model and the ideal of Christian martyrdom—Christ himself.

This technique of quasi-religious associations is extended from personages to objects. Frequently, the mere presence of certain objects associated with Lenin, especially Lenin's writings (his living word), suffices to inspire prisoners to uphold their values and faith in the face of the ultimate trials of the camps. The Communist Zaborsky, a prisoner of Kolyma in Shelest's *Kolyma Notes,* when asked by an officer of NKVD, his former comrade, to declare his most important wish about his life in the camp, says: "Give me a job in storage. I am getting old and I can hardly manage hard labor. And please, give me the six-volume edition of Lenin. I will be very grateful."[80]

On the very next page, one of Zaborsky's fellow prisoners talks about his admiration and respect for the old Bolshevik: "Well, Aleksei Ivanych was a great man. He was really important. He used to stand next to Lenin. . . . But things didn't work out too well for him. He couldn't agree with Stalin. Stalin would say one thing and Aleksei Ivanych another. Well, finally he ended up in the camp."[81]

Whereas a character associated with the figure of Lenin is almost automatically defined as positive, associations with Stalin have the opposite consequence. If contact with the word of Lenin inspires noble behavior, contact with the icon of Stalin evokes evil inspiration. For instance, Shantalov, a despotic commander of a camp presented in Aldan-Semenov's *Bas-Relief in the Rock,* wears a wristwatch with Stalin's portrait. A peculiar relationship is formed between Shantalov and his master's icon. "When the portrait gleamed in the darkness, its bluish light evoked strange happiness in Shantalov's heart," the narrator comments.[82] Shantalov draws his inspiration to do evil from this phosphorescent image of his master.

Thus, with the help of mythical narratives and quasi-apocalyptic symbolism, the world of Bolshevik dogmas becomes reconcilable with the historic trauma of real Bolshevism. The peculiar, paradoxical perception of the totalitarian experience at its worst is being filtered through ethics created by the Bolsheviks in order to justify totalitarian oppression. As a result, a peculiar vision is projected in Soviet camp literature of the late thaw. It is the vision of the martyrdom of Communist true believers in Soviet concentration camps. This martyrdom means, paradoxically, the moral victory of the Communist value system over the reality of massive oppression created by this very system.

Yet this presentation of massive historic trauma through the filter of ideology elevated to quasi-religious status produced literary statements of little value. The authors of the works of camp literature published in the Soviet Union along with Solzhenitsyn's *One Day in the Life of Ivan Denisovich,* during a brief period in the early 1960s, looked at the camp experience with their minds closed by ideological dogmas to which they gave truly religious reverence, thus turning the Bolshevik camp experience into a pseudo-apocalyptic trial of Communism. But their "apocalypse" lacks the ethical anxiety of the true Apocalypse. Theirs is an "apocalypse" written *ex post facto* by the saved. All anxiety and challenge are resolved. For these writers, the Last Judgment has already happened, and no more questions remain to be asked. This Last Judgment occurred at the Twentieth Congress of the Communist Party, where the mass terror of the Communist regime was given a verbal condemnation as a "mistake." In the conclusion of Dyakov's *The Story of What I*

Lived Through, one of the heroes recapitulates the horrors of totalitarianism: "Do you remember how restlessly we tried to understand what was at the root of this evil, and who was to be judged by whom. Now we understand. Stalin, intoxicated by his power, treated his own people as enemies, and punished them. But finally the Twentieth Party Congress came, and it transformed the whole nation and our own lives. I feel as if all these innocent victims were finally brought home by Lenin."[83]

The resolution of all the issues presented in this literature is spelled out in the same ideological and mythical language that, from the very beginning, constituted the cognitive and axiological filter impenetrable by all these authors. The world presented here is a self-contained world of ideological dogmas transformed into quasi-religious truths. The experience of Soviet concentration camps—the most radical example of the ethical horror of practical Communism—is deprived of its materiality and turned into a complex of motifs supporting the "essence" of Communism against its "appearance." Indeed, in comparison to these wordy ideological deliberations of Dyakov, Shelest, Pilyar, and Aldan-Semenov, the silence of Solzhenitsyn's semi-literate Ivan Denisovich proved to be the only voice loud enough to echo over the years to come.

5

A SLIVER IN THE THROAT OF POWER

Solzhenitsyn's One Day in the Life of Ivan Denisovich *and the Boundaries of the Soviet Public Discourse*

[Shukhov] didn't know any longer himself whether he wanted freedom or not.

—Solzhenitsyn, *One Day in the Life of Ivan Denisovich* (1962)

The revolutionary significance of Solzhenitsyn's *One Day in the Life of Ivan Denisovich* in the context of Soviet literature arose neither from the novelty of the camp topic presented in Solzhenitsyn's work nor from its alleged political message (not evident within the work). Nor can it be explained by claiming that Solzhenitsyn's account is unique in presenting the Soviet camp experience from the point of view of its victims. Georgy Shelest introduced this point of view to Soviet literature at the same time as Solzhenitsyn, and Boris Dyakov, Yuri Pilyar, and Andrei Aldan-Semenov followed suit shortly after. What differentiates Solzhenitsyn's novella from all these works is certainly its literary quality. As we have seen in the previous chapter, this difference in literary merit between Solzhenitsyn's *One Day in the Life of Ivan Denisovich* and works by other authors of Soviet late-thaw camp literature was related to peculiar ideological limitations imposed by the latter authors on their views of the Soviet camp experience. Solzhenitsyn's first published work is an example of a successful attempt to liberate literary refleetion of the Soviet camp experience from these and other ideological preconditions which reduce literary visions of the experience to mere illustrations of generalized ideological constructs projected by the authors.

What set Solzhenitsyn apart from other writers who addressed the camp topic in works published in the Soviet Union at this time was that he alone succeeded in presenting the Soviet camp experience as an open ethical problem that the reader must tackle without being coached by the author and by authors of the larger Soviet public discourse. After four decades of Soviet totalitarianism, its most emblematic experience—the horror of concentration camps—was presented in Soviet literature by Solzhenitsyn as a moral question in and of itself, not as part of an official answer to some other, abstract and allegedly more important question concerning the speed of achieving socialism, comparisons between Stalin's and Lenin's political agendas, and so on. In Solzhenitsyn's work, for the first time in Soviet literary history, Soviet readers were challenged to face, through a literary medium, the most dismal aspect of their own reality without the ideological guidance that, in all other Soviet works concerned with the camp topic, had always been there to reconcile them with this reality. In *One Day in the Life of Ivan Denisovich* Soviet readers were required to act as ethical judges and to reflect morally on a phenomenon crucial not only in terms of the Soviet social experiment, but, in a more general sense, in terms of the twentieth-century experience of "humanity *in extremis*": namely, the ultimate test of human values confronted by dehumanizing historic forces of overwhelming magnitude.

The element of ethical challenge is inseparable from the very subject matter of camp literature, whether spelled out in explicit moral terms or not. It is the very presence of the innocent victim that, once acknowledged, adds an element of ethical anxiety to any situation depicted where such a presence is noticed. The concentration camp is only a particularly vivid example of such an ethically charged situation. As we have seen in previous chapters, the main focus of Soviet literature concerned with Bolshevik victimization in general and the camp experience in particular was to provide the ethical anxiety inherent in the subject matter with an authoritative resolution, and thus either to obliterate or to neutralize the ethical challenge thereby posed. In order to do so, official Soviet camp literature, despite differences among the specific conventions employed in different periods, had one structural element in common: it always introduced a finalizing, authoritative point of view from which all ethical questions were supposed to be resolved. This finalizing point of view is represented in the texts either by the authors themselves or at least by various authorial *porte-paroles*. From this point of view the very presence of the victim (the element sufficient to create an ethical challenge) was to be explained as part of some larger, more abstract context within which the very definition of victimhood was questioned and reevaluated—hence the conventions created in the 1920s and 1930s.

Even when written from the point of view of the victim, Soviet literature managed to generate an ideologically motivated vision of the camp experience, further obliterating the ethical challenge inherent in the subject matter. The Soviet camp literature of Shelest, Dyakov, Pilyar, and Aldan-Semenov managed to reserve the right to victimhood and innocence exclusively for those victims who shared the value system of their Soviet oppressors and thus were ready to accept their own victimization as an unfortunate but justifiable part of the larger, essentially positive context of the Soviet road to Communism. Ethical anxiety, whatever it was, was resolved for the authors of these works by the Twentieth Congress of the Communist Party in its condemnation of Stalin's terror against numerous Communists. In these accounts, victims were themselves spokesmen for the official Soviet interpretation of the camp experience: they posed ideological questions and answered them in lengthy monologs, always according to the party line after the Twentieth Congress.

In this context of officially sanctioned Soviet camp literature, Solzhenitsyn's *One Day in the Life of Ivan Denisovich* is the only work that neither provides nor suggests clear authorial resolutions of the ethical problem inherent in the camp experience. The question of whether a human being is strong enough to withstand the ultimate trial of dehumanization in a camp (generally and in its particular Soviet version)—the key question of each work of camp literature, and one that

Soviet writers tried to avoid—is left by Solzhenitsyn in a state of suspension, thus challenging the reader to make his own effort to confront it. This absence of a resolution to the key moral problem of totalitarianism posed in *One Day in the Life of Ivan Denisovich* is a result of a literary strategy deployed by the author and fulfilled with uncompromising discipline. What is special about the literary form of Solzhenitsyn's novella is that it does not contain in its structure a communicative entity, a point of view or a voice, capable of representing the ultimate authorial assessment of the ethical challenge inherent in its subject matter. The narrative point of view in *One Day in the Life of Ivan Denisovich,* though rendered in the third person, is in fact closely linked to the point of view of the novella's protagonist, Ivan Denisovich Shukhov, a simple peasant-soldier serving a sentence for uncommitted crimes. His presence within the scope of the narration is constant, and the narrative point of view tends to be located behind his eyes. Thus the entire testimony of the camp experience is filtered through the single experience of this character. The only commentary in the text on the general issue of the camp experience is generated by Shukhov, a character hardly capable of, and not interested in developing, generalizing, abstract arguments in order to define his fate. Moreover, Solzhenitsyn implements this limitation of point of view by employing the narrative technique of *erlebte Rede:* the verbal account of the camp presented here is not only passed through the cognitive filter of the central character of Shukhov, but its very formulation is also colored and influenced by his linguistic competence. The language of the Russian peasant—that is, the language spoken by the "human material" of Soviet history and not by its designers—provides the main conceptual framework in which Solzhenitsyn, through the mediating presence of Shukhov, grasps the reality of the Soviet totalitarian experience. Consequently, a reader who approaches this text with the customary Soviet expectation of being guided by some general, ideological argument aimed at resolving all potential anxieties inherent in the text is headed for severe frustration. Ivan Denisovich does not speak the language of ideological generalizations, and the author himself remains silent and distant behind his protagonist.

Within this self-limiting scope of expression the reader is left alone to face the ethically challenging situation of the camp, rendered in considerable detail through the specific awareness of a victim unable to either intellectually analyze or precisely communicate his own fate. Under these circumstances, to analyze and interpret this ethical challenge becomes the reader's job. Solzhenitsyn's literary strategy implies the reader's active role in providing philosophical terms capable of defining the nature of the ethical problem presented in the novella and in resolving it. At the same time, none of these resolutions can become the final, ultimate resolution of the ethical challenge so presented. It can only remain a testimony to a dialog between a particular reader and the text, while the text itself remains open to other dialogs. Solzhenitsyn was unique in Soviet literature in establishing such a dialogical, open-ended communicative situation between the text and the reader concerning the camp experience—a topic so subversive for the Soviet authorities. If *One Day in the Life of Ivan Denisovich* is a text that is revolutionary both in its literary and its political contexts, it is so because it managed to create, in the realm of Soviet public discourse, a dialogical framework of literary communication for the topic of the Soviet camp experience.

As a literary work, *One Day in the Life of Ivan Denisovich,* because of its non-explicitness about ethical matters, poses an open challenge to the reader's quest for clear-cut ethical categories in which to frame the question of the sources and limitations of human dignity in the face of the dehumanizing trials of history. As a cultural and political text, Solzhenitsyn's work, by its very appearance in the Soviet Union, created a hole in the tightly woven Soviet public discourse, which by its authoritarian nature could not tolerate open-ended issues and their potential as sources of dissent and controversy. Since each social and human phenomenon had to be presented in the Soviet Union as fully explicable in the ideological terms of an omniscient, morally superior regime, this hole had to be patched by interpretations and explanations formulated in the language of Soviet public discourse. So *One Day in the Life of Ivan Denisovich* became a catalyst for numerous opinions presented in Soviet public discourse, all of them employing the various philosophical and rhetorical means available within the realm of that discourse to try to define and neutralize Solzhenitsyn's ethical challenge according to the ideological credo of the Soviet regime. These attempts failed, proving that the ideological resources necessary for ethical and cognitive rationalization of Bolshevik evil had already been exhausted by the regime, and that this regime remained incapable of taking a searching look at its own ethical legitimacy.

Whether approached as a literary work or as a cultural and political phenomenon, *One Day in the Life of Ivan Denisovich* should be discussed in accordance with its own projected mode of response—that is, in terms of the dialog between itself and its readers. Hence in this chapter the nature of the ethical puzzle presented by the novella will be pursued by examining several interpretive possibilities offered by the text and actually developed by its readers and critics. Special attention will be paid to distinct patterns among interpretations of *One Day in the Life of Ivan Denisovich* within the framework of the Soviet public discourse of the time, as these patterns reveal the degree to which the terms of public discourse on the topic of the camps were dependent on the ideologically based literary conventions of previous and current Soviet camp literature. After analyzing these patterns, we will move beyond the confines of the Soviet context to focus on different, fundamentally contradictory, interpretations of the ethical issues of *One Day in the Life of Ivan Denisovich*. I will show that these interpretive contradictions reflect more than the particular limitations of the Soviet response to Solzhenitsyn's work; they are in fact provoked by the ambiguities of the text itself, thus contributing to its lasting literary and cultural value.

A Cause for Anxiety

In an interview granted in March 1967 to a Slovak journalist, Pavel Licko, Solzhenitsyn outlined his own views on the principal tasks of a writer:

> By intuition and by singular vision of the world, a writer is able to discover far earlier than other people various aspects of social life and can often see them from an unexpected angle. This is the essence of talent. Talent, however, imposes certain duties. It is incumbent upon a writer to inform society of all that he is able to perceive and especially all that is unhealthy and a cause for anxiety. I was brought up with Russian literature and only circumstances prevented me from pursuing more extensive studies. . . . Russian literature has always been sensitive to human suffering.

And in a different passage of the same interview, Solzhenitsyn says:

> I know that the easiest thing for a writer is to write about himself. But I have always felt that to write about the fate of Russia was the most fascinating and impor-

tant task to be performed. Of all the drama that Russia lived through, the fate of Ivan Denisovich was the greatest tragedy.[1]

These two statements shed light on the author's intention behind his works, as well as on his awareness of his own craft. Embracing the notion of the social duty of literature (defined in ethical terms as identifying "anxiety" caused by "human suffering") and putting forth a view of Ivan Denisovich (a sufferer) as a representative type embodying the drama of historic Russian fate, Solzhenitsyn associates himself and his work with the tradition of morally committed nineteenth-century Russian realism. The significance of the issues he raises within this literary tradition is reflected not only in the concrete historical circumstances he has chosen to describe, but also in his general vision of human nature; in this sense, the actual circumstances of the concentration camp serve as justification for raising larger philosophical questions. Just as the protagonist described in *One Day in the Life of Ivan Denisovich* is a particular example of the general moral drama engulfing all of Russia, so too the drama of Russia can be seen as a particular instance of an even more general problem—that of humanity degraded by the onslaught of totalitarianism. In this sense, *One Day in the Life of Ivan Denisovich* also belongs to the great twentieth-century literary tradition of camp literature, a tradition which continually asks: How do human values stand up to the test of the totalitarian experience? What are the limits of human dignity, and what are its sources?

In order to approach the work in the light of this central ethical issue, one must confront it through interpretation of the novella's central character—Ivan Denisovich himself. Solzhenitsyn's own remarks on the character of Ivan Denisovich as a representative of Russian historic tragedy, as well as the novella's title itself, point to the obvious: the work's central issue of an ethical test of "humanity *in extremis*" becomes clearer when approached through an interpretation of the character of the protagonist.

The narration in its entirety follows all the actions of Ivan Denisovich during his waking hours on a particular winter day. He is always present within the narrative scope, while numerous other characters appear and disappear again as they come into contact with him. Yet it is not only his constant presence in the narrative that makes the character of Shukhov the center of the work's human interest. What is even more crucial is Shukhov's function as the principal medium in the narrative technique of *erlebte Rede:* the narrative point of view itself tends to find its location in Shukhov's own eyes. Although the third-person narrator is technically not identified with Shukhov's point of view, nevertheless the focus of narration, the selection of the phenomena described, and the very language that shapes the image of the camp experience presented in *One Day in the Life of Ivan Denisovich* are to a considerable degree products of the cognitive dynamics and linguistic competence of Shukhov himself. So it is not only the events of one day in the camp that constitute Solzhenitsyn's testimony to the totalitarian experience. (As a matter of fact, nothing particularly shocking or dramatic happens on that day.) What is the true repository of the novella's ethical issues is the attitude of the central protagonist to the camp experience, as reflected in the very terms of the narration. Ivan Denisovich is an insider in the dehumanizing world of the camps. As such, he is a living testimony to the long-term results of a person's confrontation with this world. After years of being subjected to the degradation and systematic reprogramming of his self-perception, his view of the camp experience and his response to it carry the potential indirect answer to the question of the sources of human victory or defeat in the face of the extreme conditions of the camp. Hence the central question that informs the ethical dimension of Solzhenitsyn's work is that of Ivan Denisovich's motivations: not only what motivates his actions, but also what motivates his perceptions.

When seen in this context, the absence of dramatic tone and the apparent lack of shocking phenomena in the image of the camp described in Solzhenitsyn's work become sources of meaningful ambiguity. In fact, hunger, cold, pain, violence, injustice, and oppression—all more than sufficient sources of shock and drama—permeate this reality. It is only their status in the eyes of the central protagonist, who tends to perceive them as elements of routine, everyday life, that deprives them of their dramatic, extraordinary impact. Shukhov, an insider in the camp, constantly understates the horror of his experience. What, then, is the motivation behind this peculiar perception of the Soviet camp experience on the part of Ivan Denisovich, a figure who should arouse our moral anxiety, as he is meant to represent not only an individual human fate but also the larger tragedy of Russia's historic fate? Is this matter-of-fact, tough-skinned perception a necessary element of the everyday struggle of an indestructible human being determined to survive and to save his dignity? Is Ivan Denisovich someone who simply cannot afford to be carried away by the dramatic rhetoric that would be quite natural coming from an outside observer of the camp but which could become psychologically disarming for a person living inside it? Or (to state the opposite possibility) are the perpetual understatement and the focus on the mundane practicalities of everyday life in the camp, to the exclusion of the element of moral shock, a reflection of an atrophied sense of ethical indignation in the central protagonist? Are they an indirect indication of Ivan's inner submission to slavery, to the point of accepting his own

victimization without a thought of protest? Are they indications of Shukhov's confusion of the wrong and the normal?[2]
Only by analyzing these questions can one answer the more
general question of whether Solzhenitsyn's novella is testimony to the victory of human dignity over totalitarian dehumanization or to its ultimate defeat.

What to Pray For?

The centrality of the question of Ivan Denisovich's capacity
to respond to the ethical challenge of Stalin's camp finds its
most direct reflection in Solzhenitsyn's work in the climactic
dialog on the bunk between Shukhov and Alyosha, a Baptist
and a victim of Stalin's religious persecution. The topic of the
conversation is, precisely, the problem of identifying sources
of human values and relating the camp experience to the
value systems of the victims. Both prisoners discuss what
their highest values in life are and how their camp experiences can be understood in light of these values. The special
character of this dialog as a key to the ethical dimension of
the novella is suggested in at least two ways. It is the first and
only major instance when Shukhov's habitual focus on the
mundane, practical aspects of his everyday existence gives
way to more "philosophical" reflection: Shukhov directly addresses the problem of ethical values in the camp, as nowhere
else in the work. Moreover, the issue of Shukhov's own motivations in his life in the camp appears here explicitly as a
theme. The second way in which the key significance of this
dialog is suggested lies in the privileged positioning of the
scene in the novella's conclusion. This gives the dialog between Shukhov and Alyosha the character of an interpretive
key to the themes and events described throughout *One Day
in the Life of Ivan Denisovich*. The philosophical issues addressed in this dialog constitute a paradigm in which the eth-

ical dimension of the phenomena described in Solzhenitsyn's work should be placed.

If Shukhov is a human puzzle because of his limited verbal competence and his reluctance to perceive his own fate in generalizing contexts, his partner Alyosha is just the opposite. The character of Alyosha personifies the notion of the individual as ethical entity—that is, as someone who defines his own fate in the camp as the ultimate test of his value system. He verbalizes his particular value system in religious terms and defines his life in terms of service to these values. Both his actions and his words show Alyosha's uncompromising observance of a fully internalized, rigid religious framework of values in which he sees his total identity. Thus, while physically confined to the camp and its dehumanizing pressures, Alyosha is spiritually free, because internally he belongs to a religious world beyond the power of the camp. This internal freedom, the source of Alyosha's human dignity in the camp, stems from his rejection of the main cause of all moral compromises in the camp—the illusory hope of survival and change of fortune. Hope that, according to Shalamov and Borowski, turns a prisoner into a slave[3] in Alyosha's case loses its tempting appeal. Within the world of the camp, hope of survival often forces a prisoner to adhere blindly to the specific pragmatics of survival and either to internalize the point of view of his oppressors, hoping for mercy or for the "clarifying of the mistake" (as in Shelest, Pilyar, Dyakov, and Aldan-Semenov) or to acquire "camp smarts" and learn to live at the expense of his fellow prisoners (the typical attitude of criminals presented in independent camp literature).[4] This notion is so foreign to Alyosha that not only does he care little for the camp pragmatics of survival; he does not even allow himself to pray for a change in his circumstances. When Shukhov tells him that in the camp praying is unlikely to shorten the time to be spent there, Alyosha replies: "You mustn't pray for that."[5] And it is this relative value of hope in the camp that becomes the key topic of the climactic dialog that sheds light on the human puzzle of the protagonist, Shukhov.

Shukhov is in many respects Alyosha's opposite. He has no clear-cut framework of verbally defined values capable of serving as a constant point of reference and a source of inner freedom in the camp. However, he indirectly expresses a need for such a point of reference external to the realm of camp experience. This point of reference appears as a traditional rhetorical entity called "God" when Shukhov, lying on his bunk in the evening, sighs: "Thank God" (p. 195). Thus Shukhov's purely rhetorical phrase opens the conversation that will provide the main ethical paradigm of the novella. "Alyoshka'd heard Shukhov thank the Lord and he turned to him. 'Look here, Ivan Denisovich, your soul wants to pray to God, so why don't you let it have its way?' " (p. 195). Shukhov answers: "I'll tell you why, Alyoshka. Because all these prayers are like the complaints we send in to the higher-ups—either they don't get there or they come back to you marked 'Rejected' " (pp. 195–196). The only desire upon which Shukhov is capable of reflecting intellectually is the hope for improvement of his circumstances, with release from the camp as the peak of this desire. But it is the futility of this hope that Shukhov realizes: "The thing is, you can pray as much as you like but they won't take anything off your sentence and you'll just have to sit it out, every day of it, from reveille to lights out" (p. 198).

Alyosha's answer opens a new dimension to Shukhov— that of a value system transcending hope. " 'You mustn't pray for that.' Alyoshka was horror-struck. 'What d'you want your freedom for? What faith you have left will be choked in thorns. Rejoice that you are in prison. Here you can think of your soul. Paul the Apostle said: 'What mean you to weep and break my heart? for I am ready not to be bound only, but also die for the name of the Lord Jesus' " (p. 198). In this climactic moment Shukhov realizes that what he thought was the source of his everyday efforts and the direction of his life in the camp was not necessarily the hope for survival and freedom. In fact, just like Alyosha, Ivan himself has already abandoned this hope and desire, and resigned himself to his fate in the camp: "Shukhov looked up at the ceiling and said nothing. He didn't know any longer himself whether he wanted freedom or not. At first he'd wanted it very much and every day he added up how long he still had to go. But then he got fed up with this. And as time went on he understood that they might let you out but they never let you home. And he didn't really know where he'd be better off. At home or in here" (p. 199). Unlike Alyosha, however, Shukhov does not know what the source of his own behavior in the camp is; in the name of what does he abandon his hope and accept fate? " 'Look, Alyoshka,' Shukhov said, 'it's all right for you. It was Christ told you to come here, and you are here because of Him. But why am *I* here?' " (p. 199).

Both Shukhov and the reader (limited by Shukhov's vision and awareness) lack direct verbal definition of the particular values for which Shukhov himself may stand in the camp. This lack of a direct, clear philosophical assessment of the nature of Shukhov's true response to the camp experience sets the principal ethical puzzle of the novella: is Shukhov's acceptance of his fate in the camp a sign of his transcending the enslaving dynamics of the camp and—as in the case of Alyosha (only unconsciously)—a sign of his inner victory over totalitarian dehumanization? (If so, a question must be addressed: what would be the source of a value more important than hope for freedom and survival itself?) Or is his abandonment of hope for freedom a reflection of the supreme victory of totalitarian slavery? Is Ivan recognizing

the camp as his true home, the only framework of his identity, including his dreams? If so, Ivan would represent a case
opposite to that of Alyosha: he would represent a Soviet version of what Tadeusz Borowski called the *Lagermensch,* a
camp prisoner whose body and spirit both become so accustomed to his circumstances that they refuse to travel beyond
the barbed wire anymore.[6] And the appearance of the *Lagermensch* may be considered totalitarianism's greatest victory
over the human spirit.

Ivan Denisovich and His Foes

This fundamental ethical issue, constituting a particular
Russian variant of the experience of "humanity *in extremis,*"
can be addressed only by a reader entering into a dialog with
the text. What is expected of the reader here is a reexamina-
tion of the text, especially the actions and attitudes of the
central character, in light of the moral paradigm suggested in
the novella's climactic dialog. In fact, the reader is expected
to provide ethical terms capable of describing the motivations behind these actions and attitudes. Thus each act of
reading and interpreting the central ethical issue of *One Day
in the Life of Ivan Denisovich* provides indirect testimony about
both the book and the reader—generated by the reader's
own particular choice of philosophical terms and priorities.

Published in November 1962 in Moscow, *One Day in the
Life of Ivan Denisovich* became an immediate focus of critical
attention and inspired a vast readership.[7] What is even more
important, the work became the focus of widespread Soviet
public discussion.[8] Given the dialogical mode of reading projected by the text, *One Day in the Life of Ivan Denisovich* became a catalyst for a whole variety of views on the issue of
the totalitarian camp experience to be expressed—but on
condition that they were compatible with the limits of dis-

sent allowed within Soviet public discourse in the Khrushchevian period. When *One Day in the Life of Ivan Denisovich* appeared in the Soviet Union, twenty-five years had passed since the topic of the Soviet camp experience had disappeared from Soviet literature.

To suggest terms by which Solzhenitsyn's ethical puzzle could be grappled with was one task, but to make these terms presentable in the Soviet public context was quite another. The latter task was especially confusing, since, up until then, each literary text referring to the topic of Bolshevik violence and camps had projected its own terms of ethical judgment, which were by definition compatible with, or representative of, the authoritative point of view presented by the regime that created the camps. But *One Day in the Life of Ivan Denisovich* came without such a set of "reading instructions." The very fact that it appeared officially in Soviet print only added to the confusion as to what the current position of the Soviet regime was on the issue of totalitarian victimization. The so-called critical debate around *One Day in the Life of Ivan Denisovich* that followed its publication could be seen as a search for a rhetorical solution to Solzhenitsyn's ethical puzzle that would be essentially compatible with the ideological basis of the Soviet authoritative point of view. In other words, it was a search for ways of presenting Solzhenitsyn's exposure of the camp experience as supportive of the system that created the camps. Shortly before the examination of *One Day in the Life of Ivan Denisovich* by the Lenin Prize Committee on 22 April 1964—the truly ironic climax of the Soviet debate about Solzhenitsyn's work—the critic Vladimir Lakshin presented in the article "Ivan Denisovich—His Friends and Foes" the whole debate as a literary expression of the political struggle between the forces of the dark Stalinist past and those of the post-Stalinist thaw.[9] Obvious as it may seem, this politically motivated dichotomy in the reception of *One Day in the Life of Ivan Denisovich* can be approached—without rejecting its political nature—from a different angle: namely, as a struggle between critics unable or unwilling to construe any terms of ethical compatibility between Solzhenitsyn's work and Soviet ideology and those who tried to prove that such compatibility is allegedly inherent in Solzhenitsyn's novella. On closer examination of both contradictory Soviet patterns of interpretations of *One Day in the Life of Ivan Denisovich,* one can detect behind them clear reflections of two Soviet literary conventions applicable to the topic of the Soviet camps: the old 1930s convention of the "beneficial reeducation of the socially ill" (introduced in "Solovki" and *Belomorkanal*) and the new late-thaw convention of "Stalinist assault against the truly Soviet values" (presented in Shelest's 1962 debut and in works by Pilyar, Dyakov, and Aldan-Semenov).

According to the convention created by Gorky and his associates in "Solovki" and *Belomorkanal,* the real ethical test posed to the prisoner by the Soviet camp is that of the prisoner's capacity to fully internalize the point of view of his oppressors (or educators) and to redefine himself and his situation according to this point of view. The ethical test is, in fact, rather simple: by remodeling his own self-identity, the prisoner acts for his own benefit and proves to everyone that he has become worthy of his new society. That, in turn, changes his status from convict to comrade-in-labor of the guards and of the whole society (even if the labor is carried out under the guns of the guards). Within this convention the degree of the prisoner's implied identification with the point of view of the regime signifies two things: it shows the author's evaluation of the prisoner's ethical progress (his sociopolitical consciousness) and, at the same time, represents the author's evaluation of how successful the camp reeducation is.

Among numerous critical interpretations of *One Day in the Life of Ivan Denisovich* based on the ethical assumptions projected by the convention of the 1930s, let us examine the most orthodox, in order to identify particular limitations imposed by this convention on the reader concerned with the theme of the Soviet camp experience. In 1970, Solzhenitsyn published in the West selected passages from letters written to him by readers of *One Day in the Life of Ivan Denisovich*.[10] The selection includes a series of the most radical testimonies of reading it through the ethical prism provided by "Solovki" and *Belomorkanal*. Judged by these standards, both Ivan Denisovich Shukhov and his camp seem to do poorly. A certain A. I. Grigorev, a reader whose opinion Solzhenitsyn himself immortalized in this peculiar collection, writes:

> The convicts' work, which is the basis of their re-education, is . . . not shown in the story. The prisoners in the story break the rules not only in their daily routine, but also while on the job. . . . The story teaches a careless attitude to socialist property—"they broke off wires to make spoons, concealing them in the corner." In our opinion, Shukhov's "days" inside the camp should not have been taken up with this kind of thing. If such negative acts on the part of the convicts did actually take place, there were constant attempts to put a stop to them, but about this the story says nothing. There were so many positive features, and still are! Surely such inadmissible acts on the part of the prisoners would not have been tolerated. The story would have had a beneficial influence if it had responded to the tasks set before corrective labor establishments.[11]

Sure enough, the horizon of expectations applied by Grigorev to the literary presentation of the Soviet camp experience in 1962 is projected by Gorky's convention from the early 1930s. Grigorev uses the very term "reeducation" in a "Gorkyite" manner. As the criterion for resolving the ethical issues attributed by this convention to the topic of the camp is only one—the degree of success—then, Grigorev asks, why does Solzhenitsyn present his camp as unsuccessful? For, to be sure, Shukhov's moral level is exceptionally low ("he breaks wires to make spoons"), which sheds dubious light on the camp crew's toleration of such attitudes. Judged by the standard of this convention, Solzhenitsyn comes across as a critical realist who exposes serious shortcomings in the educational and disciplinary work of the camp crews. The testimony of *One Day in the Life of Ivan Denisovich,* when subjected to a particular realistic verification by Grigorev, thus seems both exaggerated and unjust. In fact, Grigorev argues, the guards would be harsher and less tolerant, and prisoners would not be able to slip out of control to the point of being able to make spoons from state-owned wire. In short, the reality was brighter than suggested in Solzhenitsyn's criticism.

Sergei Ivanovich Golovin from Tselinograd agrees with Grigorev on this point. Solzhenitsyn definitely underestimates the successful efforts of the Soviet police force in their camp work. "How much unbelievable effort the Chekists put into restoring lost folk to society!," Golovin writes. "Why did he not show how our people worked for twenty-four hours at a stretch, not because of the threat of the stick, but because they knew the value of wolfram and molybdenum in wartime! In what a frenzy about a thousand people worked seventy-two hours together up to the knees and waist in cold water. Who was able to inspire such a feat of patriotism? The Chekists!" [12]

Just as Solzhenitsyn's underestimation of the efforts of the Soviet camp guards may seem a result of his exaggerated yet—perhaps—"constructive" criticism (a call for still greater effort on the part of the camp regime?), so his failure to present in a positive light the process of prisoners' gradual evolution towards an identification with their guards seems altogether suspect. "According to Solzhenitsyn, if one of the prisoners who is more conscious of his duties tells something to the authorities, then it is 'self-preservation at someone else's expense.' Some patriot, I must say! The Soviet people should say only thank you to this prisoner who has come to a proper understanding," A. F. Zakharova from Irkutsk District fumes.[13] Zakharova's mode of understanding the ethical dimension of the camp experience is determined by the convention mastered in 1934 in *Belomorkanal*. In *Belomorkanal* the internal dynamics of prisoners' evolution from confused, individualistic, conflicting identities towards a harmonious, universal, collective new identity is embodied in the gradual process of dissolution of the opposition *prisoners/guards*, from which a new opposition emerges, that of *new people/old people*, or, in a later formulation, *all people/nature*, as the humanity united by the proletarian revolution realizes the task of constructing the socialist utopia. Within these dynamics, prisoners who associate with the guards and help them oversee the internal progress of other prisoners are model figures. However, in the view of Solzhenitsyn's narrator, colored by the attitude of his central protagonist, Shukhov, this model becomes a target of unchallenged negative attitudes. A prisoner-supervisor character (a favorite hero of *Belomorkanal*) named Der is described in *One Day in the Life of Ivan Denisovich* as an evident villain. Solzhenitsyn describes a moment of confrontation between this character and other prisoners during working hours at a construction site. The prisoner-supervisor Der is about to expose a violation of the camp regulations on the part of the prisoners who are using some insulating materials in order to keep warm while working. The response of the prisoners to Der's attack is quite surprising and stops him from denouncing them to the authorities:

> God, the way the boss's face twitched all over. The way he threw his trowel on the floor and went over to Der. Der looked around. Pavlo was standing there with his shovel up. He hadn't brought it up with him for nothing. . . . And Senka, deaf as he was, had seen what it was all about. And he came out with his hands on his hips. He was strong as an ox. Der started blinking. He was worried and he looked around for a way out. The boss leaned over close to Der and said kind of quiet, but so you could hear it up there: "Times have changed for scum like you, handing out new sentences! If you say a word, you bloodsucker, you won't be alive much longer. Get it?" The boss was shaking all over and he couldn't stop.
>
> And Pavlo was looking murder at Der. He had a face like a hawk.
>
> "Take it easy, boys. Take it easy," Der said. He was all pale and he edged away from the ladder a little.
>
> The boss didn't say another word. He straightened his cap, picked up his bent trowel, and went back to his wall. (pp. 115–116)

The opposition *prisoners/guards*—which should gradually disappear according to Gorky's convention—is indestructible in *One Day in the Life of Ivan Denisovich*. No matter what the true motivations might be, a visible struggle between the prisoners and the guards is under way. In this struggle, the informer is an enemy of the prisoner treated with hostility greater than that felt by the prisoner towards the guards themselves. Thus, for a reader inclined to identify the ethical issues of Solzhenitsyn's work according to Gorky's parameters, there seems to be something fundamentally wrong with the work in question. A certain Silin writes: "Everyone knows what an informer is. In the Soviet Union these people are respected, because they are progressive, politically aware people, who help to bring into the open the enemies of Soviet power and to unmask traitors. In the camps they are those prisoners who have recognized their guilt. If there were no informers, there would be escapes. And what is a prisoner doing at liberty?" [14]

Instead of focusing on the successful reeducation of the "socially ill," either by showing their own changing point of view or by presenting the point of view of their inexhaustible "educators," as Gorky had done, Solzhenitsyn brings the reader face to face with the camp reality through the eyes of someone who is virtually unequipped to perceive his own situation within the positive larger picture but who, at the same time, dwells on each minute physical difficulty of camp life. What is the point? "Millions of Soviet people labor at felling timber and sing the praises of this form of toil, but the heroes of this story regard it with fear," Zakharova comments. [15]

The whole Soviet approach to the topic of state victimization and especially to the most systematic form of this victimization—the concentration camp—was based on one principle: a positive "larger picture" was supposed to emerge from the description of reality whose surface to an unprepared eye could appear harsh or even disturbing. To readers whose mode of response to the literary presentation of this topic was formed by Maxim Gorky and his associates in the early 1930s, no indication of the positive "larger picture" seemed identifiable in Solzhenitsyn's work. Perceived within the framework of Gorky's convention, *One Day in the Life of Ivan Denisovich* could not but seem a failure.

A certain Medne from Elgava concludes: "I would not have published this. For what reason and for whom is it? One tries to conceal his own shortcomings instead of advertising them."[16] The comment summarizes the place of Solzhenitsyn within Soviet public discourse on the camp topic as defined by Gorky. It is worth remembering that Gorky's convention allowed a certain note of criticism regarding "shortcomings" in an otherwise well-functioning system, on condition that the "shortcomings" do not exhaust the whole image. A note of "constructive criticism" toward the system fits Gorky's convention, because it illustrates the system's invulnerability to criticism and the alleged freedom of opinion within the system. At the same time, the writer's constructive role in social progress is shown as he suggests his emendations. What Solzhenitsyn is criticized for by these adherents to Gorky's view of the Soviet camp experience is not his challenge to the system as such (this seems beyond the imagination of the readers quoted here), but his failure to accompany his critique with "constructive" suggestions.

The more "inquisitive" among these readers tend to go as far as to see an almost satirical design in Solzhenitsyn's negative view of the camp. On their interpretation, the target of the satire is supposed to be the main protagonist through whose eyes we see the camp. This mode of reading, interestingly enough, seems to follow the pattern of classical satire in which the "wrong" point of view is attributed to the satire's "speaker" without even the necessity of specifying why it is wrong (the "right" point of view is assumed as obvious and unquestionable for both author and reader). The already quoted A. I. Grigorev concludes: "The principal character of the story, Shukhov, *is shown negatively,* like all others, who as the story shows, disorganized life in the camp."[17] Given the allegedly negative protagonist-prisoner determining the narrative point of view and no indication of any positive traits in his "educators," Solzhenitsyn's presentation of the camp seemed to lack an element necessary in Gorky's convention:

official optimism. And without the slightest indication of the bright future emerging from contemporary reality, the whole image—even well intended—could only be a failure.

This list of the most peculiar interpretations of *One Day in the Life of Ivan Denisovich* in the framework of Gorky's convention could be extended; the evidence is abundant. What is a crucial characteristic of these responses is their inability to follow the basic prerequisite of the mode of reading implied by the text—they are incapable of assuming the point of view of the novella's central figure, Ivan Denisovich. For within Gorky's convention, the point of view of the prisoner is wrong by definition as long as it differs essentially from the point of view of the camp regime. The only point of view entirely dominating Gorky's vision of the camp experience is that of the creators of the system. The author's personae, the voices of the state authorities (quotations from speeches and decrees), the camp guards and administrators—and finally the "conscious" prisoners themselves—are channels through which this singular, exclusively correct vision is expressed. Within this vision, the key definition of the camp experience being "social reeducation," there is no room for either victim or victimization. The prisoner's point of view becomes presentable when the barrier between the prisoner and the regime is lifted and the prisoner no longer defines himself or herself any more as a victim, but as a subject for reeducation, and so becomes a collaborator, not a victim, of the regime. This change in self-identification of the prisoner is seen as inevitable, and only a matter of time. Thus, with the time in sight when no one will identify himself in the camp as a victim, the whole notion of victimization becomes irrelevant to the topic. With the elimination of the presence of the victim, the only ethical issue left within the scope of the camp experience is that of the most efficient means to achieve the goal of fully integrating everyone in the process of labor aimed at the construction of the new, harmonious world. This is how the authors of the "letters to the author" quoted above understand the ethical problem inherent in the theme of the Soviet camp experience.

Needless to say, the ethical issue of "humanity *in extremis,*" posed by Solzhenitsyn through the ambiguities of Ivan Denisovich's response to his own victimization in the camp, cannot appear on the horizon of readers' expectations defined in terms of Gorky's convention. The question of the individual's moral victory or defeat in the confrontation with the totalitarian camp experience is understood in totally opposite ways by Solzhenitsyn and the adherents of Gorky's convention. The key issue raised by Ivan Denisovich in his conversation with Alyosha—the human capacity to transcend the camp reality by preserving or creating a source of dignity independent of the totalitarian regime—for Solzhenitsyn spells human victory over totalitarian dehumanization. Within the value system implicit in Gorky's convention, preservation (let alone creation) of an external source for an individual's self-identification is the core of all evils.

Examples of Soviet attempts to assess the ethical challenge of *One Day in the Life of Ivan Denisovich* according to Gorky's convention can only amuse today's reader, as they hopelessly miss the point. It is not their interpretive value, however, that is of interest here, but the evidence they provide of the astonishing longevity of Gorky's totalitarian convention of presenting the Soviet camp experience. The fact that this convention, already assessed by the Stalinist regime itself as ineffective and counterproductive in 1937, and henceforth absent from Soviet public discourse (together with the very topic of the camps), was unmistakably retrieved in the first instance of reintroducing the topic to literary discourse seems truly remarkable. The convention itself was proven bankrupt in the late 1930s, because its underlying belief in the imminent success of social reeducation in real Soviet life and the gradual disappearance of the camps no longer necessary in an improved society was embarrassingly frustrated as the scale of mass oppression in the camps increased. As the principal ethical argument in favor of Bolshevik oppression—its allegedly temporary character and its necessary role in building the Communist utopia—failed to withstand historic verification, the regime assessed the services of the panegyrists of concentration camps as troublesome rather than helpful and resigned itself to the ultimate recourse of banning the topic altogether. The regime simply ran out of time searching for further strategies of presenting the already well-established system of slavery and terror as something temporary. Nevertheless, the power of the descriptive convention in some instances proved greater than the power of material evidence: twenty-five years after the banishment of the camp theme, the reappearance of this topic in Soviet public discourse meant, for some, the resurrection of Gorky's vision as if time had stopped in 1934. Astonishing as it seems, the fact may serve as evidence of the power of the Soviet authoritarian and monological communicative universe. In fact, the Soviet regime did not reexamine its own fundamental ethical notions and never provided a new model for addressing the Soviet camp experience in literature in terms fully compatible with the ideological goals of the regime itself. In 1962 new attempts to reconcile the camp experience with a positive view of the Communist experiment were being made by authors of the late-thaw camp literature soon to be published. Meanwhile, however, some readers could not wait for new instructions as to how to receive the literary presentation of the camp and how not to notice the ethical challenge to the Soviet system. Contradicted by reality or not, Gorky's convention fulfilled at least one requirement: in the minds of some readers it obliterated the "cause for anxiety" inherent in Solzhenitsyn's discovery of the Soviet camp experience.

Ivan Denisovich and His Friends

Had it been for readers such as those quoted above to decide, *One Day in the Life of Ivan Denisovich* would not have entered Soviet public discourse, as it seemed incompatible with the principal foundation of that discourse—the dogma of moral superiority and infallibility of the Soviet regime and the assumption of the writer's role as a champion of this dogma. The very fact of Solzhenitsyn entering Soviet public discourse in 1962, along with the great exposure enjoyed by his *One Day in the Life of Ivan Denisovich* immediately after its publication, derived from an effort on the part of critics and readers in prominent public positions, who attempted to formulate and resolve the ethical challenge posed by the novella in terms compatible with the same dogmas of Soviet public discourse. Interestingly enough, the solutions proposed by these "friends" of Ivan Denisovich to the key ethical puzzle of Solzhenitsyn's work represented a newly developed formula for reconciling the Soviet system with its own horrors—a formula that found its literary expressions in the works of Shelest, Pilyar, Dyakov, and Aldan-Semenov. These writers abandoned Gorky's strategy of obliterating the very presence of the victim and preempting the potential ethical issues of oppression, dehumanization, struggle, and survival. In fact, as the examples of Shelest, Pilyar, and others show, the fundamental ethical issue of the testing of human values under dehumanizing pressures becomes the central focus in this approach. This ethical focus, however, proves compatible with—or rather, instrumental to—the task of championing the ethical legitimacy of the Soviet regime. This is so because of two stable elements within this view. The protagonist in the camp always passes the ethical test, and the source of this human victory over the dehumanizing impact of the camp lies in the Soviet ethical values preserved by the victim-victor. This approach is concerned with a very special type of victim, a Communist true believer, to the point of excluding other victims' points of view and redefining the very notion of victimhood as attributable exclusively to those victims who share the Communist ethical principles of their oppressors.

Thus, while the "foes" of Ivan Denisovich fumed at the work's failures, the "friends" were busy responding to Solzhenitsyn's ethical challenge by proving that *One Day in the Life of Ivan Denisovich* shows the triumph of "true Soviet values" over the confusing challenges of Soviet reality. This was how Nikita Khrushchev understood Solzhenitsyn's work when he decided to allow its publication. On 20 October 1962, Khrushchev received Aleksandr Tvardovsky and informed him of his decision. He said of *One Day in the Life of Ivan Denisovich:* "it is a life-affirming work. In fact I'll go so far as to say that it expresses the Party spirit." [18]

In the introductory note to its original publication in *Novyi mir,* Tvardovsky presented Solzhenitsyn's novella as a literary exemplification of Khrushchev's attitude to what was called the "period of the personality cult, now exposed and rejected by the Party." [19] The main purpose and cultural significance of the work were defined by Tvardovsky as the reconciliation of the Soviet order with its own horrible past. This reconciliation was pursued by Khrushchev's regime through dissociating itself in public discourse from Stalin's legacy of oppression. One of the primary strategies used to achieve this effect was breaking the taboo and thereby creating the appearance of frank openness to a public reevaluation of the past. "But whatever the past was like, we in the present must not be indifferent to it. Only by going into its consequences fully, courageously, and truthfully can we guarantee a complete and irrevocable break with all those things that cast a shadow over the past," Tvardovsky stated, commenting on the significance of Solzhenitsyn's debut. He immediately added: "This is what N. S. Khrushchev meant when he said in his memorable concluding address at the Twenty-Second Congress: 'It is our duty to go carefully into all aspects of all matters connected with the abuse of power. In time we must die, for we are all mortal, but as long as we go on working we can and must clarify many things and tell the truth to the Party and the people.' This must be done to prevent such things from happening in the future." [20]

Thanks to this rhetorical operation of Tvardovsky's, Solzhenitsyn's work was presented as an extension of the current Soviet public discourse concerned with the topic of Stalinist victimization. "This stark tale shows once again that today there is no aspect of our life that cannot be dealt with and faithfully described in Soviet literature," Tvardovsky insisted. [21]

Tvardovsky was too sensitive a reader to fail to notice that the ethical issues raised by Solzhenitsyn went too far to be waylaid by a reference to Khrushchev's speeches and to the new political line of the regime. He wrote:

One day of Ivan Denisovich Shukhov, a prisoner in a forced labor camp, as described by Aleksandr Solzhenitsyn (this is the author's first appearance in print) unfolds as a picture of exceptional vividness and truthfulness about the nature of man. It is this above all that gives the work its unique impact. The reader could easily imagine many of the people shown here in these tragic circumstances as fighting at the front or working on post-war reconstruction. They are the same sort of people, but they have been exposed by fate to a cruel ordeal—not only physical but moral. The author of this novel does not go out of his way to emphasize the arbitrary brutality that was a consequence of the breakdown of Soviet legality. He has taken a very ordinary day—from reveille to lights out—in the life of a prisoner. But this ordinary day cannot fail to fill the reader's heart with bitterness and pain at the fate of these people who come to life before his eyes and seem so close to him in the pages of the book.

Having mentioned the element of ethical challenge inalienable from *One Day in the Life of Ivan Denisovich,* Tvardovsky concluded:

The author's greatest achievement, however, is that this bitterness and pain do not convey a feeling of utter despair. On the contrary. The effect of this novel, which is so unusual for its honesty and harrowing truth, is to unburden our minds of things thus far unspoken, but which had to be said. It thereby strengthens and ennobles us.[22]

Tvardovsky's line of interpretation of *One Day in the Life of Ivan Denisovich* proved successful and influential; Solzhenitsyn's work became so highly appreciated in Soviet public discourse that it approached nomination for Lenin's Prize in 1964. During the campaign in favor of it, Soviet critics devoted to promoting it followed Tvardovsky's interpretive line and, in addition, provided specific terms describing the sources of moral victory presented in Solzhenitsyn's work. *Izvestia* published a critical essay on *One Day in the Life of Ivan Denisovich* written by V. Pallon, entitled "Hello, Captain!" Pallon relates an encounter with a former prisoner, a navy captain Boris V. Burkovsky, who admitted to being an ex-camp mate of Solzhenitsyn and who seemed to have served as the prototype for the character of Captain Buynovsky in *One Day in the Life of Ivan Denisovich*. The real captain survived the camp and subsequently assumed a post as head of a branch of the Museum of Military History on the battleship *Aurora*. Pallon quotes Burkovsky's comments on *One Day in the Life of Ivan Denisovich:*

> I read in the papers not long ago that Solzhenitsyn's story [*One Day in the Life of Ivan Denisovich*] had been nominated for the 1964 Lenin Prize. I was very excited. . . . I am no expert on literature and I won't analyse the story. . . . But if I were asked to say what I thought of it, I'd say it's a fine, truthful piece of writing. It's clear to any reader of the story that, with rare exceptions, people remained people in the camps for the very reason that they were Soviet in their hearts, and that they never identified the evil done to them with the Party, or with our regime.[23]

It is hardly possible to find a more fitting example of the effort to confront the moral issue of Ivan Denisovich by reconciling it with the Soviet ideological self-image championed by Khrushchevian policy. Both the message of this statement and its quoted source are emblematic of the new Soviet attitude to the topic of totalitarian victimization. The statement comes from the figure of a Soviet man personally associated with Solzhenitsyn in the camp, whose point of view is thus no less authoritative on this particular matter than Solzhenitsyn's own. His statement and his personal story are clear, and they complement one another. The moral victory of the Soviet man over the Soviet machine of dehumanization was accomplished thanks to the preservation of Soviet values by the victims of the camp and their refusal (or failure) to associate the evil with its only apparent source—the Soviet regime itself. Captain Burkovsky appears as living proof of this victory: he survived the ordeal of the camps and devoted the rest of his life to serving the memory of the Bolshevik cause in its most emblematic, archetypal location—the battleship *Aurora*. The Soviet thaw myth, richly illuminated in the camp literature by Shelest, Dyakov, and others, of the return to the uncorrupted sources of Leninism after the temporary misadventure of Stalinism, appears in Pallon's essay and claims Solzhenitsyn as its alleged champion.

To be sure, a simple confrontation with the text itself undermines this interpretation of the people's victory over Soviet dehumanization as due to their being "Soviet at heart." Within the linguistic universe of the work—both at the level of narration (highly dependent on Shukhov's point of view and his linguistic competence) and at the level of dialog among the personages—any "constructive" presentation of Soviet values seems strikingly out of place. In fact, it is the character of the captain who introduces this thematic and rhetorical dimension to the novella's linguistic universe in a direct way, but only to show the fundamental incongruity of this type of discourse with the human vision inherent in the linguistic universe of *One Day in the Life of Ivan Denisovich*. As the camp guards line up the prisoners at the gate on a freezing winter morning in order to strip them of any clothes not prescribed by the regulations, the captain protests:

> The Captain kicked up a fuss, just like he used to on
>   his ship—he'd only been here three months.
> "You've no right to strip people in the cold! You
>   don't know Article Nine of the Criminal Code!"
> They had the right and they knew the article. You've
>   still got a lot to learn, brother.
> "You're not Soviet people," the Captain kept on at
>   them.
> "You're not Communists!" (p. 38)

The captain's exclamation seems almost tragicomic as an expression of both helplessness and misplaced expectations. Shukhov's attitude to the captain is that of sympathy and pity; the latter seems simply a naive novice unprepared to face the reality of the camp. The captain gets ten days in the cooler for his ideologically motivated criticism. Between Shukhov (who never even mentions "Soviet values") and the captain (who attempts to apply them to the camp), Shukhov represents a point of view far more accurate and deprived of naive misconceptions. In fact, Shukhov is aware of this fundamental difference and assumes an almost fatherly attitude toward the captain. He gives the extra bowl of mush he happens to get to the captain. The narrator relates Shukhov's thoughts about the captain. "The time would come when [the captain] would learn the ropes, but as it was he didn't know his way around yet" (p. 91). The captain in Pallon's essay apparently never learned camp life as Shukhov expected him to. His assessment of the moral victory of Soviet man over Soviet dehumanization is so emblematic of the late-thaw view of the Soviet camp experience that even its wording is identical with the title of Pilyar's novel, *People Remain People*. Both Pilyar and Captain Burkovsky (according to Pallon) give the same answer to the question: "Why did people remain people in the camp?"

The thaw view of the Soviet camp experience emphasized Communist values as the source of the victory of human dignity under the impact of the camp. As to the somewhat troubling question of the origin and ethical foundation of mass victimization, the answer was: Stalin. The fundamental mystery over which the two-dimensional characters of Shelest, Dyakov, and Aldan-Semenov agonized at length was expressed in the question: Did Stalin know?— the bitter answer to which was a resounding yes.

While the issue of the source of human dignity in the dire

conditions of concentration camps was taken up as Pallon presented it, Soviet friends of Ivan Denisovich had still to determine their answer to the question of the source of the evil itself. For, of course, *One Day in the Life of Ivan Denisovich* came without a clear statement on this matter. Ivan Denisovich himself, while addressing Alyosha, asks, "Why am *I* here?" (p. 199) and thus opens the issue of the source of his misery—the source of Russia's misery. Konstantin Simonov took it upon himself to address both sides of the moral issue presented in Solzhenitsyn's work. He wrote in *Izvestia:*

> Solzhenitsyn creates one human portrait after another. Among the story's heroes there are people with wonderful human qualities, there are people who are simply good, there are people with failings, perhaps with delusions, there are stronger ones and weaker ones. But when through the power of Solzhenitsyn's artistic brush they are transformed into a portrait of a wide group of people, depicted against the leaden-grey background of one day of ordinary camp life, you, the reader, begin to feel these people, taken together, are none other than purely and simply a part of our society . . . and they remain for the most part the same people that they were before the camp—real Soviet people.

With this admission of the Soviet people's capacity to withstand the moral trials of the Soviet camp, Simonov continues:

> The consoling thought—that Stalin did not know what was happening—which some of us tried earlier to instill forcibly into ourselves has become a myth that has been destroyed. And this heavy but sober feeling flares up in the soul with new force when you read Solzhenitsyn's story—although I cannot even remember now if the name of Stalin is mentioned in it.[24]

Simonov pronounces the name Stalin as the resolution of a principal issue of *One Day in the Life of Ivan Denisovich*—the problem of the origins of totalitarian evil—in a way highly characteristic of the official Soviet approach to this question during the thaw period. Mikhail Heller describes this approach with irony: "A bad wizard came, deceived the party and the people, and made everyone serve him. Then the wizard died, and the sun started shining again." [25]

The fact that Simonov provides his interpretation without even remembering whether Stalin was mentioned in Solzhenitsyn's work is no less characteristic of the Soviet mode. To set the record straight, let us remember that Stalin *is* mentioned in *One Day in the Life of Ivan Denisovich,* but not as an issue. Perhaps even the simplest prisoner in Ivan's camp would be embarrassed to ask whether "Stalin knew" or to agonize over the alleged mystery of Stalin's decisions. A reference to Stalin is heard merely in the noise of the evening return to the barracks:

> Somebody in the room was yelling: "You think that old bastard in Moscow with the mustache is going to have mercy on *you?* He wouldn't give a damn about his own brother, never mind slobs like you!"
>
> The great thing about a penal camp was you had a hell of a lot of freedom. Back in Ust-Izhma if you said they couldn't get matches "outside" they put you in the can and slapped on another ten years. But here you could yell your head off about anything you liked and the squealers didn't even bother to tell on you. The security fellows couldn't care less. (p. 176)

Efforts to present *One Day in the Life of Ivan Denisovich* as an apotheosis of the triumph of real Soviet values tested by the experience of the "personality cult" present a peculiar spectacle of interpretive failures. It is highly interesting, and perhaps ironic, that critics, instead of promoting the main rival of *One Day in the Life of Ivan Denisovich* to the status of the central work of post-Stalinist Soviet camp literature— namely, *The Kolyma Notes* by Shelest, which reflected these ideological presumptions almost perfectly—decided to champion the ambiguous and challenging work by Solzhenitsyn. It was *The Kolyma Notes,* not *One Day in the Life of Ivan Denisovich,* that presented the "real Communists" withstanding the trial of the camp, insisted that "people remained people in the camp thanks to their being Soviet at heart," and dealt with the discovery that Stalin indeed knew. Moreover, the terms of presenting the Soviet totalitarian experience introduced in *The Kolyma Notes* were reflected in later pieces by Dyakov, Pilyar, and Aldan-Semenov, thus forming a larger literary convention fully compatible with the Soviet regime's revamped self-image. So the work which possessed all it needed to conform to the newly coined ideological image of the camp experience was overlooked in Soviet public discourse in favor of a work which was praised for "merits" it did not possess. Perhaps the real reasons for this state of affairs were never spelled out. This was typical of Soviet public discourse. Because *One Day in the Life of Ivan Denisovich* presented unmatched literary and cultural value in the Soviet context of 1962, the search for its apparent compatibility with the self-image projected by the Soviet regime may have been a purely ritualistic affair and may have served (almost surely in the cases of Tvardovsky and Lakshin) as camouflage under which the true challenge of Solzhenitsyn was introduced to Soviet public awareness.

A Symphony of Labor?

If there was an element of deception in the interpretations promoting *One Day in the Life of Ivan Denisovich* within the framework of Soviet public discourse, not everyone was willing to play the game. It was not particularly difficult to argue that if, as Solzhenitsyn's promoters insisted, *One Day in the Life of Ivan Denisovich* was intended to prove that "Soviet people never abandoned their faith in the Communist Party, in Soviet power . . . even in the most brutal conditions of Beria's terror,"[26] then Solzhenitsyn did not succeed in realizing this aim.

Such was the verdict pronounced in *Literaturnaia gazeta* on 4 June 1964. This seems to have been the moment when the hopes of the regime to "domesticate" Solzhenitsyn as a literary champion of the Khrushchevian superficial reconciliation with the Stalinist past were abandoned. In April 1964 the Lenin Prize Committee had rejected Solzhenitsyn's candidacy for the award, and a press campaign against Solzhenitsyn had begun to overshadow the voices of support. Surely, Solzhenitsyn had not only failed to provide a single, clear, authoritative proclamation of Soviet values, but he had made a fundamentally "wrong" choice about his central protagonist and the primary point of view of the novella. For it was obvious that only a Communist prisoner's point of view could in fact provide the vision of the Soviet camp experience expected by the regime. Even the notoriously limited authors of the "letters to the writer" did not fail to recognize this point. A certain Oleinik writes: "If your story is a work of art, then it should be like a rallying cry. Instead of depicting the destruction of the most loyal people in 1937, the author chose 1941, when by and large it was self-seekers who were sent to the camps. In 1937 there were no Shukhovs, and they went to their deaths grimly and in silence, wondering for whose benefit it was. . . . They did not lick food bowls there."[27] And an anonymous reader comments: "I feel no pity or sympathy for these convicts. Surely the Communists who got into trouble were not like that?"[28] These voices are echoed by the previously quoted Medne from Elgava who remarks on Solzhenitsyn: "He has practically no victims of 1937, *in other words* innocent people."[29]

The hardly sophisticated "foes" of Ivan Denisovich clarified the point his sophisticated "friends" attempted to pass over in silence: the appearance of moral legitimacy of the Bolsheviks after the "discovery" of massive victimization could be accomplished only by presenting the Bolsheviks themselves as the principal, if not exclusive, victims. By granting the status of innocent victims to other subjects of the Bolshevik oppression, one granted moral legitimacy (potential or actual) to any causes they represented. Thus the sole legitimate ideology—Communism—could become vulnerable to moral competition from other ideological and philosophical positions. By admitting the existence of moral values or philosophical frameworks of human self-identification that, although not Communist, proved capable of providing people with sources of human dignity and survival against oppression in the Soviet camps, it was inevitable that the Communist monopoly on the "right" point of view (and ethical position) would be undermined. Each of the authors of the official Soviet late-thaw camp literature, with the exception of Solzhenitsyn, resolved this potential challenge to the Communist ethical monopoly by granting the status of innocent victims exclusively to Communists or at least Soviet patriots. The camp is divided, within this dominant Soviet late-thaw view, between the Communists ("in other words—innocent people") and the rest (in Shelest's words—the "half-fascist sewage"). As for Ivan Denisovich, he is meant by the author to represent the larger historic Russian fate of the victimization of innocent people. At the same time his promoters on the Soviet literary scene were failing to show that he belonged to the "Communists or in other words innocent people." To reconcile him with the regime meant either to show him as assuming the regime's point of view or to show the regime itself voluntarily opening itself to the possibility of Ivan's moral superiority. In other words, in this confrontation between a totalitarian regime claiming supreme moral authority and an individual who finds his moral dignity outside the ideological universe of the regime, the ethical reconciliation between the regime and the individual would have to assume the moral capitulation of one or the other side.

Dramatically short of direct textual evidence of the alleged triumph of Soviet values in Solzhenitsyn's work, the "friends" of Ivan Denisovich found, nevertheless, a way of interpreting the ambiguities of *One Day in the Life of Ivan Denisovich* in favor of their claim. They suggested a specific use of Soviet conventions of public discourse in interpreting one of the most enigmatic motifs in Solzhenitsyn's work— that of the labor frenzy on the part of Ivan Denisovich and other prisoners described at the midpoint of the novella. Just as the conversation between Shukhov and Alyosha in the novella's conclusion enjoys a privileged position in the structure, so does the long scene of Brigade 104 at work, which appears as the high point of the novella's narrative tension. The narrative line of *One Day in the Life of Ivan Denisovich,* based on the dynamics of a day's routine occupations, rises following Shukhov's awakening and the growing intensity and tempo of the activities whose peak is the labor itself. "[All events] lead up to the climax [of Solzhenitsyn's work], the high point of Ivan's day: the exquisite pleasure of building a wall straight and true and not wasting any mortar," [30] Edward Brown explains, referring to the narrative dynamics of *One Day in the Life of Ivan Denisovich.* After this climax, the narrative tension descends to the point of Shukhov's falling asleep, right after the conversation with Alyosha on the bunk.

Meals, smokes, errands, conversations, and confrontations with guards provide the knots on this narrative line.

The feverish enthusiasm with which starved, freezing prisoners approach their hard, demanding physical labor at the construction site is indeed striking and begs the question of motivation. It is clear that survival in the camp requires a prisoner to save his energy by avoiding physical exertion: starved, freezing prisoners who spend the remnants of their energy on labor are endangered by a speedy decline of their physical capacity to survive. This common knowledge vanishes, however, as soon as Shukhov's brigade assume their positions at the site. Here not only are the prisoners shown as eager laborers but their attitude toward work appears as a test of their true human value. The characters presented favorably prove to be dedicated workers, while those shown in a generally negative light (like Fetyukov) tend to avoid effort. According to the logic of survival in the camp, those of Solzhenitsyn's characters who work honestly and frantically at the construction site without being forced to do so are engaged in a seemingly self-destructive activity. In order to read Solzhenitsyn's work and not find it contradictory to the standards of basic literary realism, the reader must find some motivation for this quite striking behavior of the characters. The most obvious motivation is suggested in the text itself:

You might ask why a prisoner worked so hard for ten years in a camp. Why didn't they say to hell with it and drag their feet all day long till the night, which was theirs? So simple. That's why they'd dreamed up these gangs. But it wasn't like gangs "outside," where every fellow got paid separately. In the camps they had these gangs to make the prisoners keep each other on their toes. So the fellows at the top didn't have to worry. It was like this—either you all got something extra or you all starved. ("You're not pulling your weight, you swine, and I've got to go hungry because of you. So work, you bastard!") (pp. 66–67)

But that is not all. The collective blackmail does not explain the degree of undeniable enthusiasm displayed by the prisoners. Even after the work is finished and the prisoners are expected for roll call, Ivan Denisovich is so carried away by his bricklaying work that he does not stop, by which he risks being late and receiving harsh punishment. First, he explains it to himself in a way perfectly rational everywhere but in the camp: he does not want to waste the mortar:

> If they booked you for being late, you could land in the cooler. There was a great crowd around the guardroom. Everybody was there. From the looks of it the escort had begun counting them. . . .
>
> To hell with the mortar. The boss waved his arm. "Dump it over the wall and clear out." . . .
>
> The boss had said not to worry about the mortar. ("Dump it over the wall and clear out.") But Shukhov was kind of funny about these things. And he couldn't help it even after eight years of camps. He still worried about every little thing and about all kinds of work. He couldn't stand seeing things wasted.
>
> Mortar, brick, mortar, brick . . .
>
> "That does it," Senka shouted. "Let's get the hell out of here."
>
> He grabbed the hod and went down the ladder. But Shukhov—the guards could set the dogs on him for all he cared now—ran back to have a last look. Not bad. He went up and looked over the wall from left to right. His eye was true as a level. The wall was straight as a

die. His hands were still good for something! (pp. 82–83)

Ivan's motivation is a puzzle, since there is no rational way of explaining—within the camp's logic of survival—his enthusiasm over participating in the slave-labor project. He devotes himself to his work beyond the point of self-interest and actually against his self-interest, since he puts himself at risk in order to complete well what he started.

For the ideologically focused promoters of Solzhenitsyn's work, Ivan Denisovich's attitude to his camp work spelled only one thing: unaware and lacking in eloquence as he is in speech and cognitive focus, Ivan Denisovich is, in fact, an embodiment of Soviet values, and his attitude to labor is the ultimate proof of it. At this point, Ivan Denisovich appears in a light no different from the outspoken Communist prisoners of Shelest or Dyakov, who outdid themselves in their efforts at work in the camps. According to critic Vladimir Ermilov (known for his always close adherence to the party line), Solzhenitsyn's work praises the heroes of socialist labor, and Ivan Denisovich, although in a camp, happens to be one of them:

Aleksandr Solzhenitsyn's story at times calls to mind Tolstoy's artistic power in its depiction of the national character. . . . There can be no doubt that the fight against the consequences of Stalin's personality cult, taken up by the Party and the Soviet people since the Twentieth and Twenty-Second Congresses of the CPSU, will continue to facilitate the appearance of works of art outstanding for their ever increasing artistic value, their ever deeper closeness to the people, works reflecting our contemporary life and the creative labor of our people.[31]

What Ermilov suggested in his *Pravda* review in November 1962, the Secretary of the Central Committee, Leonid Ilyichev, developed in his speech at a session of the Central Committee's Ideological Commission attended by Soviet writers and artists on 26 December of that year: "And take the novella, *One Day in the Life of Ivan Denisovich!* It speaks, as we know, about bitter things, but it is not written from a defeatist's point of view. Such literary works evoke readers' respect for the working man, and the Party supports them. To exterminate and raze all bad and negative things in people's souls, and to inspire people's readiness for heroic deeds, struggle, and creative labor: that is the way to go!" According to Ilyichev, Solzhenitsyn's work is an example of literature devoted to these purposes. He has no doubt that the central message of *One Day in the Life of Ivan Denisovich* is the praise of Soviet heroic labor represented by the character of Shukhov. Ilyichev attempts to define this alleged message: "One must admit that no cult of personality could overshadow the great and heroic labor of the Soviet people." In his praise of Solzhenitsyn as a champion of the literature of heroic Soviet labor, Ilyichev does not fail to make clear the conditions on which the subject of Stalinist oppression is permissible in such literature. He adds: "That is what we must emphasize here: it is one thing to struggle against the consequences of the cult of personality in order to reinforce the Leninist way of life, in order to strengthen our power and multiply the greatness of our people's accomplishments, and it is another thing to pretend to struggle against the consequences of the cult of personality in order to strike at our ideology and our life—in other words, at socialism and communism."[32] Solzhenitsyn's work, of course, is presented here as an example of the former type of attitude.

Both Ermilov and Ilyichev follow the automatic association of the theme of labor with Communist motivation, an association characteristic of socialist realism in general and of the Soviet conventions applied to the theme of the concentration camps in particular. For Gorky, a prisoner's devotion to labor in the camp reflects the degree of this prisoner's identification with the regime and its goals. In the works of Shelest, Dyakov, Aldan-Semenov, and Pilyar, this identification is fully internalized by victims, who do not leave any doubt as to their motivations and who provide extensive monologs about Communist values, the goals of the country, and so on. The only trouble when it comes to trying to interpret Ivan Denisovich in this way is, again, lack of direct indications of a link between Ivan's actions and the alleged ideological motivations behind them. No single proclamation of Soviet values comes from the mouths of Solzhenitsyn's alleged "heroes of socialist labor." In fact, Ermilov and Ilyichev attribute to Shukhov attitudes represented by Admiral Dushenov in Shelest's *Kolyma Notes* or by characters in Solzhenitsyn's other works (already written but not published): a naive novice Nemov in his early play *The Love-Girl and the Innocent* (Olen' i shalashovka) and, to some extent, the Communist prisoner Rubin in *The First Circle*. Yet Ivan Denisovich is neither a novice in the camp nor an ideologue who experiences the camp through the filter of ready-made ideas and values. His attitudes and motivations in the camp are evidence of a long-standing dynamic confrontation between a human independent self, a human being as a free ethical entity, and the institution established in order to destroy this independent entity. If Ivan Denisovich is, in fact, an exemplary Soviet man—excited about his tasks as a slave of the regime whose alleged goal he does not even understand—then Solzhenitsyn's work is about totalitarian victory—the creation of the *Lagermensch* whose needs and motivations are describable entirely in terms of his prison occupations.

In the scene of the conversation with Alyosha, there is a moment when Shukhov falls silent. This is the moment when the fundamental problem of Shukhov's response to his experience is spelled out: "Shukhov looked up at the ceiling and said nothing. He didn't know any longer himself whether he wanted freedom or not" (p. 199). Without confronting the issue of the human capacity to be free even under the impact of totalitarian dehumanization, we cannot address the puzzle of Ivan Denisovich.

Master of Freedom or Perfect Slave?

The key ethical issue of *One Day in the Life of Ivan Denisovich,* effectively buried in the Soviet debate following its publication, must now be dug out from under the layers of Soviet rhetoric. A circle has been drawn around the central question of Solzhenitsyn's work—who won the seminal confrontation between man and the dehumanizing system?—without giving a satisfactory answer. What the Soviet debate proved instead was the power of the conventions that, addressing as they did the Soviet camp experience in a preconceived way, aimed at making it a means of supporting the Communists' totalitarian claim to a monopoly on the cognitive and ethical terms in which to view reality. The question remained: Who is Ivan Denisovich—an indestructible, unconscious protector of human dignity or an equally unconscious perfect slave?

The issue clearly surpassed the capacities of Soviet public discourse: to provide philosophical terms in which to address the moral challenge of *One Day in the Life of Ivan Denisovich* and, at the same time, to prove the work's "message" fully compatible with the ideological self-image of the Soviet regime was an impossible task. Even when addressed in a context free from the requirements of Soviet public discourse, the ethical vision of *One Day in the Life of Ivan*

Denisovich has remained ambiguous enough to generate interpretations congruous as far as their ethical principles were concerned yet contradictory in their conclusions.

The central puzzle of Ivan Denisovich's response to his dehumanizing experience inspired Western critics—along with their Soviet colleagues—to examine the ambiguous central motif of labor, emphasized especially in the middle scene of Solzhenitsyn's work. Mikhail Heller comments on the theme of work in *One Day in the Life of Ivan Denisovich:*

> Solzhenitsyn turns to the topic of camp labor in *One Day in the Life of Ivan Denisovich.* The entire day, described in the novella, contains many minutes spent in preparation for work, the whole workday, and free minutes after work. The central event is the scene when the enthusiastic prisoners build a wall; it is a true "symphony of labor." Ivan Denisovich, it seems, understands very well that there is no point in working hard while in camp. . . . But Ivan Denisovich works hard. . . . In the scene of the construction of the wall Ivan Denisovich is simply carried away by his work to the point of working more than he was expected to. Ivan Denisovich knows that his work will be used to the advantage of the camp system, the camp administration, including [the sadistic guard] Volkovoy with his lash. But he cannot work badly.[33]

This realization leads Heller to a general interpretation of the character of Ivan Denisovich, which, in fact, presents a reverse image of the interpretation of the Soviet critics who saw in Ivan Denisovich an embodiment of the ideal Soviet man. According to Heller, Shukhov's motivation in the camp is not essentially different from that of the Communist Rubin, a character as honest and innocent as Shukhov, who enthusiastically approaches his tasks in the Soviet confinement. Heller states: "The educated Marxist Rubin consciously helps the oppressors arrest people. Semi-literate Shukhov consciously works so that the sadist Volkovoy, who whips prisoners, may receive bonuses."[34] This leads Heller to a general view: "Ivan Denisovich Shukhov and Lev Rubin are ideal material for slaves. By their lack of resistance and their enthusiasm they make the existence of the concentration camps possible. Their positive features, especially their love for work, turn into negative qualities and indicate the lack of the desire for freedom."[35]

The "lack of the desire for freedom" is understood here by Heller as a total abandonment of freedom—including both external and internal freedom. Thus Shukhov's doubts ("He didn't know any longer himself whether he wanted freedom or not . . . and he didn't really know where he'd be better off: at home or in here") are to be understood as a sign of the atrophy of Shukhov's inner capacity to embrace freedom, not only outside the camp but also inside (that is, an incapacity for self-identification anchored in an inner value system independent from the reality of the camp). On Heller's view, the camp becomes an entire universe for Shukhov, where both his misery and his happiness are rooted. Heller comments: "The ideal slave Ivan Denisovich is happy when he can count on an additional piece of bread and an additional bowl of soup. He pays for them with hard labor beyond his capacity, but his world is limited to this piece of bread and this bowl of soup."[36]

Thus, the narrative principle of the novella—its dependence on Shukhov's limited perspective and narrow linguistic competence—conveys a sense of defeat and helplessness, rather than of unspoken mystery and hope. Shukhov is unable to define his own values in the context of Alyosha's values, because Shukhov does not represent any positive human values in the camp. What he lives by are instincts, some of them—like the creative instinct of a builder—potentially positive, yet, when subjected to the pressures of the camp, they form additional causes of Ivan's enslavement. In order to serve these instincts, Ivan—according to Heller—becomes a perfect slave. Thus, Solzhenitsyn's words that "of all the drama Russia lived through, the fate of Ivan Denisovich was the greatest tragedy," are to be understood as pointing to the Soviet variant of the phenomenon called by Erich Fromm the "escape from freedom." [37] The "escape from freedom" on the part of innocent victims would, then, be "the greatest tragedy" of the totalitarian experience in Russia. In light of this interpretation, totalitarianism proves capable of turning human innocence into a destructive, enslaving tool: there is no neutral ground between a clear acceptance and a total, heroic rejection of the system. Within this interpretive view, freedom is possible only as a result of clearly defined consciousness and unconditional, self-conscious rejection of the totalitarian design.

Heller's interpretation, though consistently argued, was atypical among readings by Western critics. In precisely the same place where Heller saw the ultimate proof of the inner enslavement of Ivan Denisovich, the source of his freedom can be seen. According to Edward Brown, "The leitmotif of *One Day* is survival, not just of the physical person but of his respect for himself." [38] The climax of the novella is defined by Brown as "the exquisite pleasure of building a wall straight and true and not wasting any mortar. That climax makes of *One Day* a kind of hymn to productive labor as the quintessentially human activity, a source of satisfaction for itself alone even when performed in an evil cause." [39]

Within this interpretive context, Brown sees Ivan's enthusiasm for labor as a source of self-respect that, in turn, protects his inner self from defeat in the face of totalitarian degradation. "A most important human quality does survive in Ivan, as we have seen: love of labor and the pride of a good workman. At the high point of this work on the wall he felt himself for a moment to be independent, inner-directed, fully human and almost free." [40]

The kind of freedom referred to in this interpretation is freedom based not on conscious, consequential *rejection* of the totalitarian universe of the camp with its rules, requirements, and assumptions (as Heller suggested); it is freedom derived from the capacity to *transcend* the universe of the camp without necessarily rebelling against it. At work, Ivan enters a new context of self-identification: it is no longer his masters and him (as a subject) but the builder (master) and his material. All outside circumstances of this new context become of secondary importance to him: they are almost irrelevant to the fundamental relationship between human being (creator) and material (creation). These outside circumstances become, in fact, so unimportant that Ivan *feels free* to violate the primary rules of the physical law of survival in the camp that compels everyone to economize on energy. He forgets about the danger of being late for roll call. Finally, he removes himself from the context of the purpose of the construction at which he works. What he immerses himself in is the process—the creative act performed for its own sake and for the sake of the inner freedom it reinforces.

Edward Ericson commented as follows on the issue of the individual's ethical survival under the pressure of the camp experience in *One Day in the Life of Ivan Denisovich:*

> However much the grim environment and the need to adapt somehow to it may reduce the basic humanity of the zeks, such pressures can never eradicate the human

essence. To be sure, Shukhov is constantly and instinctively concerned with self-preservation. . . . But there is more . . . there is satisfaction in work. Ivan works poorly only when given meaningless tasks. Laying bricks well pleases him, even in prison. Constructive work brings out in him the ennobling quality of self-validation through creative effort.[41]

Thus the central and defining activity of the slave—his exploited labor—becomes a means of internally transcending the external enslavement. It becomes a realm of free actions. With no material purpose to gain in the camp, Ivan excels in construction work in order to meet his own independent inner standards, which he preserves because they reconnect him with sources of self-respect that he cannot even verbalize.[42] Ericson writes: "By definition, a process of dehumanization which is not totally successful is a failure: some humanity remains. 'There is nothing you can do to a man . . .'—except that you cannot do away with his humanity altogether."[43]

On this interpretation, Ivan comes out as the winner in his confrontation with totalitarianism. *One Day in the Life of Ivan Denisovich* becomes a testimony to the human capacity to overcome the totalitarian design. In *The Origins of Totalitarianism,* Hannah Arendt defined the fundamental confrontation represented in the totalitarian experience: "It is as though mankind had divided itself between those who believe in human omnipotence (who think that everything is possible if one knows how to organize masses for it) and those for whom powerlessness has become the major experience of their lives."[44] The inner capacity of the powerless to manage not to be transformed into material to be molded by "those who believe in human omnipotence" (by means of organization) is the main issue of Solzhenitsyn's testimony. Terrence Des Pres saw in Ivan Denisovich a testimony opposite to that proposed by Heller. He wrote:

> A powerless man may still refuse to accept his place as a victim; he may reject the benefits of abdication and, powerless, choose not to compromise—and by the fact that he exists become a reproach to the system, a sliver in the throat of power. Given the gigantic forces he confronts, his act will be painful and on a very small scale, but thereby he becomes, in his own body and person, the indispensable and life-giving proof that the human spirit will not be broken. He acts to keep faith in himself, but like the saint his example is invested with a power that moves other men to thought and inspiration. Shukhov, the simple-hearted hero of *One Day in the Life of Ivan Denisovich,* is this kind of man: "even eight years as a convict hadn't turned him into a jackal—and the longer he spent at the camp the stronger he made himself." [45]

A Genie Let Out of the Bottle

Whichever interpretation—that formulated by Heller or the one argued by Brown, Des Pres, and many others—achieves the more convincing understanding of Solzhenitsyn's 1962 testimony to the totalitarian drama is bound to remain an open question. The dialogical mode of response implied by the text projects necessary confrontations between the reader and the text and between reader and reader. This implied dialog proved to be a challenge too radical to face within the original context of the novella—that of the Soviet communicative universe. Designed as a strictly monological, authoritarian communicative universe, the Soviet system was put to the test by Solzhenitsyn's text and proved to be incapable of tolerating an open, self-examining dialog. *One Day in the Life of Ivan Denisovich* was allowed to enter the Soviet public discourse on the assumption that it would provide a new strategy for reconciling the claim to moral legitimacy by the Communist regime with the crimes committed by this regime. In other words, it was to perform in the political circumstances of the 1960s a task like that of "Solovki" and *Belomorkanal* in the 1930s. As "Ivan's foes" correctly recognized, Solzhenitsyn's work was taken for what it was not: instead of answering troubling moral questions in ethical terms supportive of the regime, it raised questions and left readers without any clear-cut answers. Moreover, the ethical paradigms within which the answers were to be sought could no longer be reduced to the ethical terms of Soviet public discourse. Ivan Denisovich and Alyosha, in that singular moment of open dialog in which they search for terms capable of making sense of their camp experience, talk about God, freedom, and hope and do not mention any of the ideological arguments so popular among the Communist prisoners of Shelest, Dyakov, Aldan-Semenov, and other official Soviet testimonies to the Stalinist past. In Solzhenitsyn's work, the dramatic opposition between those who believe in human omnipotence and those for whom "powerlessness has become the major experience of their lives" is a source of moral anxiety that cannot be resolved other than by resolving the conflict itself. Throughout its history the Soviet regime has implied only one way of resolving this opposition: by obtaining the acceptance (forced or voluntary) of human powerlessness by many, so that the grand design of omnipotence championed by a few can be implemented and tested again and again. There is nothing in *One Day in the Life of Ivan Denisovich* that would signify the continuation of this line. The alternative resolution of the opposition cannot but come to mind: the powerlessness of many can be abolished only through the abolition of the claim to omnipotence on the part of the few. And for the Soviet system—entirely based on the unexamined claim of omnipotence exercised by a few at the expense (and nominally on behalf) of others—to mention the ethical basis of Communist power without first ritually acknowledging its legitimacy would mean to expose its moral vacuousness. For only within Soviet discourse itself, isolated from reality, could the basis for Communist ethical legitimacy be found at this point. Thus testimony about Soviet camps, which lacked any direct indication of the moral superiority of the regime, was by its nature subversive to the regime.

The editors of *Literaturnaia Gazeta* had a clear understanding of this point, which they spelled out in the issue of 19 October 1963:

> A keen ideological battle is going on in the modern world. And we must not for a single moment lower our ideological and ethical standards in our assessment of literary works. It is because we respect a writer's talent that we cannot make allowances for his artistic mistakes. Soviet art knows no limitations in the choice of subject matter. All aspects of life are open to it, including the negative ones. But a socialist-realist artist handles themes from the standpoint of the communist view of the world. . . . A great danger lies in attempts to automatically adapt traditions of critical realism to the socialist reality. Soviet writers follow not formal traditions but the logic of life itself. They follow the path of a deep understanding of reality in order to emphasize the great accomplishments of the people, in the name of Communist ideals.[46]

The experiment by the Soviet regime of allowing Solzhenitsyn's work to appear in Soviet public discourse disappointed the hopes of this regime that *One Day in the Life of Ivan Denisovich* would provide a literary illustration of the principal thesis of the Khrushchevian thaw: that the existence of the horrors of the Soviet camps was a temporary anomaly in an otherwise glorious social system. "Perhaps never has the political appropriation of a work of art by state authorities backfired so dramatically and totally as in the case of *One Day*," Edward E. Ericson wrote. "Once having been catapulted into the limelight of world attention, Solzhenitsyn would not be silent. Now he had a platform, and his sense of duty urged him on. Khrushchev had let out of the bottle a genie which his successors could not put back in." [47]

It did not take Khrushchev long to realize the mistake he had made when he decided to push for the publication of *One Day in the Life of Ivan Denisovich* on Tvardovsky's request in November 1962. In his speech to the "workers in literature and art," on 8 March 1963, while still trying to "domesticate" Solzhenitsyn by ascribing to him "ideologically favorable" intentions, he spoke in a warning tone about the reappearance of the camp experience in recent Soviet literature:

> In their creative work in recent years, writers and artists have been paying great attention to that chapter in the life of Soviet society which is bound up with the Stalin personality cult. All this is quite logical and there is every reason for it. Works in which Soviet reality during those years is truthfully reflected from party positions have appeared. One could give as illustrations, among other works, Alexander Tvardovsky's *Distant Horizons,* Alexander Solzhenitsyn's *One Day in the Life of Ivan Denisovich,* some of Yevgeny Yevtushenko's poems, and Grigory Chukhrai's picture *Clear Skies.* . . . But having said this, we deem it necessary to call the attention of all creative workers to some false tendencies

visible in the works of some authors. These false tendencies are expressed by the fact that all the attention in these works is focused on instances of lawlessness, despotism, and abuse of power. . . . Those writers are wrong who one-sidedly evaluate that period in the life of our country, and who attempt to describe almost everything in dark colors. There still exist writers who like to search for subject matter on garbage heaps, and want to think that their works shed true light on the life of our nation.[48]

All in all, the theme itself appeared clearly dangerous for the Soviet regime, and the Secretary-General did not fail, finally, to notice this. "Take my word for it," said Khrushchev, "this is a very dangerous theme. It's the kind of 'stew' that'll attract flies like a carcass, enormous, fat flies, all sorts of bourgeois scum from abroad will come crawling all over it."[49] This time, Khrushchev was right on the mark. Solzhenitsyn's "discovery" of the Soviet camp experience could not be hidden from public eyes. The further proliferation of literary testimony on this subject had to be taken under stricter control. Immediately after Khrushchev's speech, rigid control was imposed on all publications dealing with this issue. At the same time, works presenting the camp experience through the filter of official Soviet ideology were introduced. Works by Dyakov, Aldan-Semenov, and Pilyar appeared in 1963 and 1964 with their "constructive" Soviet Communist messages, but nobody really treated them as a full-fledged remedy for Solzhenitsyn's ambiguities. Then the theme itself vanished quietly from a central position within Soviet public discourse. By the end of the 1960s, Russian writers and critics had stopped referring publicly to Solzhenitsyn's work, except for officially orchestrated attacks on the writer. Once again, the verbal universe created and promoted by the Soviet regime in order to shape people's perceptions of their historic experience was being saved by the only method the Soviet regime could rely on: the taboo.

After Solzhenitsyn, no one managed to create a new literary convention whereby the Soviet regime's ethical self-image would be, once again, reconciled with the creation by this regime of one of the largest, most long-lasting systems of mass oppression in history. The only way the Soviet regime managed to respond to the silent ethical challenge posed by Solzhenitsyn—the question of the Russian version of the historic confrontation between those who believed in human omnipotence achieved through mass organization and those for whom powerlessness became the defining factor of their fates—was embarrassing silence. This silence was a sign of ethical defeat and an indirect acknowledgment of the intellectual impotence of totalitarian tyranny in the lengthy period of its decline, just then beginning.

One of many lessons that may be learned from the story of the official Soviet camp literature and the roles it played in the Bolshevik experiment in totalitarian authorship is in fact a reminder about the double-edged nature of literature. Literature was expected to contribute to the task of producing a tightly woven fabric of official discourse enveloping the most emblematic experience of Soviet totalitarianism—the horror of the camps. Once again, however, literature revealed its double-edged nature. In *The Odyssey* Penelope, pressured by her suitors, spent her days weaving a burial shroud for Odysseus. The living memory of her allegedly dead husband was to be buried when the shroud was finally completed. But every night Penelope would unravel her day's work. Of course, it is not the Soviet camp literature produced in daylight that will bear the testimony of the great experiment conducted in the twentieth century in the Soviet camps. If these experiences are still remembered and reflected upon in the future, it will be thanks to works of writers consigned to the darkness of oblivion in their own time: Solzhenitsyn, Ivan Solonevich, Eugenia Ginzburg, Varlam Shalamov, Gustaw Herling-Grudzinski, and others. But this is already another subject. . . .

NOTES

Note on Russian names: When referring to original Russian texts in the notes, the names of their authors are transliterated from the Cyrillic alphabet (e.g., Gor'kii, Erenburg, Geller, D'iakov). Otherwise they are spelled in conventional English forms, sometimes chosen by the authors themselves (e.g. Gorky, Ehrenburg, Heller, Dyakov).

Chapter 1:
FICTION AND FEAR

1. Astolphe, Marquis de Custine, *Letters from Russia,* trans. by Robin Buss (New York: Penguin, 1991), p. 230. For a discussion of intellectual and artistic sources motivating de Custine's view of Russia see Irena Grudzinska-Gross, *The Scar of Revolution: Custine, Tocqueville and the Romantic Imagination* (Berkeley: University of California Press, 1991).

2. Aleksander Wat, *My Century: The Odyssey of a Polish Intellectual,* trans. by Richard Lourie, foreword by Czeslaw Milosz (Berkeley: University of California Press, 1988), pp. 173–174. Wat's statement that "the natural function of language is to ascertain the truth, or truths," leaves, of course, much room for discussion. To avoid philosophical pitfalls, one may read Wat's words in a comparative context of social discourses. As Tomas Venclova explains, Wat's assumption is that "any civilization, including that of pre-revolutionary Russia, assumes a degree

of mutual interdependence between the universe of words and the universe of things, so guaranteeing a modicum of objectivity of meaning. Hence, semantic arbitrariness is unacceptable. In the paradoxical world of Stalinism, however, the opposite obtained. Here, semantic values were elastic, changeable, and amenable to control, in accordance [with the will of the ruler]." (Tomas Venclova, *Aleksander Wat: Life and Art of an Iconoclast,* [New Haven: Yale University Press, 1996], p. 260.)

3. For instance, the documentary *Moskva-Volgostroi* (1934).

4. See A. Iu. Gorcheva, *Pressa Gulaga (1918–1955)* (Moscow: Izdatel'stvo Moskovskogo Universiteta, 1996), p. 45. The requirement that prisoners actively participate in the creation of the official fiction and behave according to it was an inherent element of the Stalinist investigation procedures. Prisoners arrested on trumped-up charges were coerced into admitting guilt: i.e., into identifying themselves with the fictitious roles ascribed to them by their interrogators. The thought reform system deployed in Chinese labor camps (*laogaidui*) shows striking similarities to the Soviet one, though it assumes far more systematic forms. In the Chinese system, the prisoner passes through three formal stages of thought reform: (1) acknowledging the crime (*jiaodai zuixing*) regardless of whether the crime has, in fact, been committed; (2) self-criticism (*pipan renshi*), which includes public confession and analysis of one's responsibility; (3) submitting to authority (*fuguan fujiao*), which includes composing a written plan for self-reform through hard labor in the camp and behaving according to this scenario until the authorities decide that the reeducation is complete (Hongda Harry Wu, *Laogai—The Chinese Gulag,* trans. Ted Slingerland [Oxford: Westview, 1992], pp. 27–33).

5. For the sake of clarity as to the nature of Bolshevik totalitarianism, it is essential to differentiate between what was attempted and what was ultimately accomplished (and to what degree). The fact that the minds of the great majority of

the Soviet population were not, in fact, completely reprogrammed and controlled in ways desired by the regime only argues the obvious: the totalitarian experiment proved to be unsuccessful. But this negative result does not alter the fact that the very process of experimentation and the methods it used determined the fates of millions of people.

6. See Mikhail Bakhtin, *The Dialogic Imagination: Four Essays by M. M. Bakhtin,* trans. Caryl Emerson and Michael Holquist (Austin: University of Texas Press, 1981).

7. Hannah Arendt, *The Origins of Totalitarianism* (New York: Harcourt, Brace & World, 1966), p. 437. Regarding the relationship between the totalitarian system inside and outside the camp, Venclova has commented: "Gulag presents itself rather not as microcosm having its own laws, but as the centre toward which the macrocosm is gravitating. The laws of the macrocosm are expressed there most clearly" (Tomas Venclova, "Prison as Communicative Phenomenon: The Literature of Gulag," *Comparative Civilizations Review* 2 [1979], pp. 66–67).

8. Wat, *My Century,* p. 175.

9. See Arendt, *Origins of Totalitarianism,* and Carl J. Friedrich (ed.), *Totalitarianism: Proceedings of a Conference Held at the American Academy of Arts and Sciences (March 1953)* (Cambridge, Mass.: Harvard University Press, 1954). Before the term "totalitarianism" was introduced on a regular basis in Western scholarship, it was used in many and various contexts. Mussolini referred to his own regime as "totalitarian," and Goebbels referred to the Nazi regime in the same manner. In the 1934 *Encyclopedia of the Social Sciences* the term was applied to single-party states, including the Soviet Union. Otto Bauer defined the Soviet Union as a "totalitarian dictatorship" in 1936 (see Henri Weber, "La Théorie du stalinisme dans l'oeuvre de Kautsky," in Evelyne Pisier (ed.), *Les Interpretations du stalinisme* [Paris: Presses Universitaires de France, 1983], p. 63). On the history of the concept of "totalitarianism" see Leonard Schapiro, *Totalitarianism* (London: Pall Mall, 1932); Karl Dietrich

Bracher, "The Disputed Concept of Totalitarianism: Experience and Actuality," in Ernest A. Kenze (ed.), *Totalitarianism Reconsidered* (London: Kennikat Press, 1981); François Furet, *La Passé d'une illusion: essai sur l'idée communiste au XXe siècle* (Paris: Laffont et Lévy, 1995), esp. ch. 6 on Communism and Fascism; and Andrzej Walicki, *Marxism and the Leap to the Kingdom of Freedom: The Rise and Fall of the Communist Utopia* (Stanford, Calif.: Stanford University Press, 1995). On intellectual sources of the Soviet totalitarian project see also Alain Besançon, *The Rise of the Gulag: Intellectual Origins of Leninism,* trans. Sarah Matthews (New York: Continuum, 1981).

10. Walicki, *Marxism and the Leap to the Kingdom of Freedom,* p. 402. In his argument, Walicki quotes from Leszek Kolakowski, "The Devil in History," in G. R. Urban (ed.), *Stalinism: Its Impact on Russia and on the World* (Cambridge, Mass.: Harvard University Press, 1987), p. 251.

11. Herbert J. Spiro, "Totalitarianism," in David L. Sills (ed.), *International Encyclopedia of the Social Sciences* (New York: Macmillan and The Free Press, 1968), vol. 16, p. 108.

12. Arendt, *Origins of Totalitarianism,* p. 438.

13. Alfred G. Meyer, "Marxism," in Sills (ed.), *International Encyclopedia of the Social Sciences,* vol. 10, p. 43.

14. Andrei Sinyavsky, *Soviet Civilization: A Cultural History,* trans. Joanne Turnbull (New York: Little, Brown and Co., 1990), pp. 31–32.

15. Merle Fainsod, "Communism (Soviet Communism)," in Sills (ed.), *International Encyclopedia of the Social Sciences,* vol. 3, p. 107.

16. *Iz istorii Vserossiiskoi Chrezvychainoi Komissii (1917–1921): Sbornik dokumentov* (Moscow, 1958), pp. 182–183.

17. Fedor Stepun, *Byvshee i nesbyvsheesia* (London: Overseas Publications Interchange, 1990), vol. 2, p. 221. See also Jozef Smaga, *Narodziny i upadek imperium: ZSSR 1917–1991* (Cracow: Znak, 1992), p. 31.

18. Cited in Sinyavsky, *Soviet Civilization,* pp. 66–67.

19. Ibid., p. 67.

20. Albert Rhys Williams, *Lenin: The Man and His Work by Albert Rhys Williams, and the Impressions of Col. Raymond Robins and Arthur Ransome* (New York: Scott and Seltzer, 1919); quoted from Mikhail Geller, *Kontsentratsionnyi mir i sovetskaia literatura* (London: Overseas Publications Interchange, 1974), p. 25. See also Robert Payne, *The Life and Death of Lenin* (New York: Simon and Schuster, 1964), p. 408.

21. Vladimir I. Lenin, *Kommunist,* no. 14 (1962), pp. 6–7, 13. See also Geller, *Kontsentratsionnyi mir i sovetskaia literatura,* p. 29.

22. Views that the NEP would have continued, had it not been for Lenin's death in 1924 and the establishment of Stalin's planned economy, are based on misconceptions. In fact, by March 1922, Lenin was calling for the abandonment of the NEP for the sake of centralized methods of controlling the economy: "We have been retreating for a year. Now we must say: Stop! The goals of our retreat have been reached" (quoted in Smaga, *Narodziny i upadek imperium,* pp. 53–54). See also R. Kosolapov, "Poslednii rabochii god Lenina," *Politicheskoe obrazovanie,* no. 17 (1989).

23. Stenographic record of a speech by Felix Dzerzhinsky at the eighth session of the All Russian Central Executive Committee, 17 February 1919. First published in *Istoricheskii arkhiv,* no. 1 (1958), pp. 6–11 (quoted in Geller, *Kontsentratsionnyi mir i sovetskaia literatura,* p. 52). In June 1929 Stalin used Dzerzhinsky's idea in his instruction, "Materials on the Usage of the Labor of the Criminal Prisoners" (*Materiialy ob ispol'zovanii truda ugolovno-zakliuchennykh*). In this instruction Stalin orders that all persons sentenced to more than three years of prison should be sent to concentration camps and put to work. New camps are to be built to accommodate this new influx of convicts. Prisoners' labor is to be used in developing remote areas and exploiting their natural resources (*Tsentral'nyi Gosudarstvennyi Arkhiv Rossiiskoi Federatsii,* F. 393 Op. 1, Eg. khr. 285, L. 31).

24. *Ocherki po istoriografii sovetskogo obshchestva* (Moscow, 1934), p. 252.

25. Geller, *Kontsentratsionnyi mir i sovetskaia literatura*, p. 30.

26. Vladimir I. Lenin, *Polnoe sobranie sochinenii* (Moscow, 1958–1965), vol. 36, p. 364.

27. Ibid., vol. 38, pp. 197–198; see also Geller, *Kontsentratsionnyi mir i sovetskaia literatura*, p. 31.

28. Sinyavsky, *Soviet Civilization*, p. 87.

29. In 1922, Lenin asked Kursky, the People's Commissar of Justice, to "find a formula which establishes a connection" between the prosecution's allegations and "the international bourgeoisie." "Propaganda or agitation *objectively* promoting the international bourgeoisie" should be, according to Lenin, punishable by death (as cited in Sinyavsky, *Soviet Civilization*, pp. 88–89).

30. Ibid., p. 88.

31. Spiro, "Totalitarianism," p. 110. See also Zbigniew Brzezinski, *The Permanent Purge: Politics in Soviet Totalitarianism* (Cambridge, Mass.: Harvard University Press, 1956).

32. Arendt, *Origins of Totalitarianism*, p. 352.

33. Wat, *My Century*, p. 174.

34. Arendt, *Origins of Totalitarianism*, p. 353.

35. Spiro, "Totalitarianism," p. 110.

36. N. Dmitieva, "Das Problem des Typischen in der bildenen Kunst," *Kunst und Literatur*, no. 1 (1953); cited from Boris Groys, *The Total Art of Stalinism: Avant-Garde, Aesthetic Dictatorship, and Beyond*, trans. Charles Rougle (Princeton, N.J.: Princeton University Press, 1992), p. 51.

37. A singular psychological insight into the connection between Jesuit and revolutionary ethics is offered in the character of Naphta in Thomas Mann's *The Magic Mountain*.

38. Cited from Sinyavsky, *Soviet Civilization*, p. 120. On the specific matter of the use of violence, Lenin stated: "We, of course, are not opposed to violence. We laugh at those who are opposed to the dictatorship of the proletariat, we laugh and say that they are fools who do not understand that there must be either the dictatorship of the proletariat or the dictatorship of the bourgeoisie. Those who think otherwise

are either idiots, or are so politically ignorant that it would be a disgrace to allow them to come anywhere near the meeting, let alone on the platform. The only alternative is either violence against Liebknecht and Luxemburg, the murder of the best leaders of the workers, or the violent suppression of the exploiters; and whoever dreams of the middle course is our most harmful and dangerous enemy" (Vladimir I. Lenin, *Collected Works* [Moscow, 1960–1970], vol. 29, pp. 71–72).

39. Yury Olesha, *Envy,* trans. T. S. Berczynski (Ann Arbor, Mich.: Ardis, 1975), p. 82.

40. Margerita Aliger, "Pechal'naia pritcha," *Znamia,* no. 10 (1987), p. 103.

41. This apparent inner consistency among cognitive, moral, and aesthetic criteria offered by the Bolshevik ideology may be seen as structurally corresponding (though in a perverted, manipulative way) to a similar pattern central to the nineteenth-century Russian literary tradition. This issue is illuminated by Alexis Klimoff's remarks on the nineteenth-century Russian literary tradition, which lead him to the following conclusion: "One can speak of a distinct set of assumptions about the nature and function of literature that was shared by the leading masters of Russian prose in the 'Golden Age' of the Russian novel (approximately 1840 to 1880). These attitudes toward literature are internally consistent and reflect the fact that Russian culture has resisted Kant's argument about the discontinuity between cognitive, moral, and esthetic spheres of intellectual endeavor. In their entire approach to their task as writers, the great Russian novelists were guided by the contrary supposition: that these three realms are linked in an intimate and indissoluble way" (Alexis Klimoff, "In Defense of the Word," in Lydia Chukovskaya, *The Deserted House,* trans. Aline B. Werth [Belmont, Mass.: Norland, 1978], p. x.) The Bolshevik model may be seen as a peculiar perversion of this unity.

42. Edward Shils, "Ideology (The Concept and Functions of Ideology)," in Sills (ed.), *International Encyclopedia of the Social*

Sciences, vol. 7, p. 69. See also Raymond Aron, *The Opium of the Intellectuals* (New York: Doubleday, 1957).

43. Geller, *Kontsentratsionnyi mir i sovetskaia literatura*, p. 30.

44. Alfred G. Meyer has commented on this point: "Although the ideology becomes primarily rationalization after the communist seizure of power, it does remain the language of politics, meaning not only a code of communications for the political elite but also the conceptual frame of reference used for cognitive and ethical self-orientation. It thus determines both analysis and action, if only negatively, that is, as ideological blinders. . . . Primarily, perhaps, the ideology functions as a legitimation device, implying not only an exercise in public relations to attain legitimacy among the citizens but, even more important, a continual attempt by the party leaders to convince themselves of their own legitimacy; more generally, it functions as an ideological exoskeleton for insecure bureaucrats in a vast and powerful administrative machine" (Meyer, "Marxism," p. 44).

45. B. Joganson, "O merakh uluchsheniia uchebno-metodicheskoi raboty v uchebnykh zavedeniiakh Akademii khudozhestv SSSR," in *Sessii Akademii khudozhestv SSSR (1,2)*, (Moscow, 1949), pp. 101–103; cited from Boris Groys, *The Total Art of Stalinism*, p. 54).

46. Cited from Groys, *Total Art of Stalinism*, p. 51.

47. Ibid., pp. 51–53.

48. Shils, "Ideology (The Concept and Functions of Ideology)," p. 68.

49. Konstantin Fedin, *Cities and Years*, trans. Michael Scammell (Westport, Conn.: Greenwood Press, 1962), p. 284; as cited in Jurij Striedter, "Journeys Through Utopia: Introductory Remarks to the Post-Revolutionary Russian Utopian Novel," *Poetics Today*, no. 1 (1982), p. 33.

50. Striedter, "Journeys Through Utopia," p. 34.

51. Ibid., p. 41.

52. Ibid.

53. This admission of the pluralistic and dialogic nature of the

human world does not represent a relativist point of view. Mikhail Bakhtin explained that the notion of the dialogic universe "has nothing in common with relativism (or with dogmatism). But it should be noted that both relativism and dogmatism equally exclude all argumentation, all authentic dialogue, by making it either unnecessary (relativism) or impossible (dogmatism)" (Mikhail Bakhtin, *Problems of Dostoevsky's Poetics*, trans. Caryl Emerson [Minneapolis: University of Minnesota Press, 1984], p. 69). See also Gary Saul Morson, "Prosaics Evolving," *Slavic and East European Journal*, vol. 41, no. 1 (Spring 1997), pp. 57–73.

54. Gary Saul Morson, *The Boundaries of Genre: Dostoevsky's "Diary of a Writer" and the Traditions of Literary Utopia* (Austin: University of Texas Press, 1981), p. 77. See also Mikhail Bakhtin, "Discourse in the Novel," in Bakhtin, *Dialogic Imagination.*

55. Striedter, "Journeys Through Utopia," p. 37.

56. Aleksandr Blok, "Krushenie gumanizma," *Znamia*, nos. 7–8 (1921) (the essay was written in March and April 1919); quoted from Aleksandr Blok, "The Collapse of Humanism", trans. John Malmstad (Cambridge, Mass.: Harvard University Core Curriculum ["Revolution and Reaction: The Rise and Fall of the Russian Avant-Garde," Course Workbook, 1992]), pp. 169, 170, 174, 176, 177.

57. Striedter, "Journeys Through Utopia," p. 33.

58. Arendt, *Origins of Totalitarianism,* p. 352.

59. Morson, *Boundaries of Genre,* p. 77.

60. Ibid., p. 96. Morson points to the connection between the magical functions of a literary utopia and those of Soviet journalism, as he refers to Herbert Marcuse, *Soviet Marxism: A Critical Analysis* (New York: Columbia University Press, 1958).

61. Morson, *Boundaries of Genre,* pp. 99, 101. For more discussion of the poetics of literary and non-literary apocalypses Morson refers to Joseph Anthony Wittreich, *Visionary Poetics: Milton's Tradition and His Legacy* (San Marino, Calif.: Huntington Library, 1979), and Frank Kermode, *The Sense of an Ending:*

Studies in the Theory of Fiction (New York: Oxford University Press, 1967). See also David M. Bethea, *The Shape of Apocalypse in Modern Russian Fiction* (Princeton N.J.: Princeton University Press, 1989).

62. Lenin spoke of himself as having been "deeply ploughed over" by Chernyshevsky. See Richard Pipes, "The Origins of Bolshevism: The Intellectual Evolution of Young Lenin," in Richard Pipes (ed.), *Revolutionary Russia* (Cambridge, Mass.: Harvard University Press, 1968), p. 32. Valentinov considers Chernyshevsky to have been the most important influence in the formation of Lenin's political views. See N. Valentinov, "Chernyshevskii i Lenin," *Novyi Zhurnal,* no. 26 (1951), pp. 192–216, and 27 (1951), pp. 225–249.

63. In the context of the present discussion of the dialogical versus authoritarian rhetorical universe, it is useful to note that both radical dogmatism and radical relativism share a common potential to generate a claim to an absolute point of view along with a claim to absolute power. The radical dogmatic rejects dialog and imposes monolog, based on his or her certainty of possessing the only truth. However, radical relativism may also be a source of radical dogmatism of its own kind. The radical relativist rejects dialog because he knows that, since there is no absolute truth, none of his potential partners in a potential dialog can represent the truth. In fact, it is his dogmatic knowledge of the truth (that there is no absolute truth) that sets the radical relativist apart from non-relativists (seen by him as lacking this awareness). The absence of ethical constraints on the part of the radical relativist may become a source of his perception of himself as uniquely suited to accomplishing grand historic tasks requiring such ethically "unconventional" means as massive human sacrifices.

64. Groys, *Total Art of Stalinism,* pp. 3–4.

65. Ibid., pp. 20–21.

66. Igor Golomstock, *Totalitarian Art in the Soviet Union, the Third*

Reich, Fascist Italy and the People's Republic of China, trans. Robert Chandler (New York: Icon Editions, Harper Collins, 1990), p. 21.

67. Sinyavsky, *Soviet Civilization*, p. 120.
68. Johann Gottfried Herder, *Ideen zur Philosophie der Geschichte der Menschheit* (1791); see part 4, ch. 4. The motif of Russia's destiny as a puzzle was emphasized by Adam Mickiewicz in his 1832 *Dziady (Forefathers' Eve) Part III*, the work that served Pushkin as a polemical point of reference to *The Bronze Horseman*. Here is a fragment of Mickiewicz's description of Russia (Adam Mickiewicz, *Dziela poetyckie* [Warsaw, 1953], vol. 3, pp. 266–268; English translation by Marjorie Beatrice Peacock in Adam Mickiewicz, *Poems*, ed. George Rapall Noyes [New York: The Polish Institute of Arts and Sciences, 1944], pp. 338–339):

This level plain lies open, waste, and white,
A wide-spread page prepared for God to write.—
Will he trace here his message from above;
And, using for his letters holy men,
Will he sketch here his writ of faith again,
That all the human race is ruled by love
And offerings remain the world's best prize?
Or will that fiend who still the Lord defies
Appear and carve with his oft-sharpened sword
That prisons should forbid mankind to rise,
And scourges are humanity's reward?
. . . .
I meet the men who dwell within this land,
. . . .
But every face is like their home, a plain,
A waste on which no inward light shines forth.
. . . .
Each body is a web, a coarse-spun roll,
In which there sleeps a caterpillar's soul,

Ere it transforms its tiny breast for flight
And weaves and tints its wings to fairy guise.
But when the sun of liberty shall rise,
What kind of insect then will greet the light?
Will a bright butterfly soar from the earth,
Or a dull moth, of dark, uncleanly birth?

69. Aleksandr Pushkin, "The Bronze Horseman," in *Pushkin Threefold: Narrative, Lyric, Polemic, and Ribald Verse,* trans. Walter Arndt (Ann Arbor, Mich.: Ardis, 1972), p. 142.
70. Nikolai Gogol, *Dead Souls,* trans. David Magarshack (New York: Penguin Classics, 1961), pp. 258–259.
71. "The Bronze Horseman," p. 43.

Chapter 2:
FROM TRAGEDY TO FESTIVAL

1. Vasily Grossman, *Forever Flowing,* trans. Thomas P. Whitney (New York: Harper & Row, 1972), p. 199.
2. Isaiah Berlin, "Russian Populism," in Isaiah Berlin, *Russian Thinkers* (New York: Penguin Books, 1986), p. 231. See also Anna Geifman, *Thou Shalt Kill: Revolutionary Terrorism in Russia, 1894–1917* (Princeton, N.J.: Princeton University Press, 1993).
3. On the role played by Russian Populist ideology in the formation of Lenin's political views, see Richard Pipes, "The Origins of Bolshevism: The Intellectual Evolution of Young Lenin," in Richard Pipes (ed.), *Revolutionary Russia* (Cambridge, Mass.: Harvard University Press, 1968), pp. 27–52.
4. Viktor Ropshin, *To, chego ne bylo* (Moscow, 1916). The English quotation is from Andrei Sinyavsky, *Soviet Civilization: A Cultural History,* trans. Joanne Turnbull (New York: Little, Brown and Co., 1990), p. 121.
5. Aleksandr Tarasov-Rodionov, *Shokolad,* 1st edn in *Molodaia gvardiia* 7–8 (1922), later published as a book in 1925 and

1927 and republished in the collective volume, *Opal'nye povesti*, ed. Vera Aleksandrova (New York: Izdatel'stvo im. Chekhova, 1955). Il'ia Erenburg, *Zhizn' i gibel' Nikolaia Kurbova*, 1st edn in *Novaia Moskva* (1923); later published in 1923 (Berlin: Gelikon) and in vol. 6 of Ehrenburg's collected works from 1925.

6. Tarasov-Rodionov, "Shokolad," in Aleksandrova (ed.), *Opal'nye povesti*, p. 375. All quotations from *Chocolate* are from this edition.

7. Ibid., p. 360. Tarasov-Rodyonov himself joined the victims of the Soviet terror. He was arrested in Stalin's purges and executed as an "enemy of the people" on 3 September 1938.

8. See Vsevolod Vishnevskii, "Optimisticheskaia tragediia," in Vsevolod Vishnevskii, *Izbrannoe* (Moscow, 1966; first published in 1933).

9. Cited in Sinyavsky, *Soviet Civilization*, p. 124.

10. Cited in ibid., p. 125.

11. Ibid.

12. Vasilii Kniazev, *Krasnoe evangelie* (Petrograd, 1918), pp. 19, 34, 40. Knyazev himself was later pronounced an "enemy of the people" and was executed on 10 November 1937.

13. Ibid., p. 15.

14. Eduard Bagritskii, *Stikhotvoreniia i poemy* (Moscow and Leningrad, 1964), p. 126.

15. Bertold Brecht, *Die Massnahme*; English quotation from Timothy Garton Ash, "Comrade Brecht," in Timothy Garton Ash, *The Uses of Adversity: Essays on the Fate of Central Europe* (New York: Random House, 1990), p. 32.

16. Cited in Tadeusz Klimowicz, *Przewodnik po wspolczesnej literaturze rosyjskiej i jej okolicach (1917–1996)* (Wroclaw: Towarzystwo Przyjaciol Polonistyki Wroclawskiej, 1996), p. 55. Viktor Kin shared the fate of Aleksandr Tarasov-Rodyonov and Vasily Knyazev: he was arrested on 3 November 1937 as an "enemy of the people" and executed probably in December 1937.

17. Yury Olesha, *Envy*, trans. T. S. Berczynski (Ann Arbor, Mich.: Ardis, 1975), p. 82.

18. Il'ia Erenburg, *Zhizn' i gibel' Nikolaia Kurbova* (Berlin: Gelikon, 1923), p. 247. The German term *erlebte Rede* has been translated into English in more than one way. Dorrit Cohn proposes the English phrase "narrated monologue," which she defines as "rendering a character's thought in his own idiom while maintaining the third-person narrative and the basic tense of narration" (Dorrit Cohn, *Transparent Minds: Narrative Modes for Presenting Consciousness in Fiction* [Princeton, N.J.: Princeton University Press, 1978], p. 100). Other English translations of the term include "indirect interior monologue" and "represented discourse." The Russian equivalent of *erlebte Rede* is *nesobstvenno-priamaia rech'* or *kosvenno-priamaia rech'*.

19. Matthew 13: 24–30.

20. On this "zoological" identification of enemies see Marc Shell, *Children of the Earth: Literature, Politics and Nationhood* (New York: Oxford University Press, 1993).

21. Tarasov-Rodionov, "Shokolad," p. 376.

22. See Mikhail Geller, *Kontsentratsionnyi mir i sovetskaia literatura* (London: Overseas Publications Interchange, 1974) p. 103.

23. Grossman, *Forever Flowing*, p. 144.

24. Isaac Babel, *The Collected Stories*, trans. Walter Morison (New York: Criterion Books, 1955), pp. 48–51. *Pan* is the Polish word for a nobleman (sir, gentleman).

25. Edward J. Brown, *Russian Literature since the Revolution* (Cambridge, Mass.: Harvard University Press, 1982), p. 91.

26. Ibid.

27. Vladimir Maiakovskii, *Izbrannye proizvedeniia v dvukh tomakh* (Moscow, 1953), vol. 2, p. 71.

28. Maksimilian Voloshin, *Stikhotvoreniia* (Paris: YMCA Press, 1982), vol. 1, p. 317.

29. Vasilii Kniazev, *Krasnoe evangelie*, pp. 18, 20, 21.

30. In Ash, *Uses of Adversity*, p. 39.

31. Leon Trotsky, *Literature and Revolution* (Ann Arbor, Mich.: University of Michigan Press, 1966), pp. 229–230.

Chapter 3:
THE GLORY OF THE GULAG

1. Leon Trotsky, *Literature and Revolution* (Ann Arbor, Mich.: University of Michigan Press, 1966), pp. 229, 230.

2. Timothy Garton Ash, *The Uses of Adversity: Essays on the Fate of Central Europe* (New York: Random House, 1990), p. 34.

3. Stalin announced at the plenum of the Party's Central Committee on 10–17 November 1929 that "mass voluntary collectivization was already happening" and pushed for its speedy completion. On 27 December 1930 a preliminary schedule for the completion of collectivization was made by the All Union Commissariat of Agriculture. On the same day, Stalin officially announced the aim of "the liquidation of the kulaks as a class." On 5 January 1929 the Central Committee made Stalin's policy official by issuing the decree on the collectivization. See Robert Conquest, *The Harvest of Sorrow: Soviet Collectivization and the Terror-Famine* (New York: Oxford University Press, 1986), pp. 112–117.

4. The process of the gradual monopolization of all artistic and cultural activities in the Soviet Union led to the Central Committee's decree of 23 April 1932, which officially disbanded all artistic and literary groups and demanded that all artists and writers be organized, according to their professions, in party-controlled "creative unions."

5. "Postanovlenie TsK VKP(b) o pervykh itogakh provedeniia samokritiki," *Pravda,* 20 August 1928.

6. Astolphe, Marquis de Custine, *Letters from Russia,* trans. Robin Buss (New York: Penguin, 1991), p. 230.

7. See Anton Makarenko, *Pedagogicheskaia poema* (Moscow, 1933–1936). Makarenko corresponded with Maxim Gorky after 1925. Gorky expressed great interest in Makarenko's experimental work with under-age, usually homeless offenders. Having visited the Maxim Gorky Colony for Minors in Kuryazh near Kharkov, Gorky encouraged Makarenko to write about his work. Makarenko wrote his novel in response to this encouragement, and dedicated it

"with devotion and love to our leader, friend, and teacher Maxim Gorky." At the time of Makarenko's rising status in official Soviet culture, an autobiographical account of inmates' experiences in the Soviet system of juvenile resocialization was published by Leonid Panteleev and Grigory Belykh (*Respublika Shkid* [Moscow, 1927]). This account, widely read in Russia, was strikingly realistic and was far from glorifying the Soviet system of juvenile resocialization. Makarenko heavily criticized Panteleev and Belykh's work.

8. Some of the footage, never shown before, was included in Maina Goldovskaya's documentary film, *Vlast' solovetskaia* (Moscow: Mosfilm, 1989).

9. Aleksandr I. Solzhenitsyn, *The Gulag Archipelago: An Experiment in Literary Investigation,* trans. Thomas P. Whitney (New York: Harper and Row, 1975), vol. 2, pp. 36–38. In order to compare the extent of political oppression practiced in Solovki before and after the revolution, some numbers may be cited. Before the Bolshevik revolution, over the entire history of the Solovki monastery, 316 people were exiled there. Soviet authorities conducted several mass executions in the Solovki camp. Dmitry Likhachev, the prominent Russian philologist and former prisoner of the Solovki camp, reminisced about one of them, in which he was supposed to be shot with others and only by a stroke of luck avoided it. He remembered the number of 300 prisoners shot on this single day. The purpose of this mass execution was purely terrorist: to discourage prisoners from attempting to escape. (See film *Vlast' solovetskaia.*)

10. Before 1923, the abbreviation stood for the Northern Special Purpose Camps (*Severnye lageria osobogo naznacheniia*). The abbreviation USLON, also associated with the Solovki camp, stood for the Administration of the Solovki (or, before 1923, Northern) Special Purpose Camps (*Upravlenie solovetskikh (severnykh) lagerei osobogo naznacheniia.*

11. See Tadeusz Borowski, *This Way for the Gas, Ladies and Gentlemen and Other Stories,* trans. Barbara Veder (New York:

Viking Press, 1967), pp. 83–84; Primo Levi, *Survival in Auschwitz*, trans. Stuart Woolf (New York: Collier Books, 1961). Stanislaw Grzesiuk, in his memoir of the Nazi camps in Dachau, Mauthausen, and Gusen, gives an account of his life in these camps as a member of a camp music band. See Stanislaw Grzesiuk, *Piec lat kacetu* (Warsaw: Ksiazka i Wiedza, 1996).

12. Solzhenitsyn, *Gulag Archipelago*, vol. 2, p. 54.

13. *Solovetskie ostrova*, nos 2–3 (1930) (newspaper edited by prisoners of the Solovki camps); quoted from Solzhenitsyn, *Gulag Archipelago*, vol. 2, p. 55.

14. Maksim Gor'kii, "Po Soiuzu Sovetov," *Nashi dostizheniia*, nos 1–6 (1929). The cycle was included in the 1949–1956 edition of Gorky's collected works (*Sobranie sochinenii*, vol. 17 [Moscow, 1952], pp. 113–233). All subsequent page references to Gorky's cycle "Po Soiuzu Sovetov," including the reportage "Solovki," are to this edition and are included in parentheses in the text.

15. Gor'kii, *Sobranie sochinenii*, vol. 17, p. 482. The letter was first published in *Pravda*, 29 March 1928.

16. See Maxim Gorky, *Untimely Thoughts: Essays on Revolution, Culture and the Bolsheviks, 1917–1918,* trans. Herman Ermolaev (New Haven: Yale University Press, 1995).

17. Vitaly Shentalinsky, *Arrested Voices: Resurrecting the Disappeared Writers of the Soviet Regime,* trans. John Crowfoot (New York: Free Press, 1996), p. 227.

18. Ibid., p. 234.

19. Gustaw Herling-Grudzinski, "Siedem smierci Maksyma Gorkiego," in Gustaw Herling-Grudzinski, *Drugie przyjscie* (Paris: Instytut Literacki, 1963), p. 225.

20. Shentalinsky, *Arrested Voices,* p. 235.

21. Ibid.

22. Ibid., p. 237.

23. Herling-Grudzinski, *Drugie przyjscie,* pp. 228–230.

24. Ibid., p. 222. See Robert Conquest, *The Great Terror: A Reassessment* (London: Hutchinson, 1990). Gorky's return to

the USSR may also be viewed as an attempt to become involved in anti-Stalin factions in the Soviet leadership. Robert Conquest, in *The Great Terror,* emphasized this side of Gorky's activities after his return.

25. Shentalinsky, *Arrested Voices,* pp. 249–250.
26. Gor'kii, *Sobranie sochinenii,* vol. 17, p. 482.
27. De Custine, *Letters from Russia,* p. 237.
28. Quoted in Adam B. Ulam, *Stalin: Man and His Era* (New York: Viking, 1973), p. 359.
29. See Lion Feuchtwanger, *Moscow 1937: My Visit Described for My Friends,* trans. Irene Josephy (New York:Viking, 1937).
30. Quoted in Mikhail Geller and Aleksandr Nekrich, *Utopiia u vlasti: Istoriia Sovetskogo. Soiuza s 1917 goda do nashikh dnei* (London: Overseas Publications Interchange, 1982), vol. 1, p. 271.
31. See Robert Conquest, *Kolyma: The Arctic Death Camps* (New York:Viking, 1978), pp. 205–208. The question of the actual deception of Western political and intellectual visitors versus the desire of many among them to be deceived is bound to remain open in many individual cases. For instance, by 1944 (the time Wallace and Lattimore visited Kolyma) ample evidence of the reality of the Soviet camps was available to Western allies in the form of testimonies by thousands of former Polish prisoners who were released by the Soviets in 1941, according to the Polish–Soviet treaty, and who then served in the Allied Forces in the West. Wallace, before his death, expressed regret at his misunderstanding of the Soviet Union. His fellow-traveler, Owen Lattimore, like many other Western intellectuals (e.g., Jean-Paul Sartre), kept denying and ignoring the evidence of Soviet atrocities. On rare occasions, enthusiastic visitors to the Soviet Union had later, unexpected opportunities to correct their views. For instance, Jerzy Gliksman had a positive impression after being shown "corrective labor establishments" for children and former prostitutes during his visit to the Soviet Union in 1935. Five

years later, he himself became a prisoner in a real Soviet camp. (See Jerzy Gliksman, *Tell the West* [New York: Gresham Press, 1948].) On the subject of Western visitors to the USSR and their ideologically motivated responses to Soviet reality, as well as on the subject of Soviet deception, see Paul Hollander, *Political Pilgrims: Travels of Western Intellectuals to the Soviet Union, China, and Cuba, 1928–1978* (Oxford: Oxford University Press, 1981); Sidney Hook, Vladimir Bukovsky, and Paul Hollander, *Soviet Hypocrisy and Western Gullibility* (Lanham, Md.: Ethics and Public Policy Center, 1987); Richard Nickson, "The Lure of Stalinism: Bernard Shaw and Company," *Midwest Quarterly* 25 (1984); Jan Gondowicz, "Teatr w wiezieniu: Reportaz w miedzywojennej Polsce szuka prawdy o ZSRR," in *Studia Litteraria Polono-Slavica*, vol. 2 (Warsaw: SOW, 1996); and François Furet, *La Passé d'une illusion: Essai sur l'idée communiste au XXe siècle* (Paris: Laffont et Lévy, 1995).

32. Solzhenitsyn, *Gulag Archipelago*, vol. 2, pp. 60–63.
33. Sergei A. Maslagov, *An Island Hell: A Soviet Prison in the Far North* (London: A. M. Philpot, 1926). Other testimonies on Soviet camps published in foreign languages shortly thereafter included W. Lipinski, R. Sliwa, and B. Kusinski (eds), *Za kratami wiezien i drutami obozow: Wspomnienia i notatki wiezniow ideowych z lat 1914–1921 (Antologia)* (Warsaw, 1927–28); Mieczyslaw Lenardowicz, *Na wyspach tortur i smierci: Pamietnik z Solowek* (Warsaw, 1930); and Ivan Solonevich, *Rossiia v kontslagere* (Paris, 1933) (in Russian and German).
34. Gor'kii, *Sobranie sochinenii*, vol. 17, pp. 483–484.
35. Regarding recent questions as to the degree of Stalin's ability to foresee the tragedy resulting from his coercive policy of collectivization, Robert Conquest refers to recently discovered documents that confirm Stalin's full awareness of the situation and his responsibility for the famine. See Robert Conquest, "Terrorists" (review of Richard Pipes [ed.], *The Unknown Lenin* [New Haven: Yale University Press, 1996], and Lars T.

Lih, Oleg V. Naumov, and Oleg V. Khlevniuk [eds], *Stalin's Letters to Molotov: 1925–1936* [New Haven:Yale University Press, 1995]), *New York Review of Books,* 6 March 1997.

36. Dmitry Donskoy was the duke of Moscow, who led the victorious Muscovite forces at the Kulikovo battle. The quotation is from Aleksandr Blok, "Narod i intelligentsiia," in Aleksandr Blok, *Sobranie sochinenii* (Moscow and Leningrad, 1962), vol. 5, p. 323. Gorky was certainly familiar with this essay, for it was commentary on Gorky's writing that constituted Blok's point of departure in this piece.

37. Trotsky, *Literature and Revolution,* p. 9.

38. Mikhail Geller, *Kontsentratsionnyi mir i sovetskaia literatura* (London: Overseas Publications Interchange, 1974), p. 138. See also Jerzy Gliksman, "Social Prophylaxis as a Form of Soviet Terror," in Carl J. Friedrich (ed.), *Totalitarianism: Proceedings of a Conference Held at the American Academy of Arts and Sciences (March 1953)* (Cambridge, Mass.: Harvard University Press, 1954).

39. The "hand of our own" does not exactly reproduce the reassuring meaning of the Russian *svoia ruka.*

40. Trotsky, *Literature and Revolution,* p. 229.

41. Il'ia Erenburg, *Zhizn' i gibel' Nikolaia Kurbova* (Berlin: Gelikon, 1923), p. 247.

42. Matthew 13: 24–30.

43. Gorky, strictly speaking, is not lying here. He seems to be describing a scene that was staged for him. However, his awareness of this staging is beyond doubt. Dmitry Likhachev, a former prisoner of Solovki, recalled a scene from Gorky's visit to Solovki: having entered the camp hospital, where he saw clean sheets and nurses dressed in white, Gorky said, "I don't like parades," and left immediately. (See film *Vlast' solovetskaia*).

44. *Literaturnoe nasledstvo,* no. 70, p. 34. See also Geller, *Kontsentratsionnyi mir i sovetskaia literatura,* p. 131.

45. *Literaturnoe nasledstvo,* no. 70, pp. 33–34.

46. *Belomorsko-Baltiiskii Kanal imeni Stalina: Istoriia stroitel'stva,* pod

redaktsiei Maksima Gor'kogo, Leopol'da Averbakha i Semena
Firina (Moscow: GIZ, 1934).This book was published in
English as *Belomor: An Account of the Construction of the New
Canal between the White Sea and the Baltic Sea,* ed. Maxim
Gorky, L. Auerbach, and S. G. Firin, prepared from the
Russian and edited, with a special introduction by Amabel
Williams-Ellis (New York: Harrison Smith and Robert Haas,
1935), and reprinted by Hyperion Press, Inc.,Westport,
Conn., 1977.The English version is much shorter, omitting
entire chapters and sections of the original (especially those
comparing the Soviet Union and the West).The English
translation of what remained after these cuts was prepared
specifically for a Western audience, and it contains many
alterations of the original. In a few instances where the
English version of the 1935 edition is faithful to the original I
quote from it, and indicate this in the notes. All other
references are to the original Soviet edition and are given in
the text in parentheses. I refer to this book by using its
shortened Russian title, *Belomorkanal.*

47. Solzhenitsyn, *Gulag Archipelago,* vol. 2, p. 103. See also A. Iu.
Gorcheva, *Pressa Gulaga (1918–1955)* (Moscow: Izdatel'stvo
Moskovskogo Universiteta, 1996).

48. The canal never became a major transportation route. It is
frozen for about half the year and, owing to its hasty
construction, is too shallow for major ships.

49. Solzhenitsyn, *Gulag Archipelago,* vol. 2, p. 81.

50. See "Zadushevnoe slovo," *Literaturnaia gazeta,* 29 August 1933,
and M. Charnyi, "Liudi i shliuzy," *Literaturnaia gazeta,* 29
August 1933. See also Greg Carleton, "Genre in Socialist
Realism," *Slavic Review* 53/4 (Winter 1994), p. 993.

51. In alphabetical order: B. Agapov, S. Alymov, L. Averbakh,
A. Berzin, S. Budantsev, S. Bulatov, S. Dikovsky, N. Dmitrev,
A. Erlich, K. Finn, E. Gabrilovich, N. Garnich, G. Gauzner,
S. Gecht, K. Gorbunov, M. Gorky,Vera Inber,Vsevolod Ivanov,
B. Jasienski,V. Kataev, Z. Khatsrevin, G. Korabelnikov,
M. Kozakov, B. Lapin, A. Lebedenko, D. Mirsky, L. Nikulin,

B. Pertsov, Y. Rykachev, V. Shklovsky, L. Slavin, A. Tikhonov,
A. Tolstoy, N. Yurgich, K. Zelinsky, M. Zoshchenko.

52. See *Literaturnaia gazeta*, 29 August, 17 October, 23 October,
23 December 1933.

53. "The Organizing Committee of the Soviet Writers' Union, as
recommended by the entire collective of the writers working
on the book about the construction of the Stalin Canal,
dedicates this book to the 17th Congress of the Bolshevik
Party. With this book, the Organizing Committee of the
Soviet Writers' Union reports to the Party Congress that the
Soviet writers are ready to serve the cause of Bolshevism and
devote their artistic works to the fight for a classless, socialist
society, in the name of Lenin's teaching" (from the dedication,
Belomorkanal, p. 1). For the circumstances and the very process
of creating *Belomorkanal* see Cynthia Ruder, "The Belomor
Canal: Fact and Fiction," paper presented at the 1993 National
Convention of the American Association for the
Advancement of Slavic Studies, in Honolulu. See also
V. Vozdvizhenskii, "Put' v kazarmu, ili eshche raz o
nasledstve," *Literaturnaia kritika*, no. 5 (1989); T. Ivanova,
"Eshche o nasledstve, o dolge i prave: Byl li Vsevolod Ivanov
zhdanovtsem?" *Knizhnoe obozrenie*, no. 34 (1989).

54. See "Kniga na stole delegata s'ezda," *Literaturnaia gazeta*, 28
January 1934; and "Chto chitaiut delegaty," *Literaturnaia
gazeta*, 12 February 1934. In the same year, 1934, Andrei
Vyshinsky, Stalin's main prosecutor, edited a collection *Ot
tiurem k vospitatel'nym uchrezhdeniiam* (From Prisons To
Educational Institutions) (Moscow: Institut ugolovnoi i
ispravitel'no-trudovoi politiki pri Prokurature SSSR i NKIu
SSSR, 1934), in which he championed the concept of the
camp as an institution of resocialization through labor.
Vyshinsky writes in the book: "the enthusiasm of the working
masses and their creative initiative have penetrated into the
places of confinement" (p. 264).

55. Ulam, *Stalin*, p. 374.

56. RAPP was the most hard-line Communist organization of

writers in the Soviet Union before the 1932 decree disbanding all writers' organizations.

57. The quick publication of the (selective) English version of *Belomorkanal* in the West in 1935 indicates that *Belomorkanal* was seen by Soviet foreign policy masters as an important element in the overall propaganda campaign aimed at preempting suspicions regarding violations of human rights in the Soviet Union.

58. See Jacques Rossi, *The GULAG Handbook: An Encyclopedia Dictionary of Soviet Penitentiary Institutions and Terms Related to the Forced Labor Camps,* trans. William A. Burhans (New York: Paragon House, 1989), pp. 517–525.

59. Andrei Sinyavsky, *Soviet Civilization: A Cultural History,* trans. Joanne Turnbull (New York: Little, Brown and Co., 1990), pp. 31–32.

60. Quoted from *Belomor: An Account of the Construction of the New Canal between the White Sea and the Baltic Sea,* pp. 59–60.

61. "Heteroglossia" is the standard English translation, introduced by Caryl Emerson and Michael Holquist, of Mikhail Bakhtin's term *raznorechie.* The term refers to the social diversity of speech types representing a multiplicity of points of view characteristic of various social groups participating in the dialogical communicative universe of the society as a whole. See Mikhail Bakhtin, "Discourse in the Novel," in Mikhail Bakhtin, *The Dialogic Imagination: Four Essays by M. M. Bakhtin,* trans. Caryl Emerson and Michael Holquist (Austin: University of Texas Press, 1981), p. 263.

62. Primo Levi, *Survival in Auschwitz: The Nazi Assault on Humanity,* trans. Stuart Woolf (London: Collier–Macmillan, 1971), p. 66.

63. Quoted from *Belomor,* p. 67.

64. Quoted with corrections from ibid., p. ix.

65. See, e.g., Katerina Clark, *The Soviet Novel: History as Ritual* (Chicago: University of Chicago Press, 1981). In her typology of the Soviet socialist-realist novel, Katerina Clark analyzes the genre in terms of its model "master plot." She sees this

"master plot" as built around the fundamental notion of the rite of passage of the central character into a universe of a higher Soviet "consciousness." The official treatment of the camp theme in Soviet "non-fiction" in the early 1930s can be viewed as a particular reflection of this larger Soviet cultural and political notion of the rite of passage. The metaphor of reforging (*perekovka*) is emblematic of this concept of initiation.

66. Trotsky, *Literature and Revolution,* p. 230.

67. During the celebrations of the finishing of the Canal, the Chief of Construction, Lazar Kogan, a high officer of the political police, spoke: "Not far off is the rally which will be the last in the camp system. . . . Not far off is that year, month and day when by and large corrective-labor camps will not be needed." "He himself was probably shot, and never did find out how sadly mistaken he was," Solzhenitsyn comments. "And maybe when he said it, he did not believe it" (Solzhenitsyn, *Gulag Archipelago,* vol. 2, p. 96).

68. None of the three editors of *Belomorkanal* lived through the subsequent spectacular wave of Stalin's purges in the party apparatus in the late 1930s. Gorky died in 1936. In the public trial against Bukharin and Yagoda the defendants were charged with assassinating Gorky. Vitaly Shentalinsky, who examined Gorky's medical record in the KGB archives, concluded that Gorky died of natural causes. The accusation against Yagoda was clearly fabricated. (See Shentalinsky, *Arrested Voices,* pp. 272–275). Averbakh, who was Yagoda's brother-in-law, was arrested in 1937. Under interrogation, he wrote a lengthy testimony in which he tried to clear himself of fabricated charges by blaming Yagoda. Averbakh was shot on 14 August 1937. Semen Firin, arrested in 1937, was executed as well. All previous positive references to the activists purged by Stalin had to be changed or, more often, removed altogether from public memory. For example, many official group photographs of Bolshevik activists were retouched for re-publication, so that some persons

disappeared from them without a trace. These persons also disappeared from many private photographs, books, and other documents. Their faces were blackened, scratched, or cut out by private citizens for fear of being associated with them. (See David King, *The Commissar Vanishes: The Falsification of Photographs and Art in Stalin's Russia* (New York: Metropolitan Books, 1997.) On the Stalinist terror of the late 1930s see Robert Conquest, *The Great Terror: A Reassessment* (London: Hutchinson, 1990).

69. *Bol'shaia Sovetskaia Entsiklopediia,* vol. 34 (Moscow: OGIZ, 1937), p. 176. Mikhail Heller comments on this encyclopedic definition: "Massive evidence and numerous documents support this definition in regard to the Soviet concentration camps, especially in places where the definition refers to the imprisonment of revolutionary and anti-fascist activists" (Geller, *Kontsentratsionnyi mir i sovetskaia literatura,* pp. 5–6). The latest publication in the Soviet press extolling resocialization through the camps was Viktor Shklovsky's " 'Perekovka' na kanale Volga-Moskva," *Bol'shevistskaia pechat'* (1937), no. 1, pp. 30–33. It should be noted that the cleansing of the Soviet libraries of literature referring to Soviet camps was, in fact, not entirely thorough. For instance, Nikolai Pogodin's socialist-realist play about the resocialization of criminals and "enemies of the people" in the Belomor Canal camp, *The Aristocrats* (*Aristokraty* [Moscow, 1935]), written at the time of the official celebration of *Belomorkanal,* remained in circulation after *Belomorkanal* disappeared.

70. Aleksander Wat, *My Century: The Odyssey of a Polish Intellectual,* trans. Richard Lourie, foreword by Czeslaw Milosz (Berkeley: University of California Press, 1988), p. 174.

Chapter 4:
HOPE BEYOND HOPE

1. *Materialy XXII S'ezda KPSS* (Moscow, 1961), p. 449.
2. The road to publication of *One Day in the Life of Ivan Denisovich* was described by Solzhenitsyn in Aleksandr I.

Solzhenitsyn, *The Oak and the Calf: Sketches of Literary Life in the Soviet Union*, trans. H. T. Willets (New York: Harper and Row, 1980), and in Solzhenitsyn's supplement to this work, *Invisible Allies*, trans. Alexis Klimoff and Michael Nicholson (Washington, D.C.: Counterpoint, 1995). See also Vladimir Lakshin, *"Novyi mir" vo vremena Khrushcheva: Dnevnik i poputnoe* (Moscow: Knizhnaia palata, 1991); Michael Scammell, *Solzhenitsyn: A Biography* (New York: Norton, 1984); and "The Road to Publication," in Alexis Klimoff (ed.), *Critical Companion to Solzhenitsyn's "One Day in the Life of Ivan Denisovich"* (Evanston, Ill.: Northwestern University Press, 1997), pp. 87–106.

3. Zhores Medvedev, *Ten Years After Ivan Denisovich*, trans. Hilary Sternberg (New York: Macmillan, 1974), p. 14.

4. *Izvestiia*, 6 November 1962, p. 6. In *The Oak and the Calf*, Solzhenitsyn gives an account of the publication of "A Nugget" by Georgy Shelest. (The title of Shelest's story in H. T. Willett's translation of *The Oak and the Calf* is rendered as "Rough Diamond.")

5. Georgii Shelest, "Kolymskie zapisi," *Znamia*, no. 9 (1964), pp. 164–180; Iurii Piliar, "Liudi ostaiutsia liud'mi," *Iunost'*, nos. 6, 7, 8 (1963) and 3, 4, 5 (1964); Boris D'iakov, "Povest' o perezhitom," *Oktiabr'*, no. 7 (1964), pp. 50–142; Andrei Aldan-Semenov, "Barel'ef na skale," *Moskva*, no. 7 (1964), pp. 68–154. At the same time, many literary works referring or alluding, in more or less indirect forms, to Soviet camp experiences were also published under Soviet censorship. Yuri Dombrovsky's novel *Khranitel' drevnostei*, *Novyi mir*, 7 (1964), deserves a special mention in this context. (English translation: Yury Dombrovsky, *The Keeper of Antiquities*, trans. Michael Glenny [New York: McGraw-Hill, 1969].)

6. Andrzej Werner, *Zwyczajna Apokalipsa* (Warsaw: Czytelnik, 1981), p. 18.

7. Ibid., pp. 18–19.

8. Elie Wiesel, *Night*, trans. Stella Rodway (New York: Hill and Wang, 1960), pp. 41–42.

9. Ibid., p. 68.
10. Ibid., p. 69.
11. Tadeusz Borowski, *This Way for the Gas, Ladies and Gentlemen and Other Stories*, trans. Barbara Veder (New York: Viking, 1967), pp. 83–84.
12. See Jan Kott, Introduction to Borowski, *This Way for the Gas.*
13. Varlam Shalamov, "Domino," in Varlam Shalamov, *Voskreshenie listvennitsy* (Moscow, 1989), p. 125. The English translation of the story, "Dominoes," in Varlam Shalamov, *Graphite*, trans. John Glad (New York: Norton, 1981), does not contain this fragment.
14. Primo Levi, *Survival in Auschwitz: The Nazi Assault on Humanity*, trans. Stuart Woolf (London: Collier–MacMillan, 1971), p. 79.
15. Ibid., pp. 80–81. "Mussulman" in the slang of Nazi camps was a word describing a prisoner apparently close to death from exhaustion and hunger. The term was the Nazi equivalent of an older word coined in Soviet camps—*dokhodiaga* (goner).
16. Ibid., p. 84. On intellectual and psychological strategies for moral survival illuminated in camp memoirs see Terrence Des Pres, *The Survivor: An Anatomy of Life in the Death Camps* (New York: Oxford University Press, 1976).
17. Varlam Shalamov, "Inzhener Kiselev," in Varlam Shalamov, *Kolymskie rasskazy* (Paris: YMCA Press, 1985), p. 338.
18. Wiesel, *Night*, pp. 94–95.
19. Ibid., pp. 102–103.
20. Ibid., pp. 107–108.
21. Ibid., p. 111.
22. Ibid., pp. 112–113.
23. Werner, *Zwyczajna Apokalipsa*, p. 22.
24. Wanda Jakubowska, *Ostatni etap (Scenariusz)* (Warsaw, 1956), pp. 17–18.
25. Seweryna Szmaglewska, *Dymy nad Birkenau* (Warsaw: Ksiazka i Wiedza, 1964), p. 22 (first published in 1946).
26. Levi, *Survival in Auschwitz*, p. 12.
27. Wiesel, *Night*, p. 114.

28. Erich Auerbach, *Mimesis: The Representation of Reality in Western Literature,* trans. Willard R. Trask (Princeton, N.J.: Princeton University Press, 1968), p. 19.

29. Janusz Nel-Siedlecki, Krystyn Olszewski, and Tadeusz Borowski, *Bylismy w Oswiecimiu* (Warsaw, 1958), pp. 6–8 (first published in 1946 in Munich). Borowski's provocative statements and his semi-identification with his narrator gave rise to personal accusations against him by readers who identified Tadeusz Borowski the survivor with Tadek the narrator. Numerous witnesses testified to Borowski's decent behavior at Auschwitz. Borowski's biography may serve as an extreme example of the impact of totalitarian theory and practice on personal fate. Born in 1922 to a Polish family in the Soviet Ukraine, he was four when his father was sent to a Soviet labor camp in Karelia for six years, where he took part in the Belomor Canal construction. When Borowski was eight, during the collectivization, his mother was exiled to Siberia for four years. In 1932 he was repatriated by the Red Cross to Poland, where the family was reunited in 1934. He was seventeen in 1939, when the Nazis invaded Poland. After four years spent in Nazi-occupied Warsaw, he was arrested and sent along with his fiancée to Auschwitz, and later transferred to the concentration camps near Stuttgart and in Dachau. Liberated by the American armed forces in 1945, he returned to then Communist Poland in 1946. His best works appeared from 1946 to 1948. In 1948 he joined the Communist Party in Poland and became an impassioned Communist propagandist. On 1 July 1951, he committed suicide at the age of twenty-nine.

30. Piliar, "Liudi ostaiutsia liud'mi," *Iunost',* no. 3 (1964), p. 22.

31. *Belomorkanal* (Moscow: G12, 1934), p. 58.

32. Piliar, "Liudi ostaiutsia liud'mi," *Iunost',* no. 3 (1964), p. 26.

33. Shelest, "Kolymskie zapisi," p. 162.

34. *Sovetskoe ugolovnoe pravo: Obshchaia chast'* (Moscow: Gosiurizdat, 1952), p. 319. See also Mikhail Geller,

Kontsentratsionnyi mir i sovetskaia literatura (London: Overseas Publications Interchange, 1974), p. 247.

35. According to official Soviet tradition, a gunshot from the battleship *Aurora* marked the beginning of the victorious Bolshevik revolution.

36. This is not necessarily just a fictitious projection. Indeed, it represents behavior documented in many testimonies of Soviet camp survivors. For instance, Ivan M. Gronsky, a Communist and the editor of *Izvestia*, purged and imprisoned in a camp, reminisced after his release that he and other prisoner-Communists used to meet in secrecy at night in a camp latrine and chorally whisper the "International." See Zinovii Papernyi, "Shutit' liubil," *Kontinent*, no. 70 (1991), p. 300.

37. Shelest, "Kolymskie zapisi," p. 173.

38. Foreword to D'iakov, "Povest' o perezhitom," *Oktiabr'*, no. 7 (1964), p. 49.

39. Shelest, "Kolymskie zapisi," p. 179.

40. Piliar, "Liudi ostaiutsia liud'mi," *Iunost'*, no. 3 (1964), p. 26.

41. Eugenia Ginzburg, *Into the Whirlwind*, trans. Paul Stevenson and Manya Harrari (London: Collins Harvill, 1989), p. 246.

42. Ibid.

43. Eugenia Ginzburg continued on this path. The second volume of her autobiographical testimony, *Krutoi marshrut* (Milan: Arnoldo Mondadori Editore, 1979), which appeared in English as *Within the Whirlwind*, trans. Ian Boland (New York: Harcourt Brace Jovanovich, 1981), was not intended for publication in the Soviet Union, and showed her profound transformation under the impact of the camp experience. She describes opening herself to the experiences of other, non-Communist prisoners, which contributed to her liberation from the confines of the ideology.

44. Shelest, "Kolymskie zapisi," p. 163.

45. D'iakov, "Povest' o perezhitom," p. 50.

46. Shelest, "Kolymskie zapisi," p. 178.

47. D'iakov, "Povest' o perezhitom," p. 54. Boris Dyakov seems to

have assumed this stance in his real life. As a secret informer of the NKVD since 1936 (pseudonym "Woodpecker"), he had every reason to view his arrest and imprisonment in 1950 as either a mistake or a cruel game. In the camp, he continued to inform on his fellow prisoners. In one of his secret reports he wrote: "This cooperation is sincerely and honestly provided and gives me the moral satisfaction of knowing that here, in unusual conditions, I am of a certain use in the common cause of fighting the enemies of the USSR." (Vitaly Shentalinsky, *Arrested Voices: Resurrecting the Disappeared Writers of the Soviet Regime*, trans. John Crowfoot [New York: Free Press, 1996], p. 165).

48. Ginzburg, *Into the Whirlwind*, p. 119.
49. Zofia Nalkowska, *Medaliony* (Warsaw: Czytelnik, 1966), p. 3.
50. Andrei Sinyavsky quotes Lenin and comments: "From this fundamental declaration, it naturally follows that a person is permitted everything, that anything is moral if it serves the interests of the working class and the good of the cause" (Andrei Sinyavsky, *Soviet Civilization: A Cultural History*, trans. Joanne Turnbull (New York: Little, Brown and Co., 1990), p. 120).
51. Arthur Koestler, *Darkness at Noon*, trans. D. Hardy (New York: Macmillan, 1941), pp. 97–99.
52. Aleksandr Tarasov-Rodionov, "Shokolad," in Vera Aleksandrova (ed.), *Opal'nye povesti* (New York: Izdatel'stvo im. Chekhova, 1955), p. 375. See also Geller, *Kontsentratsionnyi mir i sovetskaia literatura*, p. 109.
53. Werner, *Zwyczajna Apokalipsa*, p. 84.
54. Ginzburg, *Into the Whirlwind*, p. 38.
55. Sinyavsky, *Soviet Civilization*, p. 101. On Stalin's humor see also Iurii Borev, *Staliniada* (Moscow, 1990), and Z. Papernyi, "Shutit' liubil," *Kontinent*, no. 70 (1991).
56. D'iakov, "Povest' o perezhitom," p. 141.
57. Ibid., p. 66.
58. Koestler, *Darkness at Noon*, pp. 97–100.
59. Eugenia Ginzburg, *Journey into the Whirlwind*, trans. Paul

Stevenson and Max Hayward (New York: Harcourt Brace
Jovanovich, 1967), p. 214.

60. Vasily Grossman, *Forever Flowing*, trans. Thomas P. Whitney
(New York: Harper & Row, 1972), p. 105.

61. Shelest, "Kolymskie zapisi," p. 171.

62. D'iakov, "Povest' o perezhitom," p. 50.

63. Ibid., p. 52.

64. Grossman, *Forever Flowing*, pp. 107–108.

65. Ginzburg, *Into the Whirlwind*, p. 194. Nikolai Yezhov, the chief
of the NKVD during the purges of 1937, was himself purged
in 1939. His downfall began in 1938, when he was replaced
by Lavrenty Beria. Beria lasted until shortly after Stalin's death
in 1953. The degree to which the official Stalinist discourse
became ritualized can be illustrated by the fact that, according
to the announcement in *Pravda* (10 July 1953), Beria (like
Yezhov 14 years earlier) was arrested as an "enemy of the
Soviet people" and an "agent of international imperialism."

66. Varlam Shalamov, "The Life of Engineer Kipreev," in
Shalamov, *Graphite*, p. 135.

67. Borowski, *This Way for the Gas*, pp. 101–102.

68. Shalamov, "Life of Engineer Kipreev," p. 123.

69. Shelest, "Kolymskie zapisi," p. 167.

70. Ibid.

71. Ibid., pp. 168–169.

72. D'iakov, "Povest' o perezhitom," p. 52. The red flag was placed
on the building to mark the occasion of the anniversary of the
Bolshevik revolution.

73. Shelest, "Kolymskie zapisi," p. 164.

74. Sinyavsky, *Soviet Civilization*, p. 111.

75. See Lev Shestov, *Dostoevskii i Nitshe: Filosofiia tragedii* (St.
Petersburg: Tip. M. M. Stasiulevicha, 1909).

76. D'iakov, "Povest' o perezhitom," p. 66.

77. Koestler, *Darkness at Noon*, p. 60.

78. Shelest, "Kolymskie zapisi," p. 179.

79. Ibid., p. 173.

80. Ibid., p. 170.

81. Ibid., p. 171.
82. Aldan-Semenov, "Barel'ef na skale," p. 77.
83. D'iakov, "Povest' o perezhitom," p. 141.

Chapter 5:
A SLIVER IN THE THROAT OF POWER

1. "One Day with Solzhenitsyn: An Interview by Pavel Licko," in Leopold Labedz (ed.), *Solzhenitsyn: A Documentary Record* (New York: Harper and Row, 1971), pp. 13, 15. This interview was first published in *Kulturny Zivot*, 31 March 1967. For further discussion of the nature of Solzhenitsyn's literary vocation see Georges Nivat, *Soljénitsyne* (Paris: Seuil, 1980).

2. Solzhenitsyn commented directly on this subject during an editorial discussion of his text by the *Novyi mir* staff. "He who does not blunt his senses in camp will not survive," he is recorded as saying in Vladimir Lakshin's diary entry of 23 July 1962. "That's the only way I made it through. . . . If I had behaved like an intellectual, if I had been filled with inner turmoil, had fretted and taken to heart everything that took place, I would certainly have died." See Vladimir Lakshin, *"Novyi mir" vo vremena Khrushcheva: Dnevnik i poputnoe (1953–1964)* (Moscow: Knizhnaia palata, 1991), p. 67.

3. See Varlam Shalamov, "The Life of Engineer Kipreev," in Varlam Shalamov, *Graphite,* trans. John Glad (New York: Norton, 1981), pp. 123–140; and Tadeusz Borowski, *This Way for the Gas, Ladies and Gentlemen and Other Stories,* trans. Barbara Veder (New York: Viking, 1967), pp. 101–102.

4. See, for instance, Gustaw Herling-Grudzinski, *A World Apart,* trans. Andrzej Ciolkosz (New York: Penguin, 1996), and Varlam Shalamov, "On Tick," in Varlam Shalamov, *Kolyma Tales,* trans. John Glad (New York: Norton, 1980), pp. 107–112.

5. Alexander Solzhenitsyn, *One Day in the Life of Ivan Denisovich,* trans. Max Hayward and Ronald Hingley (New York: Bantam, 1990), p. 198. All subsequent references are to this edition and are included in parentheses in the text.

6. Borowski, *This Way for the Gas.*
7. The number of copies of *Novyi mir,* no. 11 (1962), where Solzhenitsyn's novella occupied pages 8–74, was increased on Tvardovsky's request by 40,000 copies. 2,200 additional copies were ordered for the enlarged Plenary Session of the Central Committee of the Communist Party of 19 November 1962. (The conspicuous presence of a newly published literary work on Soviet camps in the kiosks at the Plenary Session reminds one of a similar event twenty-eight years earlier: the conspicuous presence of *Belomorkanal* at the Seventeenth Party Congress in 1934.) In January 1963, *One Day in the Life of Ivan Denisovich* came out in the "Roman-gazeta" series in an edition of at least 750,000 copies, and in February 1963 the publishing house "Sovetskii pisatel' " published Solzhenitsyn's work in book form in an edition of 100,000 copies. See Zhores Medvedev, *Ten Years After Ivan Denisovich,* trans. Hilary Sternberg (London: Macmillan, 1973), pp. 10–16.
8. In November and December 1962 at least twenty-five reviews and articles devoted to Solzhenitsyn's work appeared in the Soviet press. In the January 1963 issue of *Novyi mir* Solzhenitsyn published two stories, "Sluchai na stantsii Krechetovka" (Incident at Krechetovka Station) and "Matrenin dvor" and (Matryona's House), and in the July issue of the same journal he contributed the story "Dlia pol'zy dela" (For the Good of the Cause). Among seventy-two reviews, articles, and other responses to Solzhenitsyn's works published in the official Soviet press in 1963, at least forty-two are concerned with *One Day in the Life of Ivan Denisovich.* At the end of 1963 it was nominated by the editorial board of *Novyi mir* and the State Archive of Literature and Art for the 1964 Lenin Prize in literature. The prize was not granted to Solzhenitsyn. In 1964, the Soviet press published forty-six responses to Solzhenitsyn's works. See Michael Nicholson, "Aleksandr Solzhenitsyn: A Bibliography of Responses in the Official Soviet Press from November 1962 to April 1973," in John B. Dunlop, Richard

Haugh, and Alexis Klimoff (eds), *Aleksandr Solzhenitsyn: Critical Essays and Documentary Materials* (Belmont, Mass.: Nordland, 1978), pp. 501–532.

9. Vladimir Lakshin, "Ivan Denisovich, ego druz'ia i nedrugi," *Novyi mir* 1 (1964), pp. 223–245.
10. *Survey*, nos 74–75 (1970); quoted in Labedz (ed.), *Solzhenitsyn: A Documentary Record*, pp. 21–37.
11. Labedz (ed.), *Solzhenitsyn: A Documentary Record*, pp. 34–35.
12. Ibid., p. 34.
13. Ibid., p. 31.
14. Ibid., p. 32.
15. Ibid., p. 30.
16. Ibid., p. 36.
17. Ibid., p. 29.
18. Vladimir Lakshin, *"Novyi mir" vo vremena Khrushcheva: Dnevnik i poputnoe* (Moscow: Knizhnaia palata, 1991). The excerpt quoted in Rebecca Park's translation from Alexis Klimoff (ed.), *Critical Companion to Solzhenitsyn's "One Day in the Life of Ivan Denisovich"* (Evanston, Ill.: Northwestern University Press, 1997), p. 99. The conversation between Khrushchev and Tvardovsky about *One Day in the Life of Ivan Denisovich* took place on the eve of the Cuban missile crisis. Solzhenitsyn comments: "Khrushchev did not, of course, know, as he chatted peacefully with Tvardovsky about literature, that blown-up photographs of Soviet rockets in Cuba were being mounted on display boards in Washington, to be shown to delegates at an O.A.S. meeting on Monday, at which Kennedy would obtain consent for his unprecedentedly bold step: inspecting Soviet ships. Only Sunday stood between Khrushchev and his week of humiliation, fear, and surrender. And it was on that very last Saturday that he issued *Ivan Denisovich's* visa." (Aleksandr Solzhenitsyn, *The Oak and the Calf: Sketches of Literary Life in the Soviet Union,* trans. H. T. Willets [New York: Harper and Row, 1980], p. 42; also quoted in Klimoff (ed.), *Critical Companion.*)
19. Aleksandr Tvardovskii, "Vmesto predisloviia," *Novyi mir,* no.

11 (1962), pp. 8–9; quoted from Tvardovsky, "Instead of a
Foreword," in Solzhenitsyn, *One Day in the Life of Ivan
Denisovich,* p. xix.

20. Ibid.

21. Ibid., p. xx. In fact, Tvardovsky was well aware of the
limitations of the Khrushchevian public discourse on the
Stalinist past. His decision to promote *One Day in the Life of
Ivan Denisovich* may be seen as a sign of both his boldness and
his caution at the same time. In 1962, besides *One Day,*
Tvardovsky received the manuscript of Lydia Chukovskaya's
short novel *Sofia Petrovna* (also known under the title *The
Deserted House*), which dealt with the Stalinist purges of 1937
in Leningrad and presented an exploration of totalitarian evil
strikingly incompatible with the limitations of the
Khrushchevian public discourse. Aware that he could not
publish both works without seriously endangering the very
existence of *Novyi Mir,* Tvardovsky dropped Chukovskaya's
work in favor of Solzhenitsyn's. In September 1962
Chukovskaya offered *Sofia Petrovna* to the publishing house
"Sovetskii pisatel'," and the manuscript was accepted for
publication. In March 1963, after Khrushchev's speech
reinforcing the boundaries on the topic of Stalinism (referred
to further in this chapter), the publication of the novel was
stopped. What followed was an event quite unprecedented in
the history of Soviet literature. Chukovskaya sued the
publisher for breach of contract and, astonishingly, won the
case and received payment of her entire honorarium. The
novel, of course, did not appear in print at that time. (See
Lidia Chukovskaia, *Protsess iskliucheniia: Ocherk literaturnykh
nravov* [Paris: YMCA Press, 1979]. See also Alexis Klimoff, "In
Defense of the Word," in Lydia Chukovskaya, *The Deserted
House,* trans. Aline B. Werth [Belmont, Mass.: Nordland,
1978], p. xx; and Aleksandr Solzhenitsyn, *Bodalsia telenok s
dubom* [Paris: YMCA Press, 1975], p. 26.)

22. Ibid., pp. xix–xx. The genre of *One Day in the Life of Ivan
Denisovich* (Russian *povest'*) is referred to in English, by

different authors, as a "novella," "tale," "short novel," or
"novel." Solzhenitsyn's work is here referred to as a "novella"
following Georg Lukács's terminological preference and
William D. Graf's English translation of Lukács's terminology.
(See Georg Lukács, *Solzhenitsyn*, trans. William D. Graf
[London: Merlin Press, 1971].) The terms "novel" and "tale"
remain in passages quoted from other English sources
according to their authors' choices.

23. V. Pallon, "Zdravstvuite, kavtorang!" *Izvestiia*, 15 January
1964; cited from Medvedev, *Ten Years After Ivan Denisovich*, pp.
22–23.

24. Konstantin Simonov, "O proshlom vo imia budushchego,"
Izvestiia, 18 November 1962; quoted from Labedz (ed.),
Solzhenitsyn: A Documentary Record, p. 17.

25. Mikhail Geller, *Kontsentratsionnyi mir i sovetskaia literatura*
(London: Overseas Publications Exchange, 1974), p. 280.

26. "Ot redaktsii," *Literaturnaia gazeta*, 4 June 1964.

27. Labedz (ed.), *Solzhenitsyn: A Documentary Record*, pp. 33–34.

28. Ibid. p. 34.

29. Ibid.

30. Edward J. Brown, *Russian Literature since the Revolution*
(Cambridge, Mass.: Harvard University Press, 1980), p. 254.

31. Vladimir Ermilov, "Vo imia pravdy, vo imia zhizni," *Pravda*, 23
November 1962; quoted from Labedz (ed.), *Solzhenitsyn: A
Documentary Record*, p. 19.

32. L. F. Il'ichev, "Sily tvorcheskoi molodezhi—na sluzhbu velikim
idealam," *Literaturnaia gazeta*, 10 January 1963.

33. Geller, *Kontsentratsionnyi mir i sovetskaia literatura*, pp. 301–302.

34. Ibid., p. 302.

35. See the Polish edition of Geller, *Kontsentratsionnyi mir i
sovetskaia literatura* (Michal Heller, *Swiat obozow koncentracyjnych
a literatura sowiecka*, trans. Michal Kaniowski, [Paris: Instytut
Literacki, 1974], p. 288). A similar, though less radical,
interpretation of the character of Ivan Denisovich was
presented by Gustaw Herling-Grudzinski in his essay, "Jegor i

Iwan Denisowicz," in Gustaw Herling-Grudzinski, *Drugie przyjscie* (Paris: Instytut Literacki, 1963), pp. 244–250.

36. Ibid., p. 290.
37. See Erich Fromm, *Escape from Freedom* (New York: Holt, Rinehart and Winston, 1976).
38. Brown, *Russian Literature since the Revolution,* p. 256.
39. Ibid., p. 254.
40. Ibid., p. 257.
41. Edward E. Ericson, *Solzhenitsyn: The Moral Vision* (Grand Rapids, Mich.: W. Eerdmans Publishing Company, 1980), p. 40.
42. In *The Gulag Archipelago* Solzhenitsyn commented on this subject: "How could Ivan Denisovich get through ten years if all he could do was curse his work day and night? After all, in that case he would have had to hang himself on the first handy hook! . . . Such is man's nature that even bitter, detested work is sometimes performed with an incomprehensible wild excitement. Having worked for two years with my hands, I encountered this strange phenomenon myself: suddenly you become absorbed in the work itself, irrespective of whether it is slave labor and offers you nothing. I experienced those strange moments at bricklaying (otherwise I wouldn't have written about it), at foundry work, carpentry, even in the fervor of breaking up old pig iron with a sledge. And so surely we can allow Ivan Denisovich not to feel his inescapable labor as a terrible burden forever, not to hate it perpetually?" See Aleksandr I. Solzhenitsyn, *The Gulag Archipelago 1918–1956: An Experiment in Literary Investigation,* trans. Thomas P. Whitney (New York: Harper and Row, 1975), vol. 2, pp. 257–258.
43. Ericson, *Solzhenitsyn: The Moral Vision,* p. 40.
44. Cited from Terrence Des Pres, "The Heroism of Survival," in Dunlop et al. (eds), *Aleksandr Solzhenitsyn: Critical Essays and Documentary Materials,* p. 48.
45. Ibid., p. 49.
46. Editorial Note in *Literaturnaia gazeta,* 19 October 1963. (The

part before the ellipsis is quoted from Labedz [ed.],
Solzhenitsyn: A Documentary Record, p. 49. The remaining part
is my own translation.)

47. Ericson, *Solzhenitsyn: The Moral Vision*, p. 36.
48. *Pravda*, 10 March 1963. (The part before the first ellipsis is
quoted from Labedz (ed.), *Solzhenitsyn: A Documentary Record*,
p. 41.) The rest is my own translation.)
49. Cited from Medvedev, *Ten Years After Ivan Denisovich*, p. 19.

INDEX

Class enemies: and Bolshevik rhetoric, xv, 23–26, 57, 164–68; and ideology, 18–19, 22–23, 94; and Soviet concentration camps, 22, 26, 100, 151, 180; and Lenin, 23–25, 80–82, 227–28, 316n29; and Stalin, 25, 82, 181, 231–32, 325n3; reeducation of, 104, 137, 142, 158–59, 163, 179, 181; and Gorky, 138–42; and *Belomorkanal,* 158–59, 181

Collectivization of farmland: and starvation, 4, 5, 21, 30–31, 126; and Stalin, 96–97, 99, 185, 325n3, 329n35; and *Belomorkanal,* 150, 164–67

Communism: and Soviet concentration camp literature, xix, 5, 211, 215, 218–20, 223, 225, 234–36, 238–39, 242–43, 246–52, 285–86, 289, 295, 297, 308, 339n36, 339–40n47; and totalitarianism, 13, 17; and ideology, 16, 237–38; and aesthetics, 30, 33; and morality, 31, 306; and teleology, 34, 145; and Russian literature, 69–71; and Bolshevik violence, 76, 148; and Stalin, 93, 185–86, 246; and Western intellectuals, 98–99; and

Gorky, 113, 119; and language, 156–57; victimization of Communists, 185, 211, 218–40, 242–45, 249–52, 256, 281, 290–91, 295

Compulsive labor. *See* Slave labor

Concentration camps: as laboratories, xi–xii; and criticism of West, 160–61, 214; and dehumanization of victim, 197, 206–7; and mind control, 312n4. *See also* Nazi concentration camps; Soviet concentration camps

De Custine, Astolphe, 1, 2, 3, 99, 113

Des Pres, Terrence, 304

Dialogal communication, 8, 41–44, 91, 258–59, 268, 304–5, 318–19n53, 320n63

Dostoevsky, Fyodor, 60, 78, 166

Dyakov, Boris: and Soviet concentration camps, xix, xx, 222; publication of, 189; ideology of, 190, 210–12, 236, 244–45, 252, 256, 265, 305; and Communism, 211, 218–19, 226, 236, 238–39, 249, 285, 289, 295, 297, 308, 339–40n47; and reality, 213; and Bolshevik violence, 214; and preconceived value systems, 217–19, 270; and

Dyakov, Boris *(continued)*
    martyrological formula,
    219–20; ethics in, 224, 229,
    232, 280; and Stalin, 231–32,
    247, 251–52, 286; and point
    of view, 254
Dzerzhinsky, Felix, 22, 68,
    100–101, 104

Economic base: and societal
    transformation, xix; and
    Bolshevik regime, 15–17,
    20, 95–96; and slave labor,
    20–22, 104–5, 150, 174–75,
    315n23; and New
    Economic Policy, 21, 95, 97,
    315n22; and Five-Year
    Plans, 97, 104, 153; and
    Gorky's account, 119,
    131–32
Ehrenburg, Ilya: and tragedy,
    xvii, xviii, 69, 71, 91, 146;
    and Bolshevik henchmen,
    66, 69, 136; and morality, 71,
    77, 87; and Bolshevik
    violence, 75; and
    dehumanization of victims,
    78–79, 136; and
    victimization, 121
Enemies of the people. *See*
    Class enemies
Ericson, Edward, 302–3, 307
Ermilov, Vladimir, 295–96, 297
Ethics: and Soviet
    concentration camps, xii, 6,
    10, 201–2, 255; and Soviet

concentration camp
    literature, xvii, xix, 67, 91,
    100, 148, 163, 211, 223–32,
    241, 251, 270–71, 278–80,
    305; and totalitarian
    authorship, xvii, 45, 52; and
    victimization, xviii, 6, 144,
    146–47, 220, 230, 256, 286;
    and totalitarian regimes,
    2–3, 14; and morality, 6–7,
    31, 72, 90, 306; of Bolshevik
    regime, 25–26, 32–33, 38,
    280–81, 309; and Bolshevik
    violence, 59, 61–65, 69–70,
    72–73, 75–77, 269; and
    Russian literature, 60–61,
    69; and Nazi concentration
    camps, 204–5, 207; and
    Solzhenitsyn, 254–59,
    261–74, 277–78, 280–81,
    283, 298–99, 302–3, 305.
    See also Utilitarian class
    ethics

Fainsod, Merle, 17
Fedin, Konstantin, 38–41
Feuchtwanger, Lion, 113
Firin, Semen, 154, 334n68
Fromm, Erich, 301

Ginzburg, Eugenia, 222–23,
    226, 230–31, 234–35, 239,
    310, 339n43
Goebbles, Joseph, 93, 313n9
Gogol, Nikolai, 53–54
Golomstock, Igor, 52

Golovin, Sergei, 272
Gorky, Maxim: and Soviet concentration camp literature, xviii, 35, 101, 105–6, 221, 232, 279, 297; and juvenile corrective colony, 101, 170, 325–26n7; and Lenin, 106–9, 130; return to Soviet Union, 110–12, 125–26; writer's journey of, 112–23, 125–27, 153; death of, 334n68
—*Belomorkanal,* 106, 151–55, 163
—*In and About the Soviet Union,* 105, 115, 118, 121–23, 125, 127, 132, 134, 144, 156
—"Solovki": and victimization, 105–6, 154–55; and ideology, 106, 118–19, 126, 132, 162–63, 180; and Solzhenitsyn, 115–17, 276; literary structure of, 118–25, 130, 133–34, 145, 156, 175–76, 182; literary motifs of, 125–31, 136–37, 139–40, 180–81; and resocialization, 134–37, 142–44, 172, 181, 221, 270, 272, 274–75, 277; and class enemies, 136–42; and ethics, 147, 270–71, 278–80, 305; post-Stalinist thaw literature compared to, 212–14; and Bolshevik regime, 244
Grigorev, A. I., 271–72, 276

Grossman, Vasily, 61–62, 82, 235–36, 239
Groys, Boris, 36, 49–51
Gulags. *See* Soviet concentration camps
Gumilev, Nikolai, 108

Heller, Mikhail, xiii, 23, 82, 133, 288, 299–302, 304, 335n69
Herder, Johann Gottfried, 53
Herling-Grudzinski, Gustaw, 310, 346n35
Hitler, Adolf, 26, 99

Ideology: and reality, xiv, xxi, 7, 29, 35, 37, 95, 148, 159, 306; and Bolshevik regime, xv, xviii–xix, 11, 17, 20, 34, 44–45, 56, 155, 259, 279, 284, 289, 298, 318n44; and experience, xvi, 35, 44; and Soviet concentration camp literature, xx, 106, 118–19, 126, 132–33, 180, 190, 192, 210–12, 216, 220, 236–37, 244, 246, 251–52, 254–56, 259–60, 265, 289, 305, 308; and terror, 15, 17–18, 20, 100; and class enemies, 18–19, 22–23, 94; and socialism, 47, 153; and avant-garde art, 51–52; and Russian literature, 59, 67–68, 71, 76; and victimization, 80–83, 94, 96,

Ideology: and reality *(continued)*
154, 220, 256; and
Solzhenitsyn, 258, 269–70,
297
Ilyichev, Leonid, 296, 297

Jakubowska, Wanda, 206–7
Jasienski, Bruno, 179

Kafka, Franz, 238
Kaganovich, Lazar, 93
Khodasevich, Vladislav, 108–9
Khrushchev, Nikita: and Soviet
concentration camp
literature, xii, xix, 185, 186,
269, 282, 307–8; and Stalin,
185–88, 281–82, 290,
345n21; and Solzhenitsyn,
281, 284, 307, 344n18
Kin, Viktor, 77–78
Knyazev, Vasily, xviii, 73–77,
87–89, 91–92, 99, 121, 146
Koestler, Arthur, 228, 233–34,
248
Kolakowski, Leszek, 13
Korolenko, Vladimir, 72
Kulaks. *See* Class enemies
Kuzemko, Y., 93

Labor camps. *See* Slave labor;
Soviet concentration camps
Lakshin, Vladimir, 269, 289
Latsis, Martin, 19
Lattimore, Owen, 114, 328n31
Lebedev, Vladimir, 188
Lenin, Vladimir I.: and

proletariat, xviii, 23–24, 229,
245; and Bolshevik violence,
17–20, 316–17n38; and class
enemies, 23–25, 80–82,
227–28, 316n29; and
morality, 31, 52, 62–63, 71,
73, 86, 90, 227, 340n50; and
points of view, 48–49; and
competition, 52; and Gorky,
106–9, 130; and
Communism, 185–86, 246,
248–50
Leninism, 13, 75, 227, 233, 285
Levi, Primo, xx, 107, 170–71,
199–201, 205, 208
Licko, Pavel, 260
Likhachev, Dmitry, 201, 326n9,
330n43
Lunacharsky, Anatoly, 72–73,
108

Makarenko, Anton, 101, 112,
325n7, 325–26n7
Malenkov, Georgy, 35–36
Mamin-Sibiryak, Dmitry, 60
Marxism, 15–16, 18, 24, 29–30,
97, 144
Marxism–Leninism, 16, 20, 89,
94, 96, 130, 156
Maslagov, Sergei, 118
Mayakovsky, Vladimir, xviii, 58,
86–88, 91–92
Morality: and totalitarianism,
xii, xx; and Soviet
concentration camp
literature, xiii, xviii, xix, xxi,

91, 109, 111, 147–48, 198,
202, 210, 227, 229–30,
245–46; and victimization,
xix, 10, 52, 132; and
Solzhenitsyn, xx, 254–55,
257, 261, 265, 268, 283–84,
287, 291–92, 298, 305;
Judeo-Christian morality,
xxi, 52, 67, 70–71, 74, 146;
and ethics, 6–7, 31, 72, 90,
306; and Lenin, 31, 52,
62–63, 71, 73, 86, 90, 227,
340n50; and Russian
literature, 37, 60, 67–78, 146,
317n41; and consistency, 45,
317n41; and preconceived
value systems, 192–93, 209;
and Borowski, 194, 196–98,
205, 209–10
Morson, Gary Saul, 41, 45–47

Nazi concentration camps:
literature of, xx, 170–71,
191–210; Soviet
concentration camps
compared to, 103, 197–98,
201, 211, 224–26, 238
Nicholas I (tsar of Russia), 2
Nietzsche, Friedrich, 50
Nikishov, Ivan, 114
Nogtev, A. P., 105

Olesha, Yuri, 31–33, 78

Pallon, V., 283–87
Peshkova, Ekaterina, 107

Pilyar, Yuri: and Soviet
concentration camps, xix,
xx; publication of, 188;
ideology of, 190, 211–12,
236, 244, 252, 256, 265; and
Communism, 211, 236, 286,
289, 297, 308; and physical
destruction, 213–15; and
preconceived value systems,
217–18, 270; and
reeducation, 221–22; ethics
in, 229, 232, 280
Plato, 33–34, 46
Points of view: and totalitarian
authorship, xiv, 8–9, 11,
39–40, 42, 45, 48–49,
320n63; and Soviet
concentration camp
literature, xx, 57, 59, 61,
91–92, 136, 148, 190–91,
208, 213, 220–21, 225,
232–33, 254–56, 269–70;
and teleology, 30–31, 33, 53;
and Solzhenitsyn, 257, 262,
276–77, 286, 290
Proletariat: as criterion of good
and evil, xviii, 23–24, 229,
245; and Bolshevik regime,
15–18, 23–24, 25;
bourgeoisie as threat to,
19–20, 26, 96, 124, 308;
proletarian psychology, 23,
26, 34; and morality, 31, 52,
227; dictatorship of, 92, 125,
131, 316–17n38; and Soviet
concentration camps, 100

Pushkin, Aleksandr, 53–55, 57, 321n68

Rachmaninoff, Sergei, 141
Reality: and Bolshevik regime, xii, xiv, 6, 27–28, 38, 42; and Soviet concentration camp literature, xiii, xv, xx, 37–45, 119–21, 123–27, 129–30, 144, 146, 148, 153, 155, 162, 175–77, 179, 190–92, 213; and totalitarian authorship, xiv, xvi–xvii, 7–9, 17, 44; and ideology, xiv, xxi, 7, 29, 35, 37, 95, 148, 159, 306; and art, xv–xvi, 36, 46, 51, 154; and Bolshevik rhetoric, xvi, 4, 7, 10, 25, 28–29, 31, 34–37, 183; and preconceived value systems, xx, 192–94, 196; and teleology, 30, 34; and Solzhenitsyn, 255, 257, 263, 272
Robins, Raymond, 20
Romain, Rolland, 130
Ropshin, Viktor, 64–65
Rossini, Gioacchino, 142
Russian literature: themes of, 12, 38–39, 60–61, 260; and morality, 37, 60, 67–78, 146, 317n41; and Bolshevik regime, 44, 56–57; and teleology, 52–53, 55–57; and Bolshevik violence, 59–60, 65–70, 73, 75, 78–80, 83–88,

94; censorship of, 60–61, 177; and Russian Populists, 62–65; and dehumanization of victims, 78–83; and conflict, 88–92, 145, 155; and Gorky, 107, 110–12, 115, 122, 131; and socialist realism, 179–80, 261, 297, 306, 335n69. *See also* Soviet concentration camp literature; *and specific authors*
Russian Populists, xvii, 62–64, 69
Rybakova, I. A., 125–26, 128

Savinkov, Boris, 64–65, 67–69, 76, 87
Shalamov, Varlam, 198, 201–2, 205, 240–41, 265, 310
Shaw, George Bernard, 113–14
Shelest, Georgy: and Soviet concentration camps, xix, xx, 222; and Stalin, 184, 286; and point of view, 187, 254; publication of, 188–89; ideology of, 190, 210–12, 236–37, 244, 252, 256, 265, 289, 305; and Communism, 211, 223, 236, 242–44, 248–50, 285, 289, 295, 297; and reality, 213; and reeducation, 214–16, 221; and preconceived value systems, 217–19, 231, 270; ethics in, 223–25, 229, 232, 280

Shestov, Lev, 245
Shils, Edward, 37
Shklovsky,Viktor, 179
Shostakovich, Dmitry, 32–33
Simonov, Konstantin, 287–88
Sinyavsky,Andrei, 16, 24–25,
    73, 163, 230–31, 340n50
Slave labor: of Soviet
    concentration camps, 4–6,
    22, 97, 104–5, 149, 315n23;
    and economic base, 20–22,
    104–5, 150, 174–75,
    315n23; and Stalin, 21, 99,
    154, 315n23; and
    reeducation, 100–101, 133,
    145–46, 150, 155, 172,
    180–81; in Nazi
    concentration camps, 103;
    and Solzhenitsyn, 104–5,
    263, 300; and *Belomorkanal*,
    160
Socialism: and totalitarianism,
    13; socialist utopia, 47, 124,
    131, 145, 153, 155, 179, 273;
    and class antagonisms, 95;
    and West, 98–99; and
    Belomorkanal, 158; socialist
    realism, 179–80, 261, 297,
    306, 335n69
Societal transformation: and
    Bolshevik regime, xiv,
    49–50, 143; and economic
    base, xix; and reality, 30; and
    avant-garde artists, 52; and
    Belomorkanal, 158–59,
    163–64, 171–72, 174; and

post-Stalinist thaw literature,
    215–16
Solonevich, Ivan, 310
Solzhenitsyn, Aleksandr, xiii,
    102–5, 115–17, 151–52,
    187, 253, 260–61, 310
    —*One Day in the Life of Ivan
    Denisovich:* and public
    discourse, xx–xxi, 268–69,
    276, 280, 282–83, 289–90,
    292, 298, 305–8, 343n8;
    publication of, 187, 189–90,
    251, 268, 281, 307, 343n7;
    and Communism, 211, 252;
    and Bolshevik violence, 214;
    and ethics, 254–59, 261–74,
    277–78, 280–81, 283,
    298–99, 302–3, 305, 309;
    and point of view, 257, 262,
    276–77, 286, 290;
    interpretations of, 257–58,
    262–63, 292–93; 300;
    literary strategy of, 259–62,
    264, 268–77, 283, 287–97,
    299–305, 308–9, 343n8; and
    reeducation, 272–75; labor
    theme of, 292–97, 299–303,
    347n42
Soviet concentration camp
    literature: and Khrushchev,
    xii, xix, 185–86, 269, 282,
    307–8; and morality, xiii,
    xviii, xix, xxi, 91, 109, 111,
    147–48, 198, 202, 210, 227,
    229–30, 245–46; and reality,
    xiii, xv, 37–45, 190–92; and

compared with, 137,
160–61, 214; and
Belomorkanal, 159–60,
162–64, 167–74, 178,
334n67
Soviet Writers' Union, 106,
153, 179, 332n53
Spiro, Herbert J., 13–14, 26–27
Stalin, Joseph: and terror, xviii,
xix, 3, 256; and
totalitarianism, 2, 12, 26;
criticism of, 3–4, 6, 185–88,
247–52, 256, 287–88,
307–8; and Bolshevik
violence, 17; and slave labor,
21, 99, 150–51, 154, 315n23;
centralized economy of, 22,
97, 315n22; and class
enemies, 25, 82, 181,
231–32, 325n3; dialectical
method of, 31, 35, 94; and
dehumanization of victims,
82; and Communism, 93,
185–86, 246; and
collectivization of farmland,
96–97, 99, 185, 325n3,
329n35; Five-Year Plans of,
97, 104, 153; and
Belomorkanal, 106, 180–82;
and Gorky, 110–11; and
Soviet concentration camp
literature, 184, 231–32, 247,
251–52, 286; and
Khrushchev, 185–88,
281–82, 290, 345n21; and
ethics, 230–31, 286

Stalinism: and mind control, xi,
312n2, 312n4; and
totalitarian model, 13; and
Fascism, 98; and
Belomorkanal, 180; criticism
of, 185, 285
Striedter, Jurij, 38–41
Szmaglewska, Seweryna,
207–8

Tarasov-Rodyonov, Aleksandr:
and tragedy, xvii, xviii, 68,
71, 99, 146; and Bolshevik
violence, 66–69, 75; and
ethics, 67, 91, 228, 232; and
morality, 77, 87; and
victimization, 80–82, 121
Teleology, 29–34, 52–57, 71,
145, 148–49, 180
Terror: and Soviet
concentration camps, xii, 97,
102–4, 326n9; and Soviet
concentration camp
literature, xiii, xix, 105–6,
121, 123, 133–34, 144–45,
148–49, 154, 180, 251–52;
and utilitarian class ethics,
xiv, 62; Red Terror, xvii, 18,
65–66, 83, 146, 212; and
Stalin, xviii, xix, 3, 185,
256; and ideology, 15,
17–18, 20, 100; and
collectivization of farmland,
20, 21, 96, 99; and Russian
literature, 61, 80, 91; and
anti-religious campaign, 77;

Bolshevik regime, 269, 284

Voloshin, Maximilian, 88

Walicki, Andrzej, 12–13

Wallace, Henry, 114, 328n31

Wat, Aleksander, 3–4, 6–7, 9–10, 28, 183, 311–12n2

Wells, H. G., 113

Werner, Andrzej, 191–92, 206, 229

West: and Solzhenitsyn, xx, 299, 301; and ethics, 2; and totalitarianism, 12, 313n9; Soviet timber exports to, 21; and teleology, 31; and dialogical universe, 42–43; socialist sympathies of,

98–99; and Gorky's account, 126–28, 131; and Soviet concentration camps, 137; opposition to, 156; and *Belomorkanal*, 157–62

White Sea–Baltic Sea Canal, 5, 150–51. *See also Belomorkanal*

Wieniawski, Henryk, 141

Wiesel, Elie, xx, 193–94, 197–99, 202–5, 207–8, 241

Yagoda, Genrikh, 181–82, 334n68

Yezhov, Nikolai, 239, 341n65

Zakharova, A. F., 273, 275

Zhdanov, Andrei, 113

Zoshchenko, Mikhail, 179

Russian Literature and Thought

Rereading Russian Poetry
Edited by Stephanie Sandler

View from the Other Shore: Essays on Herzen, Chekhov, and Bakhtin
Aileen M. Kelly

Pushkin's Historical Imagination
Svetlana Evdokimova

Liberty, Equality, and the Market: Essays by B. N. Chicherin
Edited and Translated by G. M. Hamburg

Toward Another Shore: Russian Thinkers Between Necessity and Chance
Aileen M. Kelly

Dostoevsky and Soloviev: The Art of Integral Vision
Marina Kostalevsky

Abram Tertz and the Poetics of Crime
Catharine Theimer Nepomnyashchy

Untimely Thoughts: Essays on Revolution, Culture, and the Bolsheviks, 1917–1918
Maxim Gorky

A Voice from the Chorus
Abram Tertz (Andrei Sinyavsky)

Strolls with Pushkin
Abram Tertz (Andrei Sinyavsky)

1920 Diary
Isaac Babel